in the COMPANY *of* OTHERS

Raphael Patai Series in Jewish Folklore and Anthropology

in the COMPANY *of* OTHERS

The Development of Anthropology in Israel

ORIT ABUHAV

Wayne State University Press
Detroit

19 18 17 16 15 5 4 3 2 1

Library of Congress Control Number: 2015934521

ISBN 978-0-8143-3873-5 (jacketed cloth)
ISBN 978-0-8143-3874-2 (ebook)

This book was published with the support of the Israel Science Foundation and additionally with support of the fund for the Raphael Patai Series in Jewish Folklore and Anthropology.

Designed and typeset by Morgan Laidlaw
Composed in Chaparral Pro and Palatino

CONTENTS

FOREWORD

In a speech to the Fifth Zionist Congress in Basel, December 1901, Max Nordau—the person closest to Theodor Herzl in the Zionist movement—began with these words: "'Knowledge is power.' Is this always true?" (Nordau 1941, 121). Nordau's opening seemingly challenged the famous dictum of Francis Bacon, while the purpose of his talk was to make a claim for the importance of a statistics of the Jewish people. In his day, the term "statistics" had a broad meaning. He asserted that Zionists "must know with greater precision the national material (*Volksmaterial*) with which we have to work," and mentioned anthropological, biological, economic and intellectual statistics (Hart 2000, 29–30). Historians point to this occasion as a founding moment in the development of the social scientific study of Jewish life, and it is worth keeping in mind the developments within the field of anthropology at this time.

In European anthropology, the emphasis on biological factors in understanding the characteristics and behaviors of "peoples" was gaining strength in comparison to the focus on historical and cultural factors. This trend later reached its tragic apogee within Nazi ideology but had appeared elsewhere in Europe, and not only in Germany (Massin 1996). Its prominence, and the concern about how Jews appeared in this biologized approach to human history, may be seen in the attention paid to anthropology in the *Jewish Encyclopedia* that was published in New York City in the first decade of the twentieth century (Schwartz 1991, 108–12). In Europe, there was emerging a difference between *anthropologie,* which stressed the physical side of "man," and *ethnologie,* which examined varieties of societies and culture around the world, but there still remained widespread assumptions that the physical and the behavioral were significantly intertwined in human populations.

At the same time, there were developments in anthropology that challenged the close link between biology and culture. Franz Boas (1858–1942)—who was born and educated in Germany but emigrated to the United States, partially because of his Jewish origins (e.g., Bunzl 2003 and Goldberg 2005), and became a pivotal figure in shaping anthropology there—argued vigorously against race being a significant factor in understanding human cultures. He saw culture as primarily a historical product, and while he did not seek to eliminate the topic of race from scientific investigation, he claimed that it belonged to a separate sub-discipline of physical anthropology, bearing little or no relevance to the understanding of culture (Boas 1911). A somewhat similar development emerged in Great Britain early in the twentieth century, even though there did not appear there a dominant anthropologist taking critical aim at the study of race (Barkan 1992). In England, the notion of race gradually dissipated within anthropological discourse with the crystallization of "social anthropology" based mainly on comparative ethnographic research.

Another direction of ethnography emerged, with a logic similar to that of Nordau. S. Z. Rappoport (1863–1920), a Russian-born Jew who later was better known by his pen name of S. An-sky, became committed to the ethnographic documentation of the life of Jews in the Pale of Settlement. He himself had grown up in the Pale, in Vitebsk, and in 1908 published a pioneering essay in Russian in which, with some irony, he pointed out that "there is no other people like the Jewish people, that talks about itself so much, but knows itself so little" (Deutsch 2011, 28). An-sky initiated the now famous ethnographic expedition to Volhynia, Podolia, and Kiev in 1912, the results of which have only partially come down to us because of World War I, the Bolshevik Revolution, and the subsequent policies of the Soviet Union. Even with the limited publication of the project at the time, An-sky was hewing one pillar in a tradition of Jewish ethnography and folklore that was emerging almost entirely outside of academic frameworks. Another important figure in this movement was Silesian-born Max Grunwald (1871–1953) whose foundational steps in Jewish folklore pulled it away from physical anthropology. As noted by Nathaniel Deutsch, "Grunwald viewed the collection of folklore as not only important for preserving the past but also for constructing the present, in this case, a contemporary Jewish national culture" (2011, 30–31). To many of those engaged in collecting folklore, whether narratives or descriptions of customs, the aim was to create a store of Jewish culture that could prove usable in the rapidly changing social currents of the nineteenth and twentieth centuries. This entailed various notions of Jewish peoplehood, of which Zionism was one version.

These diverse and partially conflicting streams that were internal to or intertwined with anthropology presented a dilemma for those seeking to stimulate the growth of a contemporary academic culture within the Jewish community of Mandate Palestine (the *yishuv*). Ostensibly, anthropology—dealing with the characteristics of peoples and their cultures—might have offered intellectual buttressing to the renewal of Jewish national life and Hebrew culture within the *yishuv*. But the growing racialization of the discipline in Europe surrounded the field with many question marks. One aspect of this complexity is that among Jews in Europe, who were the objects of "scientific" anti-Semitism, there emerged a counter-thrust of anthropological research that adopted the tools of "race science" to defend against attacks that "proved" Jewish inferiority, and even to claim that in certain realms Jews might enjoy biological advantages (Efron 1994).

The approaches to ethnographic study that had no connection to race also entailed dilemmas for the ethos of the emergent, Hebrew-based, national culture. Jews living in Europe, and especially in eastern Europe in recent centuries, constituted the largest segment of the Jewish people. The Yiddish language had developed among them over the course of a millennium. That language was the lynchpin of An-sky's ethnographic expedition, and—as another example—the research conducted at YIVO (Yiddish Scientific Institute; *Yidisher Visnshaftlekher Institut*), a research institute founded in Vilnius in 1925 that incorporated ethnographic projects into its program. But Yiddish was an anathema to Zionist ideology that saw the language as intimately linked to the condition of "exile" from which Jews should be liberated. Yiddish was thus avoided in the Zionist *yishuv* both in terms of everyday practice and institutional decisions.

This complex picture, with internal stress and even contortions, provides part of the background to Orit Abuhav's account of the hesitant and gradual development of anthropology in the Mandate period and in the State of Israel. Her archival research and the interviews she conducted among many of the anthropologists active in Israel spread before us the story of an academic field that always has been limited in terms of the number of its practitioners but is expansive in terms of the central questions it has placed at the doorstep of Israeli society.

The first university to formally include anthropology in its program was Tel Aviv University when it established a department of sociology and anthropology in 1963. While discussing this and later developments, Abuhav also reveals to us a fascinating "pre-history" of anthropology in the archives of the Hebrew University of Jerusalem. Among the instructive events recorded there is the report prepared by an advisory committee in 1934 (the Hartog Committee—nine years after the university opened) that proposes setting up a facility to study the biological history of the Jews, arguing—among other things—that the presence in Jerusalem of Jews from many different countries provides a special research opportunity.

Specifically, it suggests establishing a unit linked to the sociology section of the Institute of Jewish Studies, to which Arthur Ruppin was attached. Ruppin (1876–1943), known widely for his role in abetting the purchase of land in Palestine for the Zionist cause, was trained in economics and sociology but had an interest in anthropology that dated from his student days in Germany at the beginning of the century (Morris-Reich 2006). Despite Ruppin's prominence, the proposed research unit was never created.

The archives also expand our knowledge of Erich Brauer (1895–1942), a native of Berlin and friend of Gershom Scholem (1897–1982), the renowned scholar of mysticism, in his youth (Scholem 1980, 58, 71–73). Brauer was the first professionally trained ethnologist to study Jewish groups in Mandate Palestine. The troubled and complex nature of those days receives expression in that Brauer's first book (1934) on the Jews of Yemen was published in Heidelberg the year after the Nazi takeover. Brauer, like Ruppin, had an inclusive view of an anthropology-ethnology of the Jews and envisioned a special role for Jerusalem with its variety of Jewish and non-Jewish groups, but the university did not find a place for him or his plans.

Another key figure appearing in the archives is Raphael Patai (1910–96), who hoped that the Hebrew University would institutionalize anthropology within its program. Patai was born in Budapest and was educated there in programs of Jewish studies and of Semitic languages and literature. His advanced research focused on ethnological approaches to everyday life, especially as reflected in ancient texts, but he also developed an interest in ethnography. He completed his doctoral dissertation in Jerusalem and, in 1936, received the first doctoral degree awarded by the Hebrew University. In the following decade, he composed a textbook, in Hebrew, that presented the main current anthropological approaches in the United States and in England, while also reflecting the ethnological orientation of his training in Europe (Patai 1947a). At the same time, he published a monograph (a *Memoir* of the American Anthropological Association) that addressed current issues in the study of "culture contact" through the ethnographic lens of contemporary Palestine (Patai 1947b). In spite of Patai's extensive activity and links to anthropology abroad—as documented meticulously by Abuhav—the discipline remained beyond the pale in the development plans of the university.

After establishment of the state, higher education in Israel expanded rapidly, first at the Hebrew University and then in newer institutions. Sociology was included in this expansion and it began to incorporate anthropology to some extent, initially at Tel Aviv—as indicated—and subsequently in other universities. Thus anthropology always has had to find its way in the shadow of a disciplinary and institutional "big sister." Some anthropology was done in Israel before these developments, including fieldwork by researchers from abroad, and the initial favorite topics were kibbutzim, immigrant absorption in cooperative villages, and Arab (including Bedouin) communities. With time, and the formal appearance of anthropology in the universities, research foci diversified greatly (Hertzog, Abuhav, Goldberg, and Marx 2010). Intellectually, the field always was in conversation with anthropological discourse abroad; understandably, anthropology in the United States exercised a major influence (Weingrod 2004).

With not little irony and precisely at the period that recognition of anthropology in Israel was growing, the field as a whole began to absorb charges—including those made by some anthropologists—of a close connection to imperialism and colonialism. The elision of knowledge and power (e.g., Foucault 1980) had an impact in many disciplines. This formula became persuasive to critics of the old-timer "establishment" in Israel, in regard to its relationship to Jewish immigrants from Middle Eastern countries and Palestinian Arabs. A reevaluation of the early sociological knowledge produced in Israel emerged, but these discussions typically overrode the differing histories and shapes of sociological and anthropological research.

In contrast to the assumption of uniformity in the basic apperceptions and research praxis of sociology and anthropology, Orit Abuhav's interviews in this volume (carried out with a broad contextual grasp of the Israeli anthropological scene) are true to the anthropological principle of drawing a portrait that takes into account the perspective of the "objects" of research. Through them, we learn of diverse understandings among Israeli anthropologists at the individual and institutional levels, and of continuous evolution in response to changes in the discipline and within Israeli society. An image that keeps appearing is that of the anthropologist as a "nomad," a formulation reminiscent of (though not necessarily directly influenced by) Claude Lévi-Strauss's picture of his thought as anchored in the Neolithic (Lévi-Strauss 1973b, 45). Overall, the interviews yield a dynamic portrait of the acquisition, production, and ongoing modification of anthropological knowledge. Within this picture, prior awareness of positioning within fields of status or power, are only partially helpful in grasping the story of anthropology and anthropologists in the Israeli setting.

Today, many wonder about the future of anthropology in Israel and in the world generally. Societies once deemed isolated no longer exist; anthropologists do field work "at home" and not only among "the other"; and the realm of "culture" is no longer the monopoly of any specific discipline. From the interviews and ideas brought forth in this book, one may dip into the storehouse that supplied anthropological inspiration in the past, and legitimately look forward to new insights and their implications in the future.

Harvey E. Goldberg

PREFACE AND ACKNOWLEDGMENTS

This book is based on my dissertation research about the development of anthropology in Israel at the Hebrew University's department of Sociology and Anthropology. A previous version of the book was published in Hebrew (Abuhav 2010b). The current version is of potential interest to a variety of audiences: chiefly to anthropologists but also to scholars interested in the history, sociology, or anthropology of social sciences and especially anthropology.

Because of the limits inherent in any attempt to encompass the sociocultural phenomenon at the center of my work, Israeli anthropology, I have chosen three research arenas in which to focus: (1) the universities and the academic activity of research and teaching, which are the very core of the scientific discipline's activity; (2) the Israeli Anthropological Association, a voluntary institutional-professional arena; (3) life courses and careers of anthropologists—the personal arena, the inside view. The three arenas are differentiated for analytical purposes only. The anthropologist, anthropology, and the professional association operate in all three arenas simultaneously.

All three arenas are interwoven by various links. The universities allow connections between Israeli and worldwide processes to be realized. Academic institutions are affected by external factors—the state institutions on the one hand, and the overseas academy on the other. Higher education policies and state budgets, as the outcome of those policies, affect vicissitudes in the scale and orientation of research as well as the academy's autonomy in scientific decision making. In Anglo-American centers, the academy sets the agenda and establishes the frontiers of research, which affect local activity. Academic institutions are more formal and hierarchical than is the professional association. The Israeli Anthropological Association mediates between local Israeliness and cosmopolitanism in the academic centers by means of scientific discourse and exchange on research topics. The association stresses professional identity, the maintenance of the boundaries of the discipline, concern with ethical issues, and the intensification of engagement and professional accountability. It provides the dimension of democratization that is lacking at the universities, and as an association that crosscuts academic institutions, it enables dialogue among them. The academy, and less so the professional association, are frameworks for the development of the anthropologist's personal career and professional identity. The university is a work place, and a source of livelihood. Both its power and its weakness lie in the mutual dependency of the organization and its employees. At the epistemological level, the intellectual activity gives the individual the opportunity to express his/her skill and drives. In his/her vocation as an academic and as an anthropological in particular, the anthropologist takes flight on wings with which to soar into other regions: imagination, adventure, curiosity, and caring. The anthropologist expresses him/herself via ethnography, and his/her academic products are his/her intellectual calling card. The status of scientist locates him or her within the Israeli social hierarchy which is subject to the vicissitudes of the academy's own prestige.

Studies of anthropology's history have been written by both historians and anthropologists, by members of the studied community, and by anthropologists observing those communities from without. I offer a view from within, as an anthropologist who belongs to the community she studied, which has both advantages and disadvantages, as well as points of vulnerability. A research perspective, and especially one that observes from within, forces the researcher to be exposed to a particular kind of experience, a state of awareness and consciousness of the distances necessary to turn everyday friends and acquaintances into research-setting subjects and interviewees.

I am grateful to them for their consent to be "subjects" and for their cooperation. My gratitude and appreciation are extended to my two dissertation supervisors: Prof. Harvey Goldberg, who taught me, at first hand, what it means to be human and what excellent anthropology should be like. He is living proof that wisdom, modesty, and honesty are no less effective than bulldozing for paving one's path. Besides providing me keys to knowledge, Harvey also invited me into his home, where I enjoyed the warmth and friendship of Judy Goldberg and the children. I could not have imagined that one day Harvey's daughter, Ilana Goldberg, would undertake the translation of my book, and perform this task with utmost expertise, and for this I thank her. My deepest thanks are extended to my second advisor, Prof. Eyal Ben-Ari, whose common sense, experience, and focus propelled my research forward. Israeli anthropologists opened their professional and personal worlds to me, cooperated willingly and enthusiastically, and gave their seal of approval to the Hebrew version of the book.

Throughout this journey I have benefited from the generosity, wisdom, and professional experience of friends who read parts of the book and provided comments that improved it immeasurably: Prof. Esther Hertzog, Dr. Shaul Katz, Dr. Andre Levy, Prof. Emanuel Marx, the late Prof. Henry Rosenfeld, Prof. Moshe Shokeid, Dr. Anat Stavans, Prof. Alex Weingrod, and Prof. Meira Weiss. My unparalleled friends, Dr. Maya Meltzer-Geva and Dr. Varda Shiffer completed, a few years before me, a similar professional path—that of late-bloomer women. I am grateful for their example, support, encouragement, and excellent advice—in respect to both the dissertation and life in general.

During the course of research I was fortunate to receive financial support from the Hebrew University's Shaine Center and the Levi Eshkol Institute at the Faculty of the Social Sciences, as well as the Authority for Research Students. My colleagues at Beit Berl College, my place of employment and academic home for many years, constantly spurred me forward with their encouragement and support.

ONE

ANTHROPOLOGY *in* ISRAEL

A Knowledge Field in Israeli Culture and Society

Several interrelated factors have generated interest in the history of the anthropological discipline in Israel: changes in Israeli society, developments in anthropology, and the field's current status in Israel. Since the 1980s, Euro-American anthropology has undergone a crisis arising from the wake of a critical examination of the nature of anthropological knowledge and methods, issues of representations, and blurring of the distinctions between the discipline of anthropology and ethnographic research. Inspired by Anglo-American anthropology and influenced by critical and post-modern approaches in the social sciences, Israel's anthropological community became focused on examining the "colonial" orientation of Israeli anthropology; this focus offered a new perspective for understanding the history of local disciplines. Questions presently occupying Israeli anthropologists concerning how Israel's first anthropologists observed their own society have led to efforts to examine the development of anthropology in Israel. As an anthropology student in the early 1970s, and later as an active anthropologist in Israeli academe, I witnessed the crises, high and low points, and the efforts of Israeli anthropology to blaze a legitimate trail for itself within Israeli academe.

My argument here seeks to demonstrate that the presentation of Israeli anthropology as part of an oversimplified equation—with researchers representing dominant, suppressive, and exploitative power on one side, and groups of immigrants, the underprivileged, the oppressed, and powerless Mizrahim and Arabs on the other—is a formulaic, superficial, and distorted representation. The model claiming that anthropology is the "handmaiden of colonialism," as accepted in critical anthropology, mandates that the credibility of its application to local contexts be carefully examined.

Here I would like to emphasize that the "others" in the title of my book is a term indicating a methodological position, not an essentialist one in respect of the subjects of either my study or those of others. The "Other," a term commonly used in French and Lacanian philosophy, was introduced into anthropological discourse in the 1980s (Edgar and Sedgwick 2000), with the acceptance and spread of critical anthropology inspired by the writing of Edward Said.

The term has been employed in critical theory to understand and describe processes whereby societies, groups (or scientists) excluded or exoticized ethnic groups, minorities, or their own subjects. But because "others" is a frequently used word, neither it nor its linguistic derivations can be appropriated by a critical theory. A term undergoes change when introduced into a discourse and is accorded numerous, sometimes ambiguous, meanings. My use of "other" refers to methodological positioning, because research requires that its subject be in a different position than that of the researcher. Due to the blindness caused by over-proximity, distancing is mandatory in order to challenge the self-evident. I do not employ this term to signify a very distinct and discrete orientation, but only where it seems appropriate so that I cannot be suspected of defining Israeli anthropologists as different, out of an exotic or exclusionary position.

Any scientific discipline presents a variegated tapestry of elements and directions that have a history, and is comprised of people who have needs, motives, images, and identities, all of whom engage in a field shaped by local, global, social, cultural, and political forces. To augment my claims on the complexity of the power relations under discussion, I shall refer to the path taken by anthropology during the Yishuv (pre-state) period and after the establishment of the state, paying special attention to the complex relations between anthropology, the state, researchers, and research subjects. In this chapter, I shall paint the history of the discipline with broad strokes, defining periods of ebb and flow, support and neglect, until the present day.

Anthropology first circulated as a notion in local academe in the mid-1930s. However, it was not until the mid-1960s that it was accepted as a legitimate field of knowledge by Israeli universities. The prolonged deferment of this process attests to the intellectual and ideological priorities of the Yishuv, and later of the state in its first decade, and to what was declared important and deemed necessary, in contrast with other matters and pursuits that were sidelined. The volte-face regarding the discipline attests to transformations in the goals of Israeli society, in the image of anthropological knowledge, and in the availability of resources and manpower to achieve these goals. The increasing strength of the discipline can be understood against the backdrop of the high expectations it presents and the personal, social, and political agenda of its members—the group of professionals identifying themselves as Israeli anthropologists. In the 1960s, some anthropologists enlisted for research projects derived from the goals of the Zionist enterprise: settlement and the state's preparedness for absorbing and assimilating immigrants. Considered "experts on others," they were entrusted with discovering what had "gone wrong" with the processes of settlement and immigrant absorption.

They ventured out into the field. But instead of reporting back to the bodies that had commissioned them—the Jewish Agency and other institutions—the anthropologists, armed with proposals for better control of immigrant absorption, delivered sophisticated and complex ethnographies that gave a voice to the immigrants. When anthropology did not deliver the goods that the establishment had expected, the latter preferred to keep things on hold and to prevent the discipline from developing further. This decision, never explicitly stated, reflected the internal complexity of the power relations within the only university existing at the time—the Hebrew University of Jerusalem.

The breakthrough leading to anthropology's impressive presence in Israeli academe in the end of the 1960s was the outcome of external intervention—an extremely generous donation by an Anglo-Jewish magnate, Lord Bernstein. This benefactor sought to contribute to the Zionist enterprise and inadvertently discovered the kingdom of anthropology. The funds he donated for anthropological studies led to the incorporation of the discipline into Tel Aviv University, a young institution that rebelled against its older sibling—the Hebrew University. Tel Aviv was followed by the other new universities—Haifa, Bar Ilan, and Ben Gurion—all of which included anthropology in their faculties. Left with no choice, Jerusalem followed suit, bringing up the rear in the development of the discipline of anthropology.

Internationally, as in Israel, there was increased demand for higher education, and abundant resources were allocated to its promotion. Immigrant anthropologists arrived to take up academic posts and reinforce the small nucleus—no more than a handful—of local anthropologists. Israeli society opened a door for expression of ethnic diversity and withdrew, at least rhetorically, from the notion of the melting pot and "ingathering of the exiles."

There was a new willingness to look in the mirror and take stock of the country's pluralistic and multicultural image. In this new atmosphere, anthropologists, as professional practitioners in the study of human society and culture, found an opportunity to produce knowledge consistent with their personal credo, without clashing with the institutional one. The ranks of anthropology were reinforced by anthropologists who focused on immigrants and were motivated by their Jewish identity and Zionist ideology. They employed anthropology's traditional tools to study Jewish immigrants on the one hand, and native Israelis on the other. In contrast to the work produced in Anglo-American anthropology in research on immigrants and natives, motives that were nationalistic, exoticized, or romanticized were secondary. The discipline of anthropology in Israel did not dwell in isolated redoubts or ivory towers. The image of condescending, escapist, egotistical, lonely researchers, detached from their environment, had no bearing on its members. Nor were they marionettes, manipulated by forces greater than themselves (Martin 1997). Fueling their research were caring, commitment to the research subjects rather than the commissioner of the research, curiosity about the other, intellectual stimulation, and a connection to international scientific practices. These were supplemented by passion, drive, and motivation—the human factor within the anthropologist, whose devotion to scientific practice is at least as crucial as rational considerations and intentional actions. In addition, choice and serendipity played crucial roles in the strides made during this era.

In the course of the developmental stages that came in the wake of the 1970s breakthrough, anthropology became a popular major for undergraduates, and demand for its study increased. Most of the research was conducted "at home," within Israel's borders, and focused on communities that lived "across the street," so to speak. To a great degree, research could also be used in applied contexts and exploited for bureaucratic or governmental aims. At the same time, even though they were willing to be recruited as "troubleshooters," anthropologists did not conduct themselves simply as technicians in the governmental workshop. Their agenda was formulated by a combination of individual interest, topics at the cutting edge of research in anthropological centers, Israeli society's own burning issues, and research fields for which funding could be obtained. Easy communication between the local anthropological community and their colleagues in Europe and America facilitated the rapid germination of imported ideas in local soil. Although local anthropology had a decidedly dominant British hue (social anthropology) when it was first introduced into Israeli universities, it gradually began to absorb nuances of the various hues of American cultural anthropology. Simultaneously, contacts between British and American anthropology became closer; over time, the theoretical center of gravity shifted toward the American version. Israeli anthropology, which was characteristically adaptive in nature, adjusted itself to theoretical developments in Anglo-American academe, which largely paralleled changes in its society. For example, social struggles to preserve the uniqueness of ethnic groups were replaced by struggles to protect the rights of oppressed social categories, such as women, children, Palestinians, the deteriorating environment, and so forth.

Although I had not initially decided that this would be the focus of my study, at almost every turn the discussion brought up Israeli anthropology's complex relationship with nationalism and colonialism; questions relating to authority; and the exploitation, enlistment, and incorporation of anthropology into processes of nation and institution building. The concept of *giyus* (recruitment) to national, local, or other missions, is central to the discourse of collective projects in the broader Israeli context. One of the term's uses is as a symbol of personal commitment to the general Zionist enterprise, in much the same way as commitment to military service. In another context, it means volunteering—for instance, to pick apples in a kibbutz orchard—or becoming an activist in a public cause. In academic discourse centered on tensions between the collective and the individual, between the Zionist past and the post-Zionist present, the term *giyus* is accorded a different meaning. Here it represents an overall purpose (in the past) and a pointed accusation (in the present). In academic and anthropological discourse, criticism has been leveled that anthropologists enlisted themselves on behalf of the institutions of power. I would like to propose a substitute for the term: for the benefit of. Use of the latter terminology is preferable, because it represents the agency of anthropologists as social players, and the possibility of choosing the subjects of their enlistment and commitment.

In the following chapters, I shall formulate the historical-sociological-anthropological questions relating to the development of the field in its social and cultural context. I shall demarcate the boundaries of the discipline in relation to its neighboring disciplines. I shall deliberate over the most appropriate conceptual model for interpretation and analysis of the topic, and outline and explain my methodological choices. I will also indicate the research arenas I chose, and how they interlock, and will then position the Israeli case within the general context of discussion of the history of world anthropology.

My goal is to capture this evasive entity—Israeli anthropology—to draw its contours and characterize it. I seek to examine the concrete and personal context in which anthropological knowledge about Israel is produced and disseminated. This, in fact, constitutes sociology of anthropological knowledge, or perhaps its own auto-ethnology. The analysis of social and cultural processes as types of social knowledge will move along two analytical axes: first, how the production of knowledge about Israel relates to authoritative texts, career ambitions, professional practices, and institutional sites. Here, knowledge is perceived as a matrix of socially constructed skills and habits that are put into use in order to secure long-term goals. The second axis is the broad system of social distinctions and social hierarchies wherein players activate the principles enumerated above, and maneuver within them. In other words, I seek to examine how professionalization of anthropology reflects national, social, and international factors. This model, which examines how production of anthropological knowledge is embedded in worldwide social and biographical contexts, has not yet been applied to Israeli anthropology; therein lies its innovativeness.

The characterization of Israeli anthropology will focus on the following topics:

- Anthropology as a scientific field of knowledge and its boundaries: what it includes and what is defined as extraneous to it; the theoretical, methodological, and conceptual elements that underpin it; and the internal and external disciplinary factors that have influenced it
- Modes of knowledge production: How do society, science, and culture dovetail with each other? What is the scientific agenda, and what changes have taken place within this agenda and within issues at the forefront of research? What motivates people to take up anthropology as a practice, and continue to nourish it? Who shoulders the task of anthropological work, and how are anthropology's bearers perceived? What is the image of anthropological knowledge in the general public, within academe, and within the government establishment? What is the nature of anthropology as a profession? How do anthropologists' careers operate? What kind of social control or surveillance does the international anthropological community exercise on the Israeli one? Is there a "school" of Israeli anthropology; if so, what is unique about it?

- Questions concerning the encounters between anthropology and Israeli society: What is its status vis-à-vis national projects? How do anthropology and Israeli society mutually influence each other? Is the anthropology practiced in Israel solely Israeli? What are the main factors shaping Israeli society? What interests enable the discipline to exist within or outside academe or, conversely, to be neglected? What explicit or unseen principles guide it? Finally, what connections exist between the sites at which anthropology is practiced?

As a first step, I shall attempt to clarify the boundaries of the research subject I call "Israeli anthropology" and what distinguishes it from other related disciplines.

ISRAELI ANTHROPOLOGY AND ITS NEIGHBORING DISCIPLINES: COHABITION OR FENCED-OFF PLOTS?

What is anthropology? Is it a discipline, or perhaps a worldview? Is the ethnographic method its only defining factor? Is it an autonomous discipline? The importance of these questions is in the way they shape the boundaries of anthropology in the Israeli context and define it in relation to neighboring disciplines.

The most salient characteristic of anthropology in Israel is its lack of autonomy. To this day, no separate department of anthropology exists. In Israeli academic institutions, anthropology and sociology are commonly combined into one department within the universities and colleges (with the exception of Ben-Gurion University in Beersheba, where until recently it was part of behavioral sciences). The reasons for this marriage, which is uncommon in world anthropology, are many and varied. Because the influence of the centers of anthropology has shaped the image of local anthropology, I shall investigate which models it appropriated from American and British anthropology and to what extent this has been an original and unique creation.

Ever since anthropology first set foot on the soil of pre-state Israel, its identity has been troubled. When professional anthropology first came from Europe to be practiced here in the 1920s, the social and cultural were inseparable, and both were strongly linked to folklore (ethnology) on the one hand, and to the physical-biological dimension on the other. In the wake of developments in Zionist ideology and World War II and its aftermath, however, the links between the physical (racial) and the cultural and social characteristics of Jewishness were weakened and even completely severed. In Israeli anthropology, there was an organizational disconnect between the social and physical aspects of anthropology from the very time of its institutional establishment in the universities. From that time to the present day, human anatomy and physical anthropology departments are located in the medical schools, and there is only limited contact between them and the social sciences.

The 1970s, when British social anthropology was in the ascendancy, were the formative years in which the ideal model for the anthropological discipline in Israel was decided upon. As in its birthplace, the emphasis was on social anthropology. Anthropology rejected the possibilities of conjoining itself to other areas of expertise and, for epistemic and organizational reasons, preferred to be partnered with sociology. The main justification for this move derived from the temporary weakness of anthropology and the fear that the discipline would be unable to stand on its own two feet. Circumstances changed over the years, but the power of the joint model overcame any separatist tendencies.

American anthropology, since its establishment, has been home to the practice of "four fields anthropology"—a holistic, multifaceted anthropology. This approach includes specialization in linguistic anthropology, archeology, physical anthropology, and social and cultural anthropology. In Israel, the American model was adopted in toto for a number of years at the University of Haifa, but it neither maintained its position nor migrated to other university settings. A number of factors combined to prevent the adoption of this model locally. The connection between anthropology and linguistics was problematic, because this discipline was considered part of the humanities. Several valuable studies have been carried out in the field of linguistic anthropology and on the sociocultural matrix of language, but no coherent tradition has emerged in this field. The linkage between anthropology and archeology is also problematic. The two share similar research aims: archeology studies cultures, especially the material culture and technology of past societies, whereas anthropology studies current ones. In Israeli academe, however, archeology is attached to history and belongs to the humanities. In addition, for many years, Israeli anthropology neglected pre-history and was more interested in the search for instances of survival of the Jewish past. However, in recent years greater emphasis has been placed on prehistoric studies, even though the subjects of these studies are "mere humans," devoid of any national identity.

Another potential configuration joins anthropology to the study of folklore. This tradition derives from European ethnology, which viewed anthropology and folklore as a single entity. Over time, the two disciplines went their separate ways, leaving the field of folklore to the study of folk and popular culture "at home," while anthropology specialized in the study of simple/primitive/non-Western societies abroad. From the 1960s onward, a rapprochement between the two fields began, with folklore emphasizing dimensions of representation and performance, drawing attention to the importance of the context of folkloric forms, and developing theoretical viewpoints broadly adopted from anthropology. The rapprochement on anthropology's part occurred when research "at home" became more the norm, and both fields developed narrative genres and the study of life histories. It is therefore hardly surprising that of all the areas adjacent to anthropology, the folklore departments in Israel employ the largest proportion of faculty members trained as anthropologists, even though from an organizational standpoint they belong to the humanities rather than the social sciences.

Sociology was perceived then—and still is—as the most suitable candidate for accepting anthropology into its ranks. And indeed, within the organizational structure of Israeli academe these two fields are combined into one department. The proponents of this "cohabitation" justify it based on the shared subject matter, the similarity of questions posed to it, and the similarity of explanatory rhetoric. Over the past twenty years, as qualitative methods have become commonplace in sociology, these similarities have drawn the two disciplines even closer. On the other hand, the opponents of this union have underscored the great variance in research methods—differences that are not merely methodological, but essential. However, such substantive arguments have been tinged by academic politics and have never been purely disciplinary. In the early years, anthropology had no choice but to survive within the embrace of sociology, in an acceptable modus vivendi. Even today, when anthropology's power in most universities is increasing, it has not taken action to amicably separate from sociology and become autonomous. This perhaps can be explained by institutional conservatism, or by the fact that the partnership does not detract from the discipline's power but might even contribute to it, or by a combination of the factors.

It appears that anthropology's chief contender for the hearts and minds of students and researchers today is the new discipline of cultural studies. This can be deduced by the very appropriation of the concept of culture into its own title—the concept that had hitherto been the very core of the anthropological discipline. Although both fields are concerned with culture, they adopt different perspectives: cultural studies focus on texts, narratives, and their interpretation, whereas classic anthropology deals with people and with behavior. However, current anthropology embraces interpretive approaches that stand on the shoulders of literary criticism and advocate the "culture as text" approach. Moreover, in more radical anthropological practices we find an increased tendency to employ the methodology, concepts, language, representations, and research fields that are of interest to cultural studies. The emergence of cultural studies has led some anthropologists to retrench and insist that only ethnography can be at the core of anthropology (as opposed to textual interpretation), but it has also drawn others closer (for a comparison, see Lewis 2013, Ch. 9). The institutional demarcations which attach cultural studies to the humanities (at Tel Aviv University, for example), somewhat attenuate the competition between the two. At the Hebrew University, however, cultural studies are part of the faculty of social science, and the two disciplines' similarity enables their co-existence.

In describing the nature of anthropology's relations with adjacent fields, I have pointed out vectors of distancing and rapprochement, similarity and distinction, acceptance and rejection. The indistinctness of the field's boundaries and margins also enables its survival as a flexible field. It is capable of adapting to the vicissitudes of time, of absorbing significant changes, and of not disintegrating during an intergenerational transition.

THE GEOPOLITICAL BOUNDARIES OF ISRAELI ANTHROPOLOGY

When considering Israeli political and social reality, a clear distinction must be drawn between Palestinians who are citizens of the State of Israel and reside within Israel's pre-1967 borders (demarcated by what is known as "the Green Line") and Palestinians from the Palestinian Authority (PA), who reside in the territories occupied by Israel in 1967, which, according to various estimates, currently have a population of between 1.4 and 2.4 million. These two areas are separated by walls, fences, and checkpoints. Even after more than forty years of occupation, the assimilation of Palestinians from the PA into the fabric of Israeli life is only very limited, as either legal or illegal workers. On the other hand, some 350,000 Jewish Israelis live in the occupied territories, in enclaves of Jewish settlement blocs or isolated settlements. The frame of reference for this population, in any dimension, is Israel within the pre-1967 Green Line.

For those who live in Israel and do not normally cross the Green Line, the distinction between the area within and beyond the border zone is significant, even though an outside observer might gain a different impression. The policy of the Israeli government to maintain a borderless border creates an illusion, leading outside observers to believe that there is a territorial continuum between the two zones. With the exception of a number of extremist groups, the Jewish settlers living in settlements beyond the Green Line generally live routine lives, maintaining close connections with Israel within its old borders. The Palestinians, on the other hand, lead their lives within PA territory. The border zones between the two polities are zones of daily suffering for the Palestinians due to regulations, restrictions on movement, the need for permits, and the imposition of rules by Israeli authorities through the country's security services.

In determining the scope of my research (i.e., the development of Israeli anthropology), I did not include research and anthropological studies undertaken within the Palestinian Authority. It goes without saying that studies of Israeli Arabs are in the purview of my work. The reader will find more detailed and finely honed treatments of Palestinian anthropology in works by Rabinowitz (1998, 2002) and Furani and Rabinowitz (2011). This caveat notwithstanding, there are noteworthy cases of writing on border zones and crossing through them (e.g., Dalsheim 2011; Bowman 2012; and Forte 2001).

After exploring the boundaries of anthropology in Israel, and describing its research subjects, I shall examine the tools at my disposal for analyzing it.

KEYS TO INTERPRETATION AND ANALYSIS

The sociology of knowledge offers a working premise underlying any discussion of scientific knowledge, which is conditioned by society and culture while also influencing them. It is the theoretical foundation for examining the development of anthropology in a social and cultural context. Émile Durkheim (1915) laid the groundwork for thinking about the power of the social to shape systems of belief and worldviews in primitive societies, and his analysis inspired many studies that examined these contexts regarding knowledge in general and science in particular. Following Durkheim, Karl Mannheim (1952) spun a theoretical thread that attempted to reveal the various modes of representation and diverse interpretations of scientific research in social and cultural contexts, the reflections of social structures within scientific premises, and how they are affected by the characteristics of the social world in which they are produced.

When discussing the sociology of science, Robert Merton (1973) noted the connection between seventeenth-century Puritanism and the development of science in England. Puritanism was the breeding ground for a scientific ethos that valorized norms of originality, independence, humility, emotional neutrality, and impartiality. As the field of the sociology of knowledge became established, emerging insights encouraged fruitful directions of empirical research, especially in the context of the natural and life sciences (see Mulkay 1979). A later development in the sociology of science was the attention paid to the social sciences as a research subject. Sociologists and anthropologists readily accepted that underlying their supposedly value-free scientific activity are premises, beliefs, cultural worldviews, ideologies, and also social motives and personal psychological tendencies. Scientific activity, therefore, is based on sociocultural foundations in political and institutional contexts. This model enables us to look at interrelationships between the different components of the scientific, academic, social, and cultural systems—not only with respect to the effects of the social on the scientific, but also conversely: the effects of the scientific on the social.

The sociology of knowledge and science offers some keys to understanding phenomena such as Foucault's "power/knowledge regime" or Kuhn's theory of paradigm shifts. The use of a single key that provides a clear assertion—an unambiguous assertion that can be formulated in a number of statements—appears both credible and valid. But one explanatory principle cannot encompass the subtleties and complexity of reality. The illuminating power of the key may sometimes also be blinding. Anthropology in Israel is a complex reality that requires the use of a set of keys, such as feelings, talents, weaknesses, power, competition, dependency, strong egos, connections, and self-image. It is therefore incumbent upon us to consider both the micro level, which includes uncontrollable processes and randomness, and elements that organize scientific work—intellectual talent, fieldwork skills, diligence and perseverance, marketing and networking abilities—as well as the macro processes of the society in which the research is taking place.

"Realistic construction" is a concept proposed by Bourdieu (Weitman 2002: 416). As an anthropologist, Bourdieu found this concept useful for his methodological approach to documenting people's lives, or what he termed "the people behind the statistical data" or "realistic sociology with a human face." For Bourdieu, realistic construction is a methodological tool for interviewing; however, I seek to regard it as a theoretical concept of a higher order. The strength of the concept lies precisely in the internal contradiction it embodies: the tension between the personal, interpretive, subjective, and unique processes of reality construction, and its "realistic" aspects—the social facts (à la Durkheim), from which it is produced. The human meets the general, and together they form a full picture (Weitman 2002).

Foucauldian power/knowledge analysis will not yield a model that provides a credible depiction of reality. According to Foucault, techniques or practices of power are also techniques and practices of knowledge. In his view, the ideas, practices, and techniques of power have undergone changes throughout history, and any historical analysis that does not take these changes into account will be found wanting. Foucault is more interested in the transformation of power, and less in the causal connections between forms of power and social structure. The autonomy of power/knowledge is also its limitation. Like other anthropological studies seeking to understand phenomena in context, my work is concerned with the nexus of social structures and scientific edifices. Even if I discover the sought-after connection between power and knowledge in Israeli anthropology (and I certainly will), I still will not be satisfied with positing a simplistic link between them.

A Kuhnian analysis of the dynamic of the development of science cannot be an effective key for understanding Israeli anthropology, because it does not display paradigm shifts in the Kuhnian sense. Its development is evolutionary, not revolutionary. Production, dissemination, and the shattering of intellectual paradigms are conditioned by the modes of action of scientific organizations, by their dependence on or independence from state institutions, on the hierarchies pertaining to them, on the consumer public, and on strong patrons (Swidler and Arditi 1994). In recent years, Israeli anthropology has signaled the genesis of an anthropology that goes beyond fieldwork toward the more ethereal methodologies of textual analysis, but it is still too early to speak of an epistemological revolution. Israeli anthropologists were not innovators of theory, even though the Israeli arena is a special one and may require a theory of its own. In summary, I am in search of a body of knowledge comprising three components: the elements that shape the macro level of Israeli society, the elements that shape scientific work and the academic discipline, and the human materials that shape the clusters of identities and thoughts of the self.

As opposed to the one-dimensional explanation hinging on relations of power and domination, Ben-Amos (1990, 90) points to a number of factors that provide an adequate and reasonable explanation to the question of why

Judaic studies in Israel ignored folklore studies, in which historical, ideological, methodological, and social considerations intersect.

STUDYING THE HISTORY OF ANTHROPOLOGY / ANTHROPOLOGIES

The history of anthropology has developed in three directions: the biographical direction (genealogical trees of ancestors and their descendants), the contextual political-sociocultural direction (issues of modernity, colonialism, post-colonialism, and so forth), and the intellectual history direction (schools of thought, theories, methodologies, and models). As an anthropologist who studies anthropologists, I am joining a series of studies on this topic and, in my own version, make an effort to present diverse points of view, institutional and personal alike. Although my work included archival research, I prefer the anthropological perspective to the study of the history of anthropology for several reasons: its interpretive modes are suitable for a deep understanding and description of the discipline's developments; its holistic approach engages with social, cultural, and political contexts; and the reflexive mode has proved itself in extracting explanations "from the inside." I have based my account on historical documents, interviews, and observations, which are the principal methodologies for a qualitative ethnographic study.

Underlying any study of the history of Israeli anthropology is a tacit premise of the framework of the state as a unit of production and consumption of scientific knowledge. National anthropology began self-reflection in the mid-1960s. Irving Hallowell (1965) proposed a view of anthropology as part of the matrix of Western culture, and he found links between historical events, intellectual proclivities, social factors, key figures, ideas, theories, and institutions. In the early 1980s, two works were published on national anthropologies: a volume edited by Stanley Diamond (1980) that included chapters on Germany, the Soviet Union, the United States, Italy, and the Netherlands; and an article by Tomas Gerholm and Ulf Hannerz (1982) that dealt with the shaping of national anthropologists in Brazil, Poland, Sudan, Sweden, Canada, and India. These were followed by a series of publications on national anthropologies by anthropologists who had begun exploring this new area. A current representative of works surveying non-Eurocentric anthropologies is the book *Other People's Anthropologies* by Aleksander Bošković (2008).

For a national anthropology characterized by its circumscription within the boundaries of a state, the point of departure is the question of whether one can speak of the "national character" of a local anthropology. Cultural differences might produce differences between national anthropologies. For example, British empiricism as a national trait leads to functionalism; French rationalism leads to structuralism (Gerholm and Hannertz 1982); the structural origins of the survival of the functionalist paradigm in British anthropology arise from the hierarchical structure of the universities and of scientific communities (Boissevain 1974). At another level, political-sociocultural contexts affect the production and dissemination of anthropological knowledge. For example, the shift from cultural evolutionism to cultural relativism in the United States has been explained as a reaction to the events of World War II.

Broadly speaking, existing studies of national anthropologies mostly cover similar topics: the historical dimension of local anthropology alongside the contemporary issues on its agenda. These typically encompass the social and political context in which a national anthropology comes into being and is sustained; intellectual schools and traditions, genealogies, and the history of ideas; and center–periphery relations in the long-established and more recent national anthropologies.

As mentioned earlier, I am inclined to adopt the anthropological point of view for the study of the history of the discipline. Historians with differing emphases produce a complementary perspective. Among the historians, I have been inspired by the doyen of the field of history of anthropology, George Ward Stocking Jr., who contributed a wide range of studies from various points of view. These include the exploration of anthropological issues and studies of national (or regional) anthropologists, key figures, and their disciples. His work on Victorian anthropology (1987) and on British anthropology—*After Tylor* (1996)—bears special relevance to my approach. In contrast, there are the works of Marvin Harris (1968), Stanley Diamond (1980), and Alan Barnard (2000), which describe the development of local anthropologies through the prism of theoretical schools and analytical approaches. This epistemological approach, based on the history of ideas, will not be at the heart of the present book, and I leave it for future studies of the field.

National anthropologies do not exist in a vacuum. They involve active relationships with neighboring national anthropologies, as well as with the anthropological centers. In the Israeli case, the most significant ties have been to the Anglo-American center, not the neighboring anthropologies. Therefore, national anthropology may be examined with respect to the center–periphery model. This model was employed by the social sciences to explain a great many phenomena, including relations between various knowledge communities. Therefore, national anthropology may be examined with respect to the center–periphery model. It assumes hierarchical relationships between central and peripheral anthropologies, dependence of the peripheral on the center, and power relations. The nature of the relationship between peripheral and central anthropologies is influenced by international relations on the political-formal level and by international positions of academic communities on local conflicts, such as the boycott of Israeli academic activities due to its policies in the Israeli–Palestinian conflict. Brazilian anthropologist Roberto Cardoso de Oliviera (2000) enumerates a number of characteristics of peripheral anthropologies, some of which are also characteristic of Israeli anthropology: the focus on national territory, institutional weakness, dependency on foreign countries to advance professional training, lack of demand for anthropologists in the labor market, and the absence of nationally distributed scholarly journals in the local language (Cardoso de Oliviera 2000).[1]

Center–periphery relationships are chiefly based on differences in wealth between the center and periphery. By the nature of its definition, the influence of central anthropologies on local ones is crucial in defining the notion of "center–periphery" (Van Bremen 2005; Gerholm and Hannerz 1982; Gupta and Ferguson 1997). When peripheral anthropologies practice the discipline according to their own understanding, they are considered remote. When they adopt the rules of the game as it is played in the center, they are perceived by the center as imitators, and hence marginal. Bošković (2008) proposed an inverted gaze from the periphery to the center for describing national anthropologies, which he dubbed "other people's anthropologies."

A new way of thinking about links between different anthropologies is to adopt the globalization discourse proposed by Anna Tsing (2000). Labor markets, which are dependent on the global economy as well as large organizations (e.g., the American Anthropological Association [AAA]), affect the movement of people and of ideas from one country to another.

TWO

RESEARCH, TEACHING, *and* ACADEME *from the* MARGINS INWARD

An Emergent Discipline in an Emergent Society

In Israel, some small-scale anthropological research is carried out by government ministries. However, the principal anthropological activity in Israel is the research, teaching, and projects at Israel's five large universities: the Hebrew University of Jerusalem, Tel Aviv University, Haifa University, Ben Gurion University in the Negev, and Bar Ilan University. In addition to these universities, the map of anthropology in higher education includes academic institutions where anthropology courses are taught on a sporadic basis; however, the scale of this activity is minor, and those courses usually only service other central subjects taught at that institution. For example, teachers' colleges offer individual courses in anthropology within the programs in education and social science. However, in recent years, a network has developed, in which regional colleges (e.g., the Yezreel Valley College and the Kinneret and the Ashkelon colleges award undergraduate degrees in the liberal arts and multidisciplinary studies, which sometimes include courses in anthropology. Anthropological research in academic institutions outside the universities is also negligible, because the colleges are chiefly teaching institutions. However, the qualitative methods that have taken root as popular research methods in the past decade in the social sciences have beaten a path into the field of education. In the teachers' colleges, the number of studies carried out with qualitative and ethnographic methods is on the increase.

PERIODS OF DEVELOPMENT

The development of the discipline of anthropology in the areas of research and teaching will be described according to phases of historical periodization:

- Attempts to establish anthropology at the Hebrew University before the 1940s
- The period of anthropological activity that took place between the 1950s and the end of the 1960s (discussed in chapter 3), when anthropological activity outside the universities was held under the auspices of the Jewish Agency, government ministries, and Manchester University's "Bernstein Project"—a project that effectively trained the first generation of faculty anthropologists in Israel
- The period that began in the late 1960s, when anthropology was first founded and at various universities, and continued until the turn of the twenty-first century

POINTS OF VIEW ON THE DISCIPLINE

During the various periods surveyed here, I shall treat the field of academic anthropology from three points of view: (1) as an independent field in which are manifested micro-relations, interpersonal interactions and power struggles, the realization of interests, approaches and competing schools, as well as processes internal to the field; (2) as part of a broader sociocultural context, which also includes processes of institution building and self-definition, available models, collective identities, and social and cultural perceptions; and (3) via the relationships between processes in the centers of the academic world and processes within Israeli society.

I will focus on the five universities in which anthropology achieved most salience and will survey the discipline's development in each one from several points of view: processes of disciplinary development within and without the academy, the topics of research and teaching, organizational and institutional aspects of professional activity, and a general comparative view of the different universities.

It should be noted that the distinction between these aspects is merely an analytical one, as the separate treatment of each aspect allows us a systematic comparison. The advantage of treating the universities individually is that it allows one to trace internal processes within each institution and to see how these processes relate to contemporary Israeli society as well as to international anthropology. Although the academy may be viewed as an independent social field with its own circumscribed boundaries (Bourdieu 1984), it is also important to observe the context in which its activity takes place. Historical trends and processes in Israeli society and theoretical paradigm shifts in the anthropological world at large make their imprint on the sphere of academic anthropology and instigate significant change within it. The latter affect the contents of research and instruction, the scale of demand for anthropological studies, the choice of faculty and promotion patterns, the relationship between university research and external bodies that provide research budgets, budgetary research sources and their distribution, and the relationship between this sphere of activity and that of other spheres. Anthropological praxis within the universities also affects the Israeli anthropological association and is, in turn, affected by it. Another central topic, which dovetails with the previous topics—the professional careers and identities of anthropologists in Israel—is tied both to academic institutions and organizations, and to the Israel Anthropological Association, which is their professional organization.

SOURCES OF INFORMATION

This chapter is based on various sources. The search for anthropology's roots in the archives was not always a fruitful one.

At Bar Ilan University, due to its limited anthropological activity, I did not attempt to gain access to the archives.

The Hebrew University, as a pioneering and veteran institution, made available to me numerous documents, from which I learned a great deal about its history. (My work on history of anthropology at the Hebrew University before 1948, "Anthropology in Process: Hebrew University and the Human Science," appeared in the second volume of the published history of the Hebrew University [Abuhav 2005a].)

At the Tel Aviv University archives, I was allowed to examine a restricted number of files, but could not extract much information concerning the history of anthropology at that institution. It seems as though the discussions regarding the development of that area were not documented in the files to which I was given access, such as personal files or protocols of discussions in the social sciences faculty authorities. (Another explanation for the lack of documents on the topic may be that no formal discussions regarding a vision for developing the field had taken place, and the process transpired with little planning, as a response to immediate need. Yet another explanation may be that affairs were arranged amongst the anthropologists themselves in undocumented conversations.) Thus, my study of the history of anthropology at Tel Aviv University had to focus elsewhere. I held interviews with the founders of the department and with anthropologists who joined it later. Other sources of information I used are books and articles that chiefly describe the department's roots and the time of its establishment.

At Haifa University I was told that the archives were not open to researchers. Through the intervention of an anthropologist at that university, I was given access to the material, but was asked to submit my request and the list of files I was interested in to the Dean of the Social Sciences and the department chair.

At Ben Gurion University, I submitted a formal request to work in the archive, and was referred to one of the lecturers in behavioral sciences, who referred me further to the rector, and there I stopped.

Additional sources are personal interviews with anthropologists and university publications, especially yearbooks, autobiographical books and articles by Israeli anthropologists that are published occasionally, general surveys of Israeli anthropology, and issue-specific research papers that describe the development of research.

ANTHROPOLOGY AT THE HEBREW UNIVERSITY: COURTSHIP AND REJECTIONS

The historical encounter between the various versions of anthropology and the Hebrew University presents a long and complex story. This story begins with indifference and rejection during the first fifty years of institutional history, and ends with acceptance and flourishing in the following twenty-five years and until the present. One can identify two main phases in the development of anthropology at the Hebrew University:

PHASE 1	
1920s	Social and cultural research on Palestinians and a limited interest in the physical anthropology of the Jews
1930s–1940s	Social and cultural anthropology of the Jews
Early 1950s	The creation of a social science faculty, without anthropology

1960s	Limited interest; the mobilization of anthropology for nation building (settlements, absorption of immigrant); the beginnings of anthropological research in other universities in Israel
PHASE 2	
Early 1970s	Acceptance of anthropology into the department of sociology via Africanists; the absorption of immigrant anthropologists
Early 1980s	Stabilization and reduction; freezing of academic positions
Early 1990s	Growth; expansion of positions; expansion of research topics and number of students; equal status to sociology
Late 1990s	A diverse, central, recognized, and growing discipline
Late Twenty-First Century	Reduction and attrition

Attempts to Integrate Anthropology Before the Establishment of a Social Sciences Faculty

Anthropology's marginal status at the Hebrew University during its early years and the hardships of achieving recognition were a product of a number of factors. The leading factor was the multiple meanings of this discipline, and ambiguity regarding the boundaries of this field of knowledge. In Europe, which provided the model for shaping the fledgling Hebrew University, "anthropology" and "anthropologie" referred to aspects of anatomy and physiology, whereas "ethnology" and "ethnologie" referred to the study of cultural traits of ethnic groups.

During the 1930 and 40s, the term "anthropology" expanded to include the social and cultural dimensions of human life. In England, which was the main source of inspiration for Israeli anthropology in the 1960s, the term "social anthropology" was allocated to the sphere of social and cultural meaning, as distinct from physical anthropology. (By way of contrast, in the United States, the meaning of anthropology today is a multidisciplinary science that encompasses the social, cultural, physical, linguistic, and archeological fields.)

In the context of the Hebrew University, this ambiguity required that those who used the term "anthropology" clarify precisely what was intended. When the idea of promoting anthropology at the university arose, and the creation of an "anthropological institute" was proposed, the initiators had in mind the European sense of the concept: the study of the physical attributes of man. The development of anthropology at European universities to a great extent shaped the way in which the discipline was received at the Hebrew University. When anthropology was mentioned in discussions at the Zionist Congress during the university's early years, the possibility of joining or separating the biological and cultural aspects of the field was not explicitly addressed. During the 1930s and 1940s, the discussion of anthropology at the university adhered to the European sense—in other words, to the physical aspects only. Discussion of the sociocultural dimension was attached to the term "ethnology." The physical aspect, which was related to anatomy, is even today studied separately at the medical school, within the departments of anatomy. The range of meanings ascribed to the field in different periods created an obstacle to the reception of the field at the university.

Initiatives and Pioneers

As early as September 1925, at the meeting of the university's board of trustees in Munich, a proposal was presented to create an "anthropological institute." A similar idea—to establish a sociological and anthropological institute—was also proposed by the Sociological and Anthropological Association in Vienna in 1935. The proposal's initiator was most likely Arthur Ruppin, who later recommended the establishment of an institute for the study of sociology and anthropology of the Jews in Jerusalem, which, by conducting statistical and demographic research, would serve as the foundation of the Jewish social sciences. Ruppin's initiative was part of a far-ranging research effort to describe the unique physical characteristics of different Jewish groups and to compare them to each other and to non-Jewish groups. (For more on activities in the field of Jewish racial science, see Hart 2000).However, these initiatives went unheeded. A sociological and anthropological institute was never established, as it was argued that other projects should take priority.

In the mid-1930s, the Hebrew University's board of trustees appointed an external evaluation committee named the Hartog Committee, after its leader. Its findings were published in 1934 and included recommendations concerning anthropology.

> It has been suggested to us that the anthropology of the Jews should be studied in the University. It has for many years been the opinion of us . . . that there is no place so suitable for this study as Jerusalem. The opportunity is unique. Within an area of a few square miles there are to be found groups of almost every type of Jew known. Here, without expense of trouble, may be found Bokharian, Baghdadian, Yemenite, Sephardic, Ashkenasic, Karaitic and Caucasian Jews, amongst others, in such numbers as to make a survey of real statistical value. Moreover, in Palestine are to be found the allied racial groups, such as the Arabs and Samaritans, who not only themselves are worthy of study, but those relations to the Jewish groups are of utmost important. (Hartog Committee 1934, section 280, 86–87)

Several points about the committee's work should be noted: (1) The committee viewed anthropology as a field that was vital for both research and teaching. (2) The immediate task of research was to investigate the physical aspects of communities of Jews living in Jerusalem, the most diverse and fitting place for such research, in the committee's opinion. (3) The committee recommended that topics of concern to geneticists at the time should also be included.

Of the committee's recommendations, only one was implemented: the teaching of anthropology in Ruppin's lectures on the sociology of the Jews, within the Judaic Studies Institute (Ruppin 1934). Ruppin (1876–1943), who made his reputation chiefly as a Zionist leader and through his settlement activity in Palestine/Eretz Israel, also had an interest in the sociology and (physical) anthropology of the Jews. Ruppin's approach to the anthropology of the Jews integrates cultural, social, and biological aspects. It appears in retrospect to be odd, if not racist. It was wholly in keeping, however, with the scientific tradition of the "Jewish racial science" of those times. Those highly regarded studies were intensively pursued by Jewish physicians in Palestine and especially in Europe (Efron 1994). Ruppin was not content only with an armchair academic pursuit, but even sought, in the summer of 1936, to venture on an "anthropological study amongst the Jews of India and China"—an initiative that never came to fruition.

Despite the Hebrew University's official ignoring of anthropology, some limited, albeit academically valuable, social-anthropological activity took place in the field, the quality of which was only appreciated many years after its production (Rabinowitz 1998, 39–50; Zilberman 1991). The most outstanding of these studies was that of Hilma Granqvist (1890–1972), a Finnish anthropologist of Swedish origin. After completing her studies in the field of ethnology, she enrolled in "New Testament Studies" in Berlin, and traveled to Palestine in 1925 to study the life of women in the Biblical period. Granqvist belonged to a movement of Christian scholars who came to the region in the eighteenth through twentieth centuries for religious motives that harmonized well with scientific pursuits. They sought to discover in the life ways of contemporary Palestinians resemblances with the life ways of the early Christians, and assumed that the "unchanging Orient" had frozen in time and preserved life as it was lived two thousand years earlier. Granqvist stayed in the village of Artas near Bethlehem, from the middle of the 1920s and until the middle of the 1930s. Her fieldwork was inspired by her British anthropology instructors, Bronislaw Malinowski (1884–1942) and Raymond Firth (1902–2004), who had influenced her while she had stayed in England during the 1930s. True to the ways of her teachers, Granqvist wrote a richly detailed ethnography—her descriptions are extremely lively, although her theoretical insights are few.

Additional anthropological activity was conducted by Erich Brauer (1895–1942) in the field, outside of the university campus, although with the funding and support of the university. A native of Berlin, Brauer had earned his education in what was known as the "new ethnological science" in Berlin and at other German universities. His doctoral degree was awarded for a theoretical dissertation on the Herero tribe of South Africa (Brauer 1925). (For an extended discussion of Brauer, see Abuhav 2003, 2008.) In 1927, he arrived and settled in Jerusalem and began to conduct fieldwork in the Bukharian neighborhood, and then among the Jews of Yemen (in German) (Brauer 1934), and the Jews of Kurdistan (Brauer 1947 [Hebrew], 1993 [English]). His research was supported by a foundation for assistance to German refugees (until 1940), via the Hebrew University, but he was never awarded a teaching position there.

Brauer's work spanned diverse areas: he photographed and measured his research subjects, collected everyday artifacts and Judaica, described their daily life ways in their countries of origin in detail, and even drew their portraits and scenes of their everyday life in Israel. Brauer had been trained by the Kulturkreis school, which was based on Frobenius' notion of culture "circles." According to this theory, every geographical region had its appropriate cultural type, which both influenced and was influenced by neighboring cultural regions with which it came in contact. Brauer attempted to persuade the Hebrew University administrators of the need to study the ethnology of the Jews, and one of the memos he sent in 1938 contains his vision for establishing an ethnographic museum.[1] In a discussion held in 1939 by the university senate concerning Jewish ethnology and pre-history, it was stated that:

> The senate does not find it advisable that the research on the ethnology of the Jews of Orient or in pre-history should be terminated. As for Jewish ethnology, there is an urgent need to collect and preserve the ethnological lacunae that are slipping out of our hands . . . in respect to both cases, they are of importance due to being part of the *Eretzisraeli* science, and also as long as no other institution exist to take upon themselves the cultivation of this science it is the honorable duty of the university to sustain it under its auspices . . . if teaching in this area expands in the future in the direction of the study of contemporary Jewry, Jewish ethnology will have an important place in this framework.[2]

The committee's statement suggested that the "original" or "authentic" culture that Jewish groups brought from their countries of origin was disappearing in wake of their encounter with other groups and with a new reality; it pointed to an urgent need for "salvage research" in order to document the past and the present before the culture disappeared entirely.

In a eulogy for Erich Brauer, S. D. Goitein, one of the important Orientalists of the time, pointed to Brauer's failure at realizing his vision and noted that "because of the coincidence of various circumstances, Brauer was not always rewarded in the way that he deserved. But in appreciating his life's work today, we can affirm whole-heartedly the declaration that the deceased made two days before his passing—'I will be the ethnologist of the people of Israel—even if the people of Israel does not want it.'" Brauer was poised to have become a pioneer of holistic anthropology in the American tradition, which Israeli universities later made efforts to adopt.

The passing of both Brauer and Ruppin, within a brief time interval, left Raphael Patai (1910–1996) as the only acting ethnologist in the area. (For an expanded discussion of Patai, see Abuhav 2003, 2005c; Schrire 2010.)[3] A native of Budapest, Patai had been ordained there as a rabbi and also received his first doctoral degree in Semitic languages and literatures. After immigrating to Palestine, he was awarded a second doctoral degree from the Hebrew University for a comparative study of water in Jewish sources (Patai 1936). Patai published scores of articles, essays, and reviews in Hebrew, Hungarian, German, and English, in a variety of fields: Hebrew literature, folklore, the Bible, and Hebrew poetry. His chief interest was in the Jews of the Orient, and especially in the folklore of groups of Jews from Iran and Afghanistan, and he published several articles on this topic in journals and newspapers. After applying to the Hebrew University for the position of a folklore scholar, which was refused, he was awarded a number of research grants. But the major part of his research was financed from family funds.

In his attempts to convince the university administrators of the urgency of ethnological research of Jewish ethnic groups, Patai formulated his personal anthropological credo.[4] It expressed his aspiration that a monograph be written for each ethnic group in Israel, and that ethnology should describe the "material and spiritual culture and the social structure of the human group . . . the environment, and the history of the local Jewish settlement. Next, attention should be paid to the physical types of the ethnic group." Patai's chief contribution to the anthropology of the time was the establishment of the "Eretzisraeli Institute for Folklore and Ethnology" together with the second president of Israel, Yitzhak Ben Zvi, and a few known folklorists. The Institute published the journal *Edot*, which came out in the years 1944–1947, providing a platform for publications on folklore and anthropology, while also serving as a two-way mirror between the world of anthropology and Palestine. In addition, Patai wrote an introduction to anthropology in Hebrew (Patai 1947a) and edited Brauer's book on the Jews of Kurdistan, arranging to have it published posthumously in Hebrew (Brauer 1947) and in English in 1993.

At the end of 1946, Patai realized that the Hebrew University was planning to establish a faculty of social sciences. He identified the opportunity to integrate anthropology (or ethnology) in university teaching. His arguments in favor of anthropology stressed two elements: the first was that the research methods of anthropology were as legitimate as those of other research traditions in the social sciences, and the second was the possibility of creating a connection between anthropology and Judaism. It should be noted that it was precisely the two topics that Patai brought up—methodology, and the links to Judaism—which would later become a liability for anthropology at the university and give rise to controversy. Well before the institutionalization of academic anthropology in Israel, Patai (1946) proclaimed in a report about the local anthropological activity in the journal *American Anthropologist* that he had taken it upon himself to be the middleman between "the great world" and the periphery in Palestine. The report appeared in the middle of World War II as part of a series dealing with the state of anthropology worldwide; it surveyed research in the fields of cultural anthropology, physical anthropology, archeology, linguistics, and folklore. The article describes the activity of the Eretzisraeli Institute for Folklore and Ethnology that Patai had established two years earlier, as well as that of the Society for Palestinian Folklore and the Museum of Jewish Antiquities. Patai's review opened a window for communication between the local periphery and the anthropological center in America, by means of which he hoped to enlist support for the neglected anthropological activity.

Patai made a connection with the American anthropologist Melville Herskovits (1895–1963), one of Franz Boas' students, through which he was exposed to the theoretical influences of the Boasian school of American anthropology. Patai's links to American anthropology enabled his quick integration into America and the university career he developed there, after emigrating there at the end of the 1940s, following his failure to find a place for himself within Israeli anthropology and at the Hebrew University.

The university was then in contact with David Bidney, an anthropologist and philosopher of Jewish background who served as the secretary of the Viking Foundation, an anthropological charitable fund that later became the Wenner-Gren foundation. The university submitted a request—which was rejected—for funds to establish a chair in general and in Jewish anthropology and for the ongoing funding of research on the topic. This led to a discussion among the university's highest authorities. Martin Buber supported the proposal and suggested that the chair be devoted to the research and teaching on "the ethnology of Oriental Jews and the ethnology of Near Eastern people."[5] S. D. Goitein challenged this view, alluding to the problems concerning the boundaries of the discipline:

> "the science of man" in the broad sense of the term, which includes its languages, cultures, economic and social transformations—it is difficult to view this as a scientific discipline, because it in fact includes all the branches of the humanities. Therefore, my suggestion is that the proposal to establish a chair for anthropology at the Hebrew University will clearly define the compass of the profession, with attention to what is available and desirable at our [institution].[6]

In light of the university leadership's statement in the 1930s and 1940s, its reservations about housing the disciplines of anthropology and ethnology are clear. Moreover, even if the attitude to anthropology at the Hebrew University had been more favorable, it would have been difficult to incorporate it into the university from an organizational standpoint. The institutions and departments that might have potentially incorporated anthropology were the institute for the Study of Oriental Jewish Communities in the Middle East, the Institute for Judaic Studies, and the Institute for Oriental Studies.

Yitzhak Ben Zvi (1884–1963) served as the director of the Study of Oriental Jewish Communities in the Middle East from the time of its establishment until he took the office of the State presidency in 1952. Ben Zvi was interested in the Jewish communities in the Palestine and in the Ottoman Empire,[7] and he investigated these groups' connections to the Jewish settlement in Palestine and to Zionism. He and his colleagues were interested in and focused chiefly on history, documents, and texts from the Jewish Oriental communities, but not on anthropology.

At the Institute for Judaic Studies, the incorporation of anthropology was even more problematic. The connection between Judaism and anthropology was a complex one, even at other academic centers around the world. Scholars such as Goldberg (1995, 2002) have offered a number of explanations for the disconnect between anthropology and Judaism, as well as for anthropology's hesitancy with respect to the study of Jewish folklore. (1) Anthropology began as a research field that was focused on the biological and physical traits of mankind; in respect to Judaism, its main concern was with the question of the very existence of the "Jewish race" and the physical characteristics of Jewish groups, and it ignored the cultural achievements and the sociocultural aspect that is at the center of the field of Judaic studies. (2) The main anthropological schools that dominated anthropology from the 1930s through the 1950s limited the analysis of social phenomena to the ethnographic presence, and their ahistorical perspective was anathema to the analytical spirit of Judaic studies. (3) Because of the linking between anthropology (the study of the "primitive") and Biblical and Judaic studies, there was resistance to the use of anthropological concepts in a Jewish context. (4) Those who were concerned with Jewish studies recoiled from what were perceived as the "lower" elements of daily human life: dress, food, dwelling, and even legends and folktales (Katz 1998). Similarly, in the essay arguing for the rejection of the field of Jewish folklore (Ben-Amos 1990), three aspects were delineated: the historical, the social, and the methodological. The German school that dominated Judaic studies ignored the importance of the social aspect of Judaism and believed that the contemporary study of Jewish groups could not aid the understanding of Judaism, because Jews who were influenced by the culture of their non-Jewish neighbors had distanced themselves from authentic Judaism. German folklore scholars saw Judaic studies as a means for integrating Jews into German society, as opposed to the familiar use of folklore as a tool for strengthening a unique national identity. Folklore as a comparative science did not limit itself only to the use of Jewish sources; on the contrary, it presented Judaism as one of several possible cultural models that shaped the patterns of behavior and thought of the Jews. As opposed to the stance of the Judaic scholars, the pioneers of anthropology in Palestine/Eretz Israel made the case that it was important to collect Jewish quotidian artifacts and not just ritual Judaic objects.

The Institute for Oriental Studies did not include an ethnological specialization. Although the pioneers of ethnography mentioned previously—Brauer and Patai—had been trained in Europe in the discipline of Oriental studies, their actual engagement in research on Jewish groups, and especially contemporary ones, prevented any association with this institute. As a research institute with a regional focus, its members were chiefly concerned with historical and linguistic studies. And, as within Judaic studies, texts took priority over the lives of the people who created them.

My research indicates that the institutes at the Hebrew University with the potential for the incorporation of anthropology—the Institutes of Oriental Studies, Judaic Studies, and the Study of Jewish Communities of the Middle East refused to serve as a host for the discipline of anthropology. The other possible site for anthropology to inhabit might have been the faculty of social science; however, here too, anthropology was not received as a guest of honor initially and was forced to wait on the sidelines for some twenty years before the discipline's name was paired with sociology in the department's title.

Anthropology in the Faculty of Social Sciences

In 1950, the time became ripe for the Hebrew University's leadership to directly discuss the issue of anthropology. This discussion brought up the need to recruit anthropologists from abroad, due to the scarcity of local anthropologists. One potential source was from America. (The university's contacts with American anthropologists, it should be noted, began as early as 1928, when Paul Radin [1883–1959] was interested in developing the topic of the "sociology of the Jews and Arab" at the Hebrew University. But, for lack of budgetary sources, the proposal was rejected.) Another target for potential recruitment were Jewish anthropologists of South African origin who had immigrated to England and helped establish anthropology there. The links between South African Jewry and Israeli anthropology is longstanding, meaningful, and variegated—a chapter of Israeli anthropology yet to be written. Among the South Africans in England of interest were Hilda Kuper (1911–1992), Max Gluckman (1911–1975), and Meyer Fortes (1906–1983). Fortes' name had come up as a possible candidate at Tel Aviv University, and he even contributed the article on the development of social anthropology for the Encyclopedia Hebraica (Fortes 1968). In addition, when Brauer had become discouraged from his attempts to establish an ethnology chair in 1940, he approached S. Z. Schocken and asked him, when traveling abroad in the United States, to make contact "with Prof. Franz Boas, to tell him about my work in the field of Jewish ethnology via the university . . . I think Prof. Boas understands the importance of these researches, and also knows that not many people can yet appreciate their importance. That is the fate of every new science."[8] The idea remained a virtual one, and had no practical outcomes.

When, at the end of 1950s, the university discussed the place of anthropology, the importance of employing an anthropologist was justified in reference to the mass immigration, which provided "a non-recurring opportunity to research the ethnography and anthropometry of the different groups, and the changes caused by the contact between them in our state."[9] Following this discussion, it was recommended that the teaching of anthropology be instituted in the department of sociology, within the newly established social sciences faculty, and the search for a suitable candidate began. The preference was for a scholar who would lecture both on physical and social anthropology, but when it became clear that it would be difficult to identify a multidisciplinary candidate, the search focused on a social anthropologist. The idea came up to invite Robert Redfield (1897–1958), the head of the anthropology department at the University of Chicago, for a limited time. Redfield was described as "a Christian, a man of excellence who is interested in Israel . . . and if we succeed in winning his heart—he can bring us much benefit and arouse others as well."[10] Two years later, the candidacy of Mark Zborowski (1908–1990) was considered. Zborowski was a member of the interdisciplinary team headed by Margaret Mead (Mead and Metraux 1953), in the context of which he had created a reconstruction of life in the Jewish European shtetl (Zborowski and Herzog 1952). Despite concern that it would be difficult to recruit candidates due to the security situation and economic circumstances, the faculty of the social sciences demanded the employment of anthropologists specializing in social anthropology so that they could both assist the absorption of the mass immigration and devote themselves to the study of the Jewish immigrant groups as a rich research field. At the same time, the faculty heads believed that it was necessary to deal with the "anthropometrics"—the discipline of anthropological physical measurements, which at that time was thought of as a line of inquiry parallel to social anthropology. The formulation of this policy would have provided employment for many anthropologists with diverse research interests. But, as we shall see shortly, a variety of factors delayed the incorporation of anthropology until the 1970s.

The dynamics within the department of sociology had a crucial influence on the development of anthropology, its location, and marginality. Outstanding disciples of Martin Buber (head of the sociology department) included Yonina Talmon-Gerber, for whom anthropology was not a foreign notion (whose influence, however, was limited), and S. N. Eisenstadt, who then served as department chair. For many years, Eisenstadt had voiced his opposition to integrating anthropology into the department, and some view him as the chief obstacle in this respect. Eisenstadt chose to respond to the university's anthropological initiative in an article published in a scholarly journal (Eisenstadt 1949), a strategy that served him again some fifteen years later, when he published an additional article on the topic. His chief argument was to cast doubt on anthropology's right to exist as separate from sociology, in the context of the social sciences. To his thinking, the only justification for researching peoples considered primitive was for the use of comparison (in sociological terms) to European and American culture and society. An attempt to counter Eisenstadt's view, also in a scientific journal, was made by the anthropologist Dorothy Willner (1956) in *Megamot*. Willner, who was employed during the 1950s in the Jewish Agency Settlement Department and conducted research on immigrant moshavim, presented the discipline as well as its possible contribution to solving the problems of absorbing immigrants. At any rate, when such was the perspective of the dominant department chair, the chances that anthropology would grow or develop as an independent field were slim. In another article, published in 1964, Eisenstadt (1964) weighed in against the uniqueness of social anthropology as a separate discipline and pointed to the difficulties that anthropologists encounter in their attempts to explain the social distribution of labor or in analyzing social change. In his view, anthropology's *raison d'etre* could only be in its service to sociological theory, and, therefore, it should not be allocated a domain separate from sociology, but should continue to be kept under the wing of sociology. (The publication of a journal article as a tactic for debating with colleagues is not unknown to Israeli anthropology. Topel [1996] has shown how Israeli anthropologists used scientific journals as an arena for ideological and political struggles in the context of Israeli anthropology.)

The Search for Anthropological Candidates

The search began for a candidate who would be able to teach physical, social, and culture anthropology together. In 1954 a suitable candidate seemed to have been found—the scholar Henry (Yehezkel) Sonnabend (1901–1956), who was born in Germany and specialized in sociology and demography. After his studies in Italy, he immigrated to South Africa, where he taught sociology and conducted field research in the subjects of education, demography, urban planning, social services (chiefly in relation to black populations), and also on the topic of "race relations." He immigrated to Israel in 1952, and settled in Ashkelon, where he also held office as mayor and volunteered to teach courses in ethnography and anthropometrics at the university for symbolic pay. However, before he was able to carry out his plans, he died unexpectedly and the window of opportunity for instituting a multidisciplinary anthropology was closed once again.

Another opportunity for anthropological development—in a different direction—arose in the 1960s, following the strengthening of ties between Israel and France. This "francophone turn" occurred as a result of the convergence of local and international circumstances. The military and political ties between Israel and the French government became closer. Israeli experts were sent to Africa as part of an Israeli foreign aid program directed at former French colonies. Finally, a factor that has not been sufficiently emphasized came into play: the mass immigration of North African Jews under French rule, and their exposure to French culture. In 1960, the university established the Institute of Asian and African Studies, which offered regional courses on developing countries. The institute's program stated clearly that the emphasis would not be on the study of language and culture, but rather on anthropology, modern history, and problems of modernization. To actualize the plans, the university approached the French government and the university's Friends Association in Paris to help establish a chair in social anthropology at the Hebrew University (which was to be named after Marcel Mauss). In justifying the request, an emphasis was placed on the large proportion of North

African immigrants who lived under French occupation and who had brought with them an important cultural heritage. The letter stressed the importance of conducting anthropological research among them. Simultaneously, the significance of understanding the peoples and cultures of Africa was emphasized.[11] In response, the name of a Protestant French minister was raised—Father Louis Molet, who had focused on Biblical studies as a graduate student at the Sorbonne and had spent a number of years in Madagascar as a missionary, where he had carried out ethnographic research. However, this proposal was never followed through. The tendency to connect with French anthropology might have opened up a new international orientation for Israeli anthropology, both from the perspective of the researchers' identity and from the perspective of the Asian and African fields of study.

In the 1950s and the beginning of the 1960s, there were many failed attempts by the Hebrew University to integrate lecturers in anthropology; among them Henry Rosenfeld (1925–2007), who later founded anthropology at Haifa University, and Alex Weingrod, later among the founding faculty of anthropology at Ben Gurion University. At the university's board meetings, the name of Max Gluckman was brought up. Gluckman was already then a well-known figure in British anthropology. During his visits to Jerusalem in 1959 and 1963, the Hebrew University met with him to discuss joining the university. Speculations about the reasons why Gluckman was not invited to hold a position in the department were offered by local sociologists and anthropologists. According to them, it was difficult for Eisenstadt to share control of the department with someone of Gluckman's charisma and power; in addition, there were monetary disputes between Gluckman and the university about the conditions of his employment. According to Don Handelman, when Eisenstadt was asked when there would be a department of anthropology at the Hebrew University, he replied: "When Claude Lévi-Strauss immigrates to Israel."

This period of time could have been a breakthrough era for Israeli anthropology due to the interest in the research arenas of the kibbutzim and moshavim in those decades. But when the Hebrew University's search for an anthropologist who would suit the multidisciplinary model—whose professional skill set included the physical, cultural, and social fields of anthropology—failed, and such a candidate could not be found, the university abandoned its efforts to promote anthropology in any form. The window of opportunity that the kibbutzim research projects might have afforded was closed.

FOREIGN FIELDS AND IMMIGRANTS: ANTHROPOLOGICAL ACTIVITY OUTSIDE THE ACADEMY

Between 1948 and the end of the 1960, anthropological activity within Israeli academia existed on a very small scale—the field was kept afloat by a handful of anthropologists outside the academy. Activity outside the university setting took place in the following arenas: the Center for Anthropological Research, the Ministry of Health, the Jewish Agency Settlement Department, kibbutzim research projects, and the Bernstein Project.

Center for Anthropological Research

The Center for Anthropological Research, during the years in which it was active (1956–1964), was the principal extra-academic framework of activity for anthropologists in the country at the time. Henry Rosenfeld, the center's founder and director, received assistance from a foundation that obtained its funding from Vera Rubin, an American anthropologist and a former colleague of his from their student days together at Columbia University. A small and intimate group of anthropologists who were in the country at the time formed around this center, and its activity was mainly research oriented.[12]

At the Center for Anthropological Research, anthropologists and folklorists could find partners for discussion of professional matters, at a time when they felt alienated and misunderstood by the academic establishment. The center's founders modeled it on the vision of an extra-academic research institute, which together with other extra-academic institutions such as museums or applied anthropological projects, would coexist with the universities and colleges, without depending on them financially, and would constitute an alternative field of activity to the academy.

After eight years of research and professional activity, the center's activity ceased in 1964 due to the dispersal of its members. A number of the members left and went overseas, and others changed their career paths.

Phyllis Palgi at the Ministry of Health

Anthropologists would have been likely candidates for incorporation into government ministries, in order to implement their specialized knowledge. In Israel, however, they had no significant presence in public institutions. One exception was Phyllis Palgi, who was active for some 40 years in the field of health and mental health. Palgi was born in South Africa in the mid-1920s and came to Israel at the end of the 1940s. Appointed as an anthropologist in the department of mental health in the Ministry of Health in 1953, she was the first, and for many years the only, anthropologist who was recruited to assist in the needs of the day: the austerity policy, cultural diversity, and the various problems created by immigration that required solutions in the fields of medical and nursing systems. In order to overcome resistance to anthropology and its goals within the government administration, which was based on the view that a focus on ethnic differences would encourage stigmatization and derail integration efforts, Palgi drew on Margaret Mead, the most famous American anthropologist of her time. She had developed a close personal relationship with Mead during her times as a student. Palgi invited her mentor in 1956 to a professional visit in Israel, which included meetings with ministers, decision makers, policymakers, medical staff, and local government leaders (Mead 1956, 1960). Among others, Mead met with Labor Minister Golda Meir and with Education Minister Zalman Aran, with whom an acerbic exchange took place (Palgi, pers. interview). Mead made it clear that a brief three-week visit was not enough to collect deep and thorough knowledge; however, she recommended to the Ministry of Health that an anthropologist be appointed as part of the decision-making team, and that anthropologists and experienced fieldworkers be included as part of the ministry's various activities. According to Mead, the role of the applied anthropologist in situations of rapid and directed change was not only to provide knowledge about the present situation, but also to make a commitment to adopt an active role in every change that comes about.

Had Mead's recommendations been accepted in the 1950s, there would have been no shortage of employment for anthropologists in government ministries; however, that was not how things turned out. Mead's recommendations probably disappointed those who had invited her, especially her critique of the governmental ministries' basic policies, even if her words came sugarcoated as encouragement. In an evaluation of Mead's visit, Lev and Cohen suggest that decision makers were impervious to her recommendations because they were captive to "Israel-centric" ideology and thinking. "The story of Mead's visits—apart from its being a constitutive moment in the history of the racialization of public discourse in Israel—was not a remedial moment, but remained a mutation that neither reached fruition nor motivated [what might have been] an important development movement in the history of the relationship between the Israeli political establishment and practitioners of anthropology" (Lev and Cohen 2010, 238).

The Jewish Agency Settlement Department (JASD) and Moshavim Study

The Jewish Agency was the organizational framework that financed and planned the settlement of the thousands of immigrants who arrived in Israel during the first decade of the state's existence. The Jewish Agency took responsibility for transporting the immigrants into the country and for settling them in new settlements throughout Israel; this activity was accompanied by the Center for Social Research in the Settlement Department, whose job was to advise the policymakers in the organization. The research center played a key role in social research during that period and in anthropology's contribution to the shaping of this research. The first directors of the center were the anthropologists Dorothy Willner and Alex Weingrod. The research team included sociologists, who in practice carried out anthropological field research (and some of whom were later accredited as anthropologists). In fact, the center served as an incubator for the future development of anthropology. The information about the anthropological activity in the Jewish Agency Settlement Department is based on interviews I conducted with anthropologists who then worked within this framework, and a few written sources (Shapira 1972; Schwartz 1995; Gluckman 1971).

In 1955, American anthropologist Dorothy Willner was appointed as director of the Center. Willner had been trained in Chicago, where the tradition of community research had developed under the leadership of anthropologists such as Robert Redfield (e.g., Redfield 1955)—a tradition well suited to the perception of the moshav or kibbutz as a small community. In the JASD, researchers were expected to contribute anthropological insights about the immigrant moshavim, their social and economic problems, and their contact with Israeli bureaucracy and with the Jewish Agency's counselors. (Willner 1969). Although her work earned the respect of anthropologists and sociologists, she resigned from the position after a number of years and left the country, and Alex Weingrod was appointed as her replacement in 1959. Weingrod had also been trained by the Chicago School and had conducted his own field research at a moshav in the Negev, which had been settled with Moroccan immigrants. His book on this moshav (Weingrod 1966) pointed to processes of change that had taken place and was concerned with the interaction between the residents and the settling agencies. The sociologists who worked in the department did not accompany the process of settling the moshavim from the outset, but only after the moshavim had been "implanted in their soil," whereupon they were called in to find out why the "seedling had not taken root properly." (The metaphor is borrowed from Weingrod's work, in which he makes use of the image of "implanted settlements.") According to Moshe Shokeid's testimony, for example: "My specific work led me to [the moshav] Nevatim . . . the regional counselor invited me to join him on a visit, complained to me about the processes of social deterioration, reduction of agricultural activity, and desertion" (Shokeid 2002, 52). Of another moshav, which was "populated by former residents of the Atlas Mountains: I was asked by the regional direction to look into why the settlers in this village are constantly in a state of dispute, and refuse to receive their farms" (Shokeid 2002, 35). Like many of his colleagues on the team of sociologists, after having fulfilled this role for a number of years, Shokeid left to pursue his doctorate in anthropology in Manchester, England.

The product of each researcher's field research was a report submitted to the JASD. What effect did the research reports written by sociologist-anthropologists have on Jewish Agency policies? According to Weingrod, the goals of the researchers did not conform to the goals of their directors. The researchers strived to develop academic theorizations, to go beyond the mundane problem-solving requirements, and to point to the social and cultural issues arising from the field. However, the directors at the JASD used the reports for implementing ad-hominem changes and for achieving internal political and extra-organizational goals. Yet the reports had some value in terms of operational decisions—for example, in regards to the dilemma concerning the policy of marketing agricultural produce. In light of the report, a reform was instituted that enabled a measure of private (rather than collective) marketing. Shlomo Deshen, a regional sociologist in the southern part of the country, sharply criticized the agency's bureaucracy: "The bureaucrats at the Jewish Agency did not read the reports and therefore did not expel the sociologists from their work roles." Deshen had a clear sense that he was expected to serve the interests of the agency. But, in practice, the problems that required solutions were, in his words, "all nonsense": "When I came to moshav Berekhiya because of the issue of organized marketing, I found that the moshav had rebelled against the agency. All of its members were working as employees in Ashkelon. I could look at what truly interested me, because the agency clerks were not interested in what I wrote."

Shokeid made a distinction between the contributions of the sociologists versus those of the anthropologists in the Jewish Agency Settlement Department. The anthropologists' point of departure was sympathy for and curiosity about cultural diversity, and they regarded the honoring of the immigrants' cultural tradition as an important task, but the public mood was not receptive to this attitude. According to Weingrod, "We were young and full of enthusiasm; we saw this work as a challenge of participating in an historical moment. We could develop a new and non-institutionalized anthropology, we were involved with the issues, and we could bring our realistic voices to what was happening on the ground." Of the meetings of the department's directorship, he said, "I felt as though I were representing the settlers." In analyzing the roles of the anthropologists compared to those of the sociologists, Schwartz claimed that the anthropologists protested against the accepted stereotypes about Mizrahi Jews and pointed out the rational elements of their behavior and their processes of decision making. The unique contribution of the anthropologists, he argued, was their ability to point to the lack of fit between the organizational structure of the moshav and the cultural background of the immigrants. The anthropological approach to understanding the moshav as a social system was humanistic and yet realistic: humanistic because it distanced itself from the bureaucracy's condescending attitude. The clerks, although they were sincerely interested in the condition and economic needs of the settlers and worked for their welfare, classified, categorized them, and labeled them as "human material." The bureaucracy's goal was to see how quickly the immigrants could fit in, modernize, and adapt to moshav life. Their attitude was realistic, because they identified the political, symbolic, and economic interests within the moshav, and tempered the ideological enthusiasm of those who attempted to create an instant melting pot. These claims, as voiced by a sociologist, were challenged later by academic and public discourses about the research on the immigrants from Middle Eastern countries.

The aforementioned research studies were carried out within a joint, designated framework co-created by the academy and the JASD, which included a joint seminar in which JASD sociologists and university faculty with an interest in the subject could participate. Within the department of sociology at the Hebrew University, there developed a specialization in the study of moshavim, which attempted to translate the theoretical framework developed by S. N. Eisenstadt for the analysis of absorption processes, into what they called "rural sociology" (Eisenstadt 1954). The Israeli case was of interest to the international sociological community, by virtue of Israel's being in the process of institution building, and because the country was perceived as a laboratory or a model for the problems of Third World countries. The

UN (UNESCO) and the U.S. Department of Agriculture provided part of the funding for these studies. Because the moshavim were cohesive communities of immigrants, a pattern that was perceived as structurally analogous to peasant/rural societies around the world, they could have become classical anthropological field sites. However, this opportunity was never realized, among other things, due to Eisenstadt's resistance, as leader of the department of sociology at the Hebrew University, to the disciplinary premises of anthropology. Moreover, the practical translation of theories of modernization and development, which were the guideline for the study of the moshavim (and for the study of absorption issues in the development towns), did not suit the realities in the field.

Moreover, the sociologists who went into the field clearly believed that the situation *was* amenable to an holistic approach, the hallmark of anthropological research. The informal ties between the researchers and the settlers, and the researchers' participation in the private and public events in moshav life, were characteristic of the kinds of relationships anthropologists routinely develop in a classic field situation. In most cases, the researchers were aware of the tension between the commissioning party (the JASD), which had presented them with a problem to be solved, and their own commitment to scientific autonomy, which should guarantee the researcher a free choice of research focus. These are some of the various aspects of the discussion about the complex relations between anthropological research and scientific activity that took place at the JASD in the early 1960s.

Study of the Kibbutzim by Non-Israeli Researchers

The kibbutzim, "a social experiment that has not yet failed," as Buber described them, were a drawing point for researchers from around the world and from many different disciplines. They were also perceived as a prototype of a community that could be conveniently investigated with anthropological concepts, for they were small communities, with defined boundaries (or so they were imagined), characterized by collectivism and social cohesiveness, and also amenable to intensive anthropological fieldwork. This being the case, a study comparing kibbutzim with communities sharing some of these characteristics—in tribal or industrial societies—could be undertaken.

The kibbutz, therefore, drew anthropologists who were interested in this form of settlement both as researchers and as members. From the 1930s onward, this settlement form was studied by sociologists (e.g., Landshut

1944). Stanley Diamond, for example, visited Israel in 1951–1953 and carried out fieldwork at Kibbutz Kiryat Anavim. Diamond (1922–1991) had trained at Columbia University together with the Israeli anthropologist Henry Rosenfeld, with whom he came to Israel for both professional and ideological motivations. Diamond's study had an impact chiefly because of the comparison he carried out between the kibbutz and the Eastern European shtetl (Diamond 1957). Another American anthropologist who studied the kibbutz was Melford Spiro (b. 1920). His research on the Beit-Alfa kibbutz in the mid-1950s—carried out jointly with his wife Audrey, a psychologist—engendered a book that became a canonical monograph of the kibbutz (Spiro 1963, 1972). His observations of family sleeping arrangements, socialization, marriage ties between peer age groups, and other topics challenged some of the basic taken-for-granted assumptions about the universality of the family and its role as an agent of socialization. A number of anthropologists of Jewish American origin, who viewed the kibbutz as a Zionist, pioneering social experiment, were attracted to experience it while simultaneously researching it, based on the socialist liberal traditions that attracted young Jewish intellectuals during the Cold War period. According to Schwartz, kibbutz society in particular and Zionist society in general were perceived as the antithesis of their societies of origin (Schwartz 1995, 20).

Study of the Kibbutz by University Researchers

In the mid-1960s, the kibbutz topic drew widespread interest, and a team of researchers at the Hebrew University came together under the direction of Yoninah Talmon-Gerber (1970). The members of this team eventually became the leading anthropologists in Israel's universities. The chief contribution to the study of the kibbutz by anthropologists and sociologist at that time was in removing the veil of idealism from it and investigating what was going on under the mantle of ideology—for example, by underscoring inequality, stratification, or the importance of family loyalties over and against the collective. Later, the kibbutz was also studied by anthropologists who were kibbutz members: Joseph Shepher (Shepher and Tiger 1975), Israel Shepher (1983), Gideon Kressel (1974, 1983), and Reuven Shapira (1990).

A comparative survey of settlement patterns in Israel, which was carried out by anthropologists Don Handelman and Shlomo Deshen (Handelman and Deshen 1975; Handelman 1975), identified a number of characteristic focal points of tension in the kibbutz. These tensions included the conflict between the values the founders were raised on (in the Eastern European shtetl) and kibbutz values, pioneering versus parasitism, equality versus hierarchy, and modesty and thriftiness versus bourgeois values.

The Bernstein Project: Max Gluckman and Manchester University

The thrust to establish Israeli anthropology received a shot in the arm from the Jewish British Lord Sidney Bernstein (1899–1993), who for Zionist motivations created the most significant anthropological project in the country, under the title "The Bernstein Project."[13] Bernstein, a Jewish magnate who owned the popular television channel "Granada," had a special connection to anthropology and Israel. Based on the popularity of social anthropology in Britain, he believed that anthropological studies of social processes taking place in Israel could assist the young state. Bernstein funded ten anthropological doctoral research projects, on various topics, to be conducted in Israel.

For academic sponsorship and oversight, Bernstein chose Max Gluckman (1911–1975), the head of the anthropology department at Manchester University. Gluckman had been born into a well-known Zionist family in South Africa, where he had studied anthropology. He later immigrated to England and contributed greatly to British anthropology. As a theoretical innovator, and as part of his critique of the classic functionalist-structuralist approach in British social anthropology, he enriched theory by introducing dimensions of conflict and change into it. Together with other colleagues at Manchester he founded the "Manchester School," whose influence reached several corners of the world—for example, the Rhodes-Livingstone research institute (RLI) that he founded in Zimbabwe, which focused on the research of central African societies (Schumaker 2001; Handelman and Evens 2006).

As head of the project in Israel, Gluckman appointed Emanuel Marx, who had established anthropology at the new department of sociology and anthropology at Tel Aviv University. The participants in the project, some from Israel and some from the United States, underwent a training period at Manchester and then conducted their fieldwork in Israel.

The goals of the project were diverse: comparative studies of family and kinship in different ethnic groups, community studies focused on issues of political organization and leadership, studies of inter-group relations between different ethnic groups in urban and industrial contexts, and studies of the historical nature of the old Jewish communities and non-Jewish communities, with an eye on processes of change (Marx 1975).

The ten doctoral dissertations produced in the first stage of the Bernstein Project were all developed into book publications: Jay Abarbanel wrote about collective farming and the nation state (Abarbanel 1972), Myron Aronoff wrote about the new "border city" (Aronoff 1974), Elaine Baldwin researched differentiation and collectivism in a veteran moshav (Baldwin 1972), Shlomo Deshen wrote about immigrant voters in Israel (Deshen 1970), Terry Evens focused on democracy on the kibbutz and intergenerational tensions (Evens 1995), Don Handelman wrote about work and play among the elderly at a handicraft workshop (Yad LaKashish) in Jerusalem (Handelman 1977), Leonard Mars examined a moshav (Mars 1980); Emanuel Marx wrote about the social context of violence (Marx 1976), Moshe Shokeid analyzed the double heritage in a moshav of Moroccan immigrants (Shokeid 1971a), and Israel Shepher wrote an anthropological study of a kibbutz (Shepher 1983).

During the project's second phase, several more studies, such as those on the Ashdod port, the regional council in the Sharon province, and on Mapai (The Israel Workers' Party), were undertaken.

At Tel Aviv University, Emanuel Marx organized a seminar that accompanied the researchers as they deliberated about their topics, and provided them with an innovative and challenging theoretical framework. Gluckman, who pioneered the study of social change in Africa, especially in urban and industrial contexts, proposed that in Israel the same sort of questions be posed as those asked about African societies. He sought to understand the ways in which the behavior of immigrants from different groups changed after they were absorbed into their new environment. However, the project participants were not directed to focus only on immigrant communities; in fact, research was also conducted on some veteran communities of Israel. The formulation of research questions dictated the nature of the research fields, which, it was decided, were all to be small communities or small organizations.

Shokeid, a member of this group of researchers, characterized the theoretical basis upon which the studies were conducted as an "extended case study" focused on a chain of events, from which one was to derive an insight that was distinctively different from the immediate interpretation of each separate event. Scholars using this theoretical school, claimed Shokeid, were adept at developing sensitivity to the cultural world and everyday life of their research subjects, most of whom came from Muslim countries. This method enabled anthropologists to recognize the point of view of the immigrants' pain and their adaptation to a new reality, as opposed to the institutional sociologists, who were interested in the woes of Western bureaucracy (Shokeid 2002).

The Bernstein Project was perceived by those who participated in it as the antithesis of the Hebrew University studies on the immigrant moshavim, and as an alternative to the research model shaped by the theory and methodology practiced at the Hebrew University's department of sociology. The project aimed to describe Israeli society from a close vantage point. A series of localized studies were meant to provide a portrait that was as close as possible to existential reality—as opposed to the portrait figured through the classic sociological studies at the Hebrew University's sociology department, which was captive to "Parsonian functionalism" (Shokeid 2003, 72–73).

The chief contribution of the Bernstein Project was, therefore, through its exposure of new research paradigms and strategies, accompanied by a revolutionary spirit and dedication to the cause. This direction of development was in tune with new trends in world centers of anthropology—the engagement with theories of conflict on the one hand, and the ethno-methodological and phenomenological directions on the other. Thanks to Gluckman's efforts and reputation, Israeli anthropology received international recognition and was no longer just a passive object of field research for foreign anthropologists. The monographs produced in wake of the Bernstein studies became an anthropological and literary memento of Israel at the end of the 1960s and the early 1970s. Articles by the project's participants were published in a collected volume (Marx 1980b). However, the ambitious goal of providing an overall view of Israeli society by putting together a kaleidoscopic view taken from narrow angles and sections turned out to be problematic because of the difficulty of drawing a coherent portrait of Israeli society. Instead, Marx proposed that the state be seen as collection of multiple entities with a variety of interrelationships.

Some of the participants in the project created the infrastructure for establishing anthropology at Israeli universities, while others stayed in Israel for a limited time and then returned to their homelands abroad. The Hebrew University faculty was joined by two Africanists anthropologists, Uri Almagor and Yitzhak Eilam, who were Manchester graduates—but not participants in the Bernstein Project—and were also influenced by Gluckman and his school.

Shokeid has summarized Gluckman's contribution to Israeli anthropology in one brief statement: "For all practical reasons Israeli Anthropology was founded through Max [Gluckman]")Shokeid 1992, 237). Max Gluckman passed away in 1975 while on Sabbatical in Jerusalem.

ANTHROPOLOGY AT THE UNIVERSITIES AFTER THE MID-1960S: A LEGITIMATE PAIRING

The developments of anthropology that occurred outside the universities led to the marriage of the problematic discipline and the academic establishment.[14] Anthropology was accepted into the universities and developed its own special color and character at each institution. Where did the merging actually occur? What was this marriage like? Who preserved the relationship, and who attempted to hamper it? Were there better alternatives? These questions will be discussed next, describing the situation at each university separately. Although the Hebrew University was the last institution to recognize the legitimacy of anthropology, I present it first, because of its primogeniture on the map of Israeli academia.

The Hebrew University: The Departments of Sociology and Social Anthropology

At the Hebrew University, anthropology cleared the last obstacle of resistance within Israeli academia: In 1971, the department of sociology presented, at the university senate, a proposal to include the study of anthropology and to open a program in social anthropology.

The transformation of the university's attitude toward anthropology can be attributed to a number of factors—both intra- and extra-institutional. Israeli sociology had opened up to new theoretical trends, which had revitalized the uniform functionalism that had dominated the department up until then. Structuralism, as spearheaded by Lévi-Strauss, had disseminated beyond France and had influenced other national anthropologies; ethno-scientific approaches spread out through Europe and America (Barnard 2000, 135–8.) These joined in with the Manchester school, which was already well established among Israeli anthropologists. The diversity of perspectives and the very multivocality of the field allowed for an expansion of the field and its overflow into a number of university settings. The entry of anthropology into the newer universities prompted the older Hebrew University to follow suit. The replacement of the powerful and influential department chair, S. N. Eisenstadt, who had impeded the merging of anthropology into his department, enabled new ideas to be presented and developed in other directions.

A master's program was started, and the department submitted a plan to establish an anthropological institute, which would allow representation to the university's other institutes in the fields of Jewish studies, Asian and African studies, Ibero-Latin American studies, folklore, and archeology.

The program in anthropology was able to establish itself securely due to the recruitment of lecturers into the department's faculty. Among the anthropologists who joined the department at the end of the 1960s were two natives of Israel who had earned Ph.D.s in anthropology at Manchester University and had carried out fieldwork in East Africa. The first was Yitzhak Eilam, who had conducted fieldwork in the Uganda (Eilam 1972); the second was Uri Almagor, whose fieldwork was carried out in Ethiopia (Almagor 1978). Eilam and Almagor had completed their undergraduate degrees in the department of sociology and, upon returning from Africa and England to the university in the early 1970s, they found the Hebrew University had made room for a new academic agenda, which allowed them to find their way into the department as well as in African studies.

In the mid-1970s Eilam turned his interest to the study of Georgian immigrants. A collection of his writings on the subject (Eilam 1980) were published by the department after his premature death in 1978, at the age of 43. There was much speculation about the circumstances of his death at the time; some claimed it was a suicide, due to the hardships of earning tenure and being promoting at the university. The suicide rumors (later disproven) stirred up debates about promotion and micro-politics at the university, a discourse that is as lively and vital today as at the time. Eilam left behind a research legacy that was carried out by his students: Pnina Motzafi-Haller wrote her doctorate about Botswana (Motzafi-Haller 1988) and Maya Melzer-Geva wrote on Georgian Jewry (Melzer-Geva 1983, 2012). (For more on Eilam, see Deshen 1979, as well as Eilam 1980).

In 1972, Harvey Goldberg joined the department in Jerusalem. Goldberg was a native of New York City. In an autobiographical article, Goldberg described his youth in the United States and the circumstances that led him into anthropology (Goldberg 1985). In the mid-1960s, he had carried out fieldwork among Libyan Jews in Porat, a moshav in the Sharon region (Goldberg 1972). His lifelong research on Libyan Jews encompassed many and varied areas of their lives overseas and in Israel (e.g., Goldberg 1990, 1993a, 1993b, 2010).

Don Handelman, a native of Canada who had participated in the Bernstein Project—in the process of which he conducted fieldwork on an occupational center for the elderly in Jerusalem (Handelman 1977)—made his home in Jerusalem and joined the Hebrew University faculty.

The department was also strengthened by the recruitment of another anthropologist—the sociologist Eric Cohen, a native of Zagreb, who moved between the worlds of anthropology and sociology. At Gluckman's invitation, Cohen spent a year of sabbatical leave in Manchester and, following in his mentor's footsteps, began a process of conversion into ethnographic research (Cohen 1971).

From the mid-1970s on, the department was gradually enriched by lecturers, courses, and students who chose to enroll in the anthropology program. The handful of anthropologists developed close relationships with each other and with the few students who expressed an interest in the new field. They were bound together by a sense of distinction from their sociologist colleagues—a sense that was sharpened by anthropology's marginality in sociology—and the pioneering spirit of developing a new area.

During the anthropology program's first decade, the department's anthropologists focused mainly on African societies (Rosenfeld, Almagor, and Eilam), Jewish North African groups (Goldberg and later Bilu), Arab and Bedouin societies of the Middle East (Rosenfeld, Cohen, and Kressel), and on classical anthropological issues typical of the study of tribal societies: kinship, religion and religious revival movements, rites of passage, socialization, systems of symbolization and abstraction, and so on. Courses in research methods and anthropological theory dealt with the theories that then prevailed in England and the United States: the Gluckman style "improved" functionalism, structuralism, ethno-methodology, culture and personality, and phenomenology. There was also a growing interest in subjects such as ethnicity, the absorption of immigrants (Goldberg, Weil, and Eilam), socialization (Goldberg), expressive behavior, and ritual (Handelman). New areas were the study of psychiatry and culture, communication and play, and bureaucracy.

Toward the end of the 1970s, the department also developed joint courses of anthropology and sociology, teaching topics such as society and culture, the social structure of Israel, and major theoretical issues. In 1979, there was another unsuccessful attempt to introduce physical anthropology into the curriculum (in a course on heredity and society), which was preceded by an attempt to offer a course on gender difference from an interdisciplinary perspective. The openness to integrating courses in sociology and anthropology with other disciplines (students were advised to take electives from the departments of folklore, Asian and African studies, and Middle Eastern studies), was a refreshing change from the faculty's policy of the previous two decades. Students began to pursue master's and doctoral degrees in anthropology, and Ph.D.s who graduated the department eventually developed careers in the discipline. The first Ph.D. in anthropology was awarded to Yoram Bilu, who became a leading figure in the Jerusalem school of anthropology, devoting his research to the modes of traditional psychiatry among Moroccan immigrants in moshavim in the Jerusalem region. He was followed by Eileen Basker, who studied the culture of fertility in Israel. Both were supervised by Harvey Goldberg. The department also assisted students who wished to pursue their doctorate overseas—for example, Eyal Ben-Ari studied at Cambridge and carried out his field research in Japan (and later joined the department as a faculty member).

In the mid-1980s, the expansion of the department came to a stop and was even curtailed somewhat. The university as a whole was subject to reductions, no new positions were created, and, in general, the path to development was blocked. Many candidates competed for the same tenure-track positions. These factors were accompanied by internal changes in the department. Although sociologists of the second generation had no objection in principle to anthropology, its influence waned somewhat because the leading figures in the community of anthropologists did not push for its growth. There were some who also cast new doubts on the discipline's uniqueness vis-à-vis sociology, because sociology gradually began to adopt qualitative approaches. In practice, in 1983, anthropology was studied only in the second and third (final) years of the undergraduate program, and only in courses with an empirical focus.

It was precisely during those years, when anthropology was on the ebb, that Raphael Patai promoted an initiative, from far abroad and behind the scenes, to establish a chair in anthropology at the university. Ever since he had emigrated to the United States, he had attempted now and again to renew his connection with the Hebrew University. When he retired in the 1980s, he sought to come to the university for a sabbatical leave in the department of sociology and anthropology or in the department of folklore, making do with a modest financial compensation. The faculty of social sciences rejected his overtures, claiming that it was not capable of supporting even these minor expenses.[15] Patai, however, did not despair; in 1984, he asked to donate USD 150,000 for a chair in anthropology that would bear his name. His generous offer was blocked at the outset and never even came to the knowledge of the department chair, Harvey Goldberg, who learned of it for the first time after I discovered it while perusing the university's archives.

A revival of the discipline occurred at the end of the 1980s and the early 1990s. Anthropologists who arrived from the outside challenged the premises of the local anthropologists who were practicing anthropology "at home." Views from the outside were provided by, for example, Virginia Dominguez, who wondered about the essence and definition of "Israeliness" (Dominguez 1989); Robert Paine, who asked about the nature of "tradition" (Paine 1989); the late Lisa Gilad, who studied Jewish women in a new Israeli town (Gilad 1982, 1989); Herbert Lewis, who had an interest in Yemenite in Israel (Lewis 1989); Sumi Colligan, who conducted fieldwork among the Karaites (Colligan 1980); and Shifra Epstein (1983), who studied the Purim Shpil. All led to a fresh view from the inside. It provided a stimulus for reflexivity and for posing questions about what had been taken for granted, and also contributed to the expansion of the research fields and methods. The department recruited a number of anthropologists who were prepared to take on the task of developing the discipline. The strengthening of anthropology within the social sciences in research centers overseas also made its mark on Israeli anthropology. New approaches were being aired; there were innovative schools and theoretical shifts as Israeli anthropologists who had gone abroad for post-docs or sabbaticals came back with fresh notions. The members of the second generation, such as Eyal Ben-Ari and Yoram Bilu, were already appointed to positions that enabled them to make an impact. The first generation had invested in allowing them to grow—by supporting their student careers and accepting them as department faculty members—and they paid back their credit dues in full.

Events taking place in Israeli society entered anthropology's agenda: the immigration of Jews from the Soviet Union and from Ethiopia to Israel, wars (which were a constant part of reality), and up and downs in relations with the Palestinians and with Israeli Arabs. The department hired Anatoly Khazanov, an anthropologist who arrived from the Soviet Union in the mid-1980s and was an expert on nomadic societies, but he left for the United States after several years of activity. For the first time in years, the department funded fieldwork overseas, a study carried out by André Levy in Casablanca.

Following the intensive waves of immigration by Ethiopian Jews to Israeli in "Operation Solomon" in the early 1990s, interest in this community increased and inundated academic discourse—especially the social sciences, and anthropology in particular. Extra-academic, academic, and nonprofit organizations offered generous research funds to study the "peculiar tribe" that had immigrated to Israel. At the Hebrew University, this topic was researched by Hagar Salamon, then a doctoral student in the department of sociology and anthropology, and currently a member of the faculty of the folklore department; and by Shalva Weil, an anthropologist who came from England and, after studying Indian Jewry, turned to the study of Ethiopian Jewry within the framework of the School of Education.

Not surprisingly, the army and the war—whose presence was so significant in the Israeli experience—were a central subject of study in Israeli anthropology pioneered at the Hebrew University, and they remain a continuing topic of interest to anthropologists and sociologists today. The topic's chief scholars were the students of Eyal Ben-Ari and Edna Lomsky-Feder (Lomsky-Feder and Ben-Ari 1999).

The department was also joined by Meira Weiss, whose studies focused on the anthropology of disease and of the body (Weiss 1994, 2002). Weiss joined Yoram Bilu, whose research embodied the nexus of psychology and anthropology in his well-known studies of folk healing, saint worship, and pilgrimage (Bilu and Ben-Ari 1997; Bilu 2000). Tamar El-Or—whose focus was on issues of gender, religion, and literacy—also joined the department, contributing groundbreaking studies on topics that later became fashionable (El-Or 1994): various aspects of gender and religiosity (Wasserfall 2010), born-again Jews, newly secular Jews, the ultra-Orthodox community, and settlers. The department also included Dan Rabinowitz, a graduate of Cambridge University, whose studies dealt with Palestinians in Israel (Rabinowitz 1997). Rabinowitz moved to the parallel department at Tel Aviv University in 2000.

Personal ties between the founding generation and the second generation were characterized by mutual appreciation and a joint attempt to push the discipline forward and earn it supporters and followers. Most of the sociologists viewed anthropology as a sister discipline whose value was no less than that of their own. The process of rapprochement between the two, which had begun about a decade earlier, now received a new impetus, thanks especially to the widespread entry of qualitative methods in other social science disciplines, such as psychology and education, which in the past had been considered positivist. The graduate of recent years is a socio-anthropological or anthro-sociological creature, depending on one's emphasis. The symbiosis between the two fields is a complementary relationship, unlike the state of affairs during the department's early years, when one partner (sociology) contained the other (anthropology).

The most impressive growth in anthropology in the era beginning in the 1990s is in the field of research and the openness to new intellectual fields. More studies now deal with the middle class—the "us." Focus shifted from

African tribal societies in the 1970s to immigrant societies in the 1980s and from there to the members of the urban, secular middle class and their worlds. Such, for example, was Handelman's study of bureaucratic rituals as part of his concerns with topics of play and theory of ritual (Handelman 1998, 2004; Shamgar-Handelman and Handelman 2010).

This shift in focus has brought with it the adoption of new theoretical approaches. This trend is evident in the course offerings and in the papers given at various conferences in Israel and abroad. The junior and senior faculty's habit of using their sabbatical leave and professional development funds for traveling abroad increases the impact on local anthropology through the import of new ideas, such as interpretive approaches and identity politics. The blend of moderate post-modernism and critical approaches has filtered into the ranks of the Hebrew University's department, which had formerly been considered the most conservative of Israeli anthropology departments. The faculty is composed of scholars of a variety of intellectual stripes. Some of the faculty derived from European traditions (especially England), others from American traditions, and lastly from Israel.

The department has accepted into its ranks anthropologists promoting a feminist agenda, especially Meira Weiss, Eyal Ben-Ari, and Tamar El-Or. Since the 1980s, the field of medical-psychological anthropology has been explored under the influence of Yoram Bilu, who has supervised doctoral students (e.g., Yehuda Goodman) working on related topics (see Bilu and Goodman 2010). The latter's concern with the connection between Judaism, anthropology, and psychology tied in with Harvey Goldberg's interest in the anthropology of Judaism and with Meira Weiss' and Don Seaman's focus on the anthropology of illness and of the body. (Seaman lately moved to Bar Ilan University.) The question of Israelis' attachment to place and territory was a concern of a small group in the department, who published a collection of articles on this issue (Bilu and Ben-Ari 1997). A prominent figure in the pioneering field of tourism, and one of its leaders in world anthropology, was Eric Cohen (Cohen 2000, 2007). His students undertook the study of Israeli backpackers, a topic of interest to young students who experienced it at first hand. Nir Avieli studied food in Vietnam and Daria Maoz studied Israeli backpackers in India (Maoz 2002). The popularity of Africa in the 1970s was supplanted by an attraction to Asia in the 1990s. Interest in Southeast Asia increased with the opening of the Anglo-American world to China, and with the technological and economic growth of those countries—and possibly also as a result of Asia having becoming a popular destination for young Israeli travelers.

Toward the end of the 1990s, interest in Haredi (ultra-Orthodox) society was on the rise. Studies by Yoram Bilu and Harvey Goldberg from a decade earlier led to the opening of a new research field ten years later. The increase in power of the Shas (religious Mizrahi) movement, the power and prominence of Haredi society, and the continuing attempt to study "at home" led to a series of studies on the topic—Nurit Stadler on Haredim and Sarit Barzilay on those questioning their faith and leaving the fold of Haredi society. This turn occurred on the threshold of the Second (Al-Aqsa) Intifada, just before 2000, when the place of Arab society as a fascinating and fashionable research field was replaced by Haredi society.

The shift occurred following changes in the national agenda, and the efforts at peacemaking with the Palestinians: the Arab was no longer a threat, but rather one who ought to be understood. His slot was therefore taken up by the threatening and intriguing Haredi, whose power had risen both within the Green Line (the pre-1967 border line) and outside of it Stadler (2007). At the same time, one cannot conclude that studies dealing with Arab society completely ceased. Efrat Ben Ze'ev studied the collective memory of Palestinian villages in Israel (Ben Ze'ev 2000).

At the same time, an interest in Judaism and the links between anthropology and Judaism continued as a theme in the work of Goldberg, who continued to illuminate this issue from a variety of angles, and who trained students specializing in Judaics who had chosen anthropology as their preferred methodological approach (Goldberg 1987, 2001, 2002, 2003; Goldberg, Cohen, and Kopelowitz, 2012; Werczberger 2012; Fischer 2012).

From the beginning of the 1990s, one can discern among the Jerusalem cohort the signs of the reflexive turn that had taken place in anthropological centers already in the 1970s. This turn was tied to post-modern trends in the social sciences and humanities, and in anthropology in particular. In anthropology, post-modern methodology poses questions regarding the very practice of the discipline, the place of the researcher in the study, the relation between the researcher and his/her subjects, the researcher's authority as well as that of the research subjects, and more. This trend is apparent in some works of prominent anthropologies: the work of Bilu on his relations with his Tzadikkim, their cultural mediators, and their believers (Bilu 1990); El-Or, especially in the book on Haredi poor Mizrahi women (El-Or 2006); Ben-Ari on his military service in the occupied territories (Ben-Ari 2010); and others. Students (especially at the graduate level) were now offered courses dealing with subject-object relations, fieldwork and post-modernism, critical thought, and more. At the same time, there arose new lines of thinking that challenged colonialism, Orientalism, Zionism, and modernity. These issues were intensively discussed at the turn of the previous century and quickly appeared on the Israeli anthropological (and Jerusalemite) agenda as well.

From the methodological perspective, the genre of "life narratives" that had taken root in fields adjacent to anthropology also affected this discipline. The narrative turn in the social sciences produced a great many studies in the fields of education and psychology that emphasized the contribution of the life narrative to general social insights, and, from the mid-1990s onward, many anthropological studies of this genre were written. The first studies of this kind were Lomsky-Feder's dissertation on life narrative of Israeli male combat soldiers, Bilu's study of the Jewish Moroccan saint Yaakov Wazana (Bilu 2000), Sarit Barzilai's study of the life stories of people who have abandoned religious observance (Barzilai 2004), and Gabriela Spector-Mersel's publication of the life stories of Palmah veterans (Spector-Mersel 2006). Several anthropologists joined the ranks of other university departments (Frank Stewart in Middle Eastern studies, Hagar Salamon in folklore, and Shalva Weil in the School of Education).

The process of expansion of the faculty, the broadening of research topics, and promotion opportunities at the Hebrew University—which reached a peak during the first decade of the twenty-first century—became stymied toward the end. The department fell into a crisis: a university-wide budget cut occurred as part of the governmental policy to gradually reduce the investments in higher education, science, and academia. This led to a reduction of faculty positions, teaching hours, research budgets, and employment opportunities at the department; the retirement of a number of older faculty members; as well as a failure to integrate young faculty. This all resulted in a significant reduction of course offerings, especially in anthropology.

Alongside the organization crisis, at the end of the first decade of the twenty-first century, several crises occurred surrounding departmental personalities . Weiss left the department in 2005 in wake of a conflict with the university management concerning the credibility of her research. A second crisis occurred around Eyal Ben-Ari's departure, following student accusations of abuse of authority. The implications of these events weakened the department and the central place it had held hitherto. Nevertheless, the reputation of its academic excellence was recognized when Yoram Bilu was awarded the Israel Prize in Sociology and Anthropology in 2013.

Anthropology at Tel Aviv University: A New Home

The establishment of Tel Aviv University in general, including its department of sociology and anthropology, was an act of rebellion against the Hebrew University in Jerusalem. The department was created within the faculty of social sciences by faculty members who decided to break away from their *alma mater* and create an independent and autonomous estate. Moshe Shokeid described the separation from Jerusalem as an act of divorce (Shokeid 1992). Two metaphors from the world of kinship—that of a rebellious youth, and that of a couple's break-up—reflect the mode of affairs during the department's early years, and affected the shape of its later evolution to no small degree.

Four chief phases can be identified in the development of anthropology in Tel Aviv:

1. Separation from Jerusalem and self-construction as an independent entity (mid-1960 until the early 1970s)
2. Establishment with the assistance of the Bernstein Project (end of the 1960s until the end of the 1970s)
3. Expansion and maintenance (the 1980s)
4. Reduction in the 1990s and a considerable revival into new directions in the first decade of the 2000s

Tel Aviv University's roots lie in the mid-1930s, when the Tel Aviv municipality gradually founded small academic institutes to serve the city's residents. Though the institutes had not yet coalesced into an independent university, the leaders of the Hebrew University objected to the creation of a competing academic institution in the center of the country. Tel Aviv had its own School of Law and Economics, which was established in 1935 and was designed to train experts in these areas. For years, it battled the government mandate to receive academic accreditation. In the beginning of 1959, talks began between the Hebrew University and the Tel Aviv municipality. Only in 1963, after the new university in Tel Aviv had persuaded the higher echelons of government of its necessity, was a faculty of social sciences recognized and established. Tel Aviv University was able to stand on its own feet, but not because of renowned scientists and professors who had fled Europe to reach Palestine, nor because of the leadership of Zionist visionaries. Unlike the Hebrew University, it was founded by people with political and strategic acumen (Shokeid 2002).

The social sciences faculty included the departments of sociology, political science, and economics and statistics; a department of developing countries was later added. Emanuel Marx, who had received his Ph.D. in anthropology at Manchester, was asked to set up a department of anthropology. To strengthen it, he suggested creating a joint department of sociology and anthropology. After a number of years, Marx recruited Shlomo Deshen, and Moshe Shokeid, graduates of the Bernstein Project, and this triad formed the main pillar of the department during its first decade.

Because the three were disciples of the Manchester theoretical school, this approach was, for many years, characteristic of Tel Aviv, making anthropology at Tel Aviv University a kind of alternative to the Hebrew University. The formative experiences (which affect the Tel Aviv department to this day) were two intertwined rebellions: the first against S. N. Eisenstadt as the dominant father figure and founder of the department of the Hebrew University in Jerusalem, and the second against the functionalist sociology that he represented. As opposed to the theoretically driven Jerusalem, the Tel Aviv researchers foregrounded an attitude of "respect for facts, and suspicion of works that were empirically thin but attractively packaged in language that entices the innocent reader" (Shokeid, personal interview). The Tel Aviv anthropologists envisioned themselves as a rebellious, innovative, and energetic alternative to the conservative, frozen, and rigid Jerusalem, which could not support a diversity of approaches. For many, this was a liberating and redeeming experience that shaped the academy (in terms of anthropology) and shaped their own Israeli careers for many years after the fact.

The leader of this movement, Emanuel Marx, was a native of Germany who had arrived in Israel in 1949, completed his bachelor's degree at Jerusalem, and had written his M.A. thesis on the Bedouin of the Negev under Eisenstadt's supervision. This formative experience led him to fundamentally question the ability of the Jerusalem school to represent reality as lived, and he sought alternative ways to do so. After leaving for Manchester to pursue his doctorate, he returned to found the field of anthropology within the department of sociology and anthropology.[16] The department had generous resources, and new opportunities to fashion a strong academic anthropology were born. Moshe Shokeid and Shlomo Deshen soon joined the department's faculty. According to Shokeid's testimony, he was drawn to Tel Aviv because it promised something new and free and, in contrast to the Hebrew University in Jerusalem, there was no "parental control." This was accompanied by the enthusiastic pioneering spirit that came as part of creating something new. As opposed to the situation in Jerusalem at that time, the power of the Tel Aviv anthropologists was no less than that of their sociologist counterparts. Tel Aviv anthropology stressed fieldwork and empirical research and took into account the concrete and individual theory arising from fieldwork, through the "extended case study" and some other concepts derived from the Manchester school. It based itself on a more incisive and more pragmatist approach than had hitherto been practiced.

Teaching during the first years focused on an introduction to social anthropology and a methodological course. The introductory course was structured as a lecture, accompanied by sections that followed Raymond Firth's text on the Tikopia (Firth 1936). This method was transferred to Tel Aviv University by the Manchester disciples. (By way of contrast, at the Hebrew University, Itzhak Eilam, also a Manchester graduate, taught the introductory course in anthropology as the story of the Hima culture, which he himself had studied.) In the private mythology of Tel Aviv University graduates, the Tikopia are known as the basis of knowledge in social anthropology. In 1971, the department received authorization to award master's degrees, and a year later the department was renamed as the department of sociology and anthropology. Over time, it became clear that the sources for recruiting anthropologists were more limited than those for sociologists. Nevertheless, the anthropologists produced more, and, for a long time, the team of Tel Aviv anthropologists was considered the leading group of Israeli scholars by academics outside Israel. At the same time, recruiting efforts did not stop. Long before the first student was sent by the Hebrew University to carry out fieldwork abroad, Tel Aviv sent several students to pursue their doctorates overseas, and a small number of them were awarded positions in the department. Later, the department adopted a policy of locating candidates from an external pool, excluding their own graduates, and even preferred those who had obtained their Ph.D.s abroad.

Emanuel Marx devoted his apprenticeship in anthropology to research on the Negev Bedouin (Marx 1967). Later, his interests broadened to include the Bedouin of Sinai, a topic he continued to follow throughout his career (Marx 2001, 2006, 2013). (An homage to Marx's attraction to nomads appeared in a festschrift in honor of his eightieth birthday [Hazan and Hertzog 2012].) At the same time, Marx focused on social relations and bureaucracy, an interest that emerged from his research on violence in an immigrant town (Marx 1976). This trend inspired students who pursued a similar interest in bureaucratic relations.

Shlomo Deshen was born in Germany, and studied Jewish history and sociology at the Hebrew University. He was recruited as a researcher in the department of settlement at the Jewish Agency. He later went on to pursue his Ph.D. as part of the Bernstein Project (see Deshen 1970); his research focused on elections at an immigrant town in southern Israel. His studies of Jews from southern Tunisia were published in a collection on North African Jews that he edited jointly with Moshe Shokeid (Deshen and Shokeid 1974). Deshen, an observant Jew working in a secular establishment (while successfully, to his mind, keeping these aspects apart), invested a great deal of effort in the study of religion in general, and religious aspects of Mizrahi Jewry in particular (Deshen et al. 1995). Later, he studied the blind in Israel (Deshen 1992), as well as the history of Ashkenazi communities.

Like Deshen, Moshe Shokeid, his colleague and partner to many publications, began his career with the study of a moshav of immigrants from Morocco (Shokeid 1971a), with whom his identification was such that it led him to adopt a new Hebrew surname based on the name of the moshav. Subsequently, he expanded his range of interests to North African immigrants in general, and later shifted his research focus to Israelis who immigrated to the United States (Shokeid 1988), and to a gay synagogue in New York (Shokeid 1995). Shokeid also wrote extensively on fieldwork and on various aspects of Israeli anthropology, including autobiographical works (Shokeid 2001, 2012).

During the period of its flourishing, in the late 1970s and 1980s, the department produced a number of Ph.D.s. Haim Hazan, who trained as a doctoral student in England, became a central anthropologist in the department and in the faculty of social sciences. Hazan was born in Jerusalem and studied at Tel Aviv University, which supported his Ph.D. studies at London's University College. From there he returned to the department, and was the director of the Institute for Social Research, the Horowitz Institute, and the Herczig Center for the Study of Aging. Hazan focused his research on old age as a cultural phenomenon (see, e.g., Hazan 1992, 1994, etc.).

Over the years, courses were offered dealing with Israeli society as well as with contents and approaches proper to social anthropology. Study topics included theoreticians such as Lévi-Strauss and Goffman, qualitative research methods, rural and urban communities, social categories (old age and the elderly), family and kinship, bureaucracy and violence, religion and symbolic system, immigration and ethnic identity, nomadic societies, ecology, energy and environment, Thai society, play, and communications. Attempts by junior anthropologists to obtain a tenure-track appointment at a university are part of the career trajectory at all institutions of higher learning; it seems, however, that in Tel Aviv University the traffic is more lively than elsewhere. The teaching ranks are beefed up also by inviting visiting scholars from abroad to spend a sabbatical at the department.

After anthropology established itself academically at the department, anthropologists began to be exposed to new intellectual influences. The classic foundations of social anthropology in the British tradition were laid down by Deshen, Marx, and Shokeid in the "Introduction to Anthropology" course, and, for this purpose, they published an anthology in Hebrew (Shokeid, Marx, and Deshen 1980) that included classical texts in anthropology alongside articles of their own (the first edition was later updated [Shokeid and Deshen 1999]). During the same year, a book edited by Marx appeared (Marx 1980b), painting a portrait of Israeli society. New winds were blowing from the North American continents, such as Victor Turner's studies of symbols, ritual, and religion in the early 1980s (Turner 1980) and Clifford Geertz's interpretive anthropology in the 1970s (Geertz 1973/1990)—which also affected Tel Aviv anthropology. Shokeid remarked that Geertz allowed one to attempt to understand what was prohibited at Manchester: emotions, feeling, and so on. The content of the courses offered began to change little by little, and listings on topics such anthropology of health and the body, visual anthropology, bureaucracy and violence, nature and culture, and more began to appear. Judaism as a topic of anthropological research also received a more significant place at the end of the 1990s. Gender, inequality, the state, and the environment all became central issues during the first decade of the 2000s.

In the eyes of some of the anthropologists in the department, especially the more veteran ones, some of the methodological directions that characterized the late 1980s and the early 1990s were perceived as straying far beyond the boundaries of the discipline, as an undermining of its borders, and as damaging to its resilience. In my interview with him, Deshen felt that the development of new genres of textual research was a discovery of a new field for research, but he questioned the role of the anthropologist as one to engage in it: "Those who study texts are scholars of literature and history, and they have the tools to do so: anthropologists do not. The department should make an effort to support ethnographic anthropology. There are not that many students doing ethnography—it should be seen as in need of fostering, and as an object of affirmative action. If we want others to continue in our path—a way needs to be found to help and encourage ethnography." Shokeid shares his view: "Since the 1960s, anthropology has been undergoing dramatic changes. The number of anthropologists has grown wondrously, but the classic research fields have diminished" (Shokeid 2002, 195). He expressed concern that the new methodological direction would take over the safe and traditional ethnographic fieldwork. Shokeid even devoted a special article to discussing the dangers of these new trends (Shokeid 2003). On the other hand, Haim Hazan spoke favorably of the dissolution of the boundaries of anthropology and the meshing with neighboring disciplines, especially cultural studies, geography, archeology, Oriental studies, and history. The blurring of boundaries and the bleeding of research methods from one discipline to the next (ethnography out of anthropology, and textual analysis into anthropology) were perceived by him as a positive development that ought to be encouraged. Such debates were not unique to anthropology at Tel Aviv. Many veteran anthropologists have voiced a wariness of abandoning ethnography and opening anthropology to other directions, the chief redirection today being toward cultural studies. (For a discussion of these debates, see Barnard 2000, 168–177.)

At the beginning of the 2000s, the department was undergoing a generational shift—Shlomo Deshen, Moshe Shokeid, and Emanuel Marx retired. (Marx's contribution to the field had already been recognized in 1998 with Israel Prize in Sociology.) The generation of founders made way for the second generation, the most outstanding of whom were Haim Hazan, Ofra Goldstein-Gidoni, and Dan Rabinowitz. Goldstein-Gidoni began her career with fieldwork on weddings in Japan (Goldstein-Gidoni 1997, 2005). Rabinowitz began his interest in the Palestinian by writing on the Arabic Nazareth (Rabinowitz 1997). Later, he composed the most comprehensive and outstanding work that reviews research on Palestinians in Israel (Rabinowitz 1998) and the beginnings of Israeli research on Palestinians (Rabinowitz 2002)—to which Henry Rosenfeld (2002) responded with a critical rejoinder. New dimensions were added to this topic when Khaled Furani joined Rabinowitz in his research (Furani and Rabinowitz 2011). Rabinowitz focuses currently on social research of environmental issues.

Anthropology in Tel Aviv also exists outside of the department of sociology and anthropology. The medical school includes a department of behavioral sciences that was founded many years earlier by Phyllis Palgi, who was later succeeded by Henry Abramowitz. This department could have potentially become a center for research in medical anthropology, but instead it only taught "Introduction to Anthropology" to medical and nursing students. At the same time, the medical school contains a department of anatomy and physical anthropology (which has not come under the compass of this study, and which is devoted exclusively to social and cultural anthropology).

Over the years, a group emerged that, according to Shokeid, was diligent and had impressive academic achievements. However, alongside the achievements, academic and personal conflicts caused a split. In his view, the reasons were partly due to the limitations on recruiting new anthropologists, and were partly tied to interpersonal relations "over which we had no control," as well as the lack of an anthropological research institute, which was a disadvantage. In addition to these factors, other circumstances handicapped any attempt to reinforce anthropology. A group of sociologists in the department who specialized in sophisticated statistical methodologies found it difficult to support an anthropology that followed qualitative methods. The conflict in the department between those who supported the existence of a separate discipline (vis-à-vis cultural studies) and those who negated this position, and wished to define the boundaries of anthropology by narrative genres, is a divisive one, making it difficult for the anthropologists to function within the department.

The divisions caused by the theoretical controversies were compounded by personal rivalries. The rival factions—Moshe Shokeid, Shlomo Deshen, and their disciples on one hand, and Emanuel Marx, Haim Hazan, and their disciples on the other—are at combat in a crowded, resource-scarce, and passion-intense arena. The rivalries create mutual paralysis in which each side interferes with the other's progress, among other things, by intercepting and blocking the rivals' successors. The inner-departmental struggle among the sociologists explains, among other things, the impossibility of producing heirs within the department.

Perhaps now, with the incorporation of a number of new faculty members, one can see signs of recovery. The horizon for the development of anthropology in Tel Aviv, according to Dan Rabinowitz, will emerge from the new management regime at the university, which grants budgetary autonomy to the individual departments but obliges them to be profitable. This will enhance the degree of the faculty members' involvement in marketing academic programs and making them attractive. This characteristic is not unique to Tel Aviv University; in recent years, the Hebrew University has been dealing with similar managerial and budgetary problems. The labor market today encourages employees of middle rank and higher to obtain a master's degree, even in anthropology.

Haifa University: Four-Field Anthropology and Anthropology Abroad

Haifa University began as the "Haifa University-Institution," which was a branch of the Hebrew University in 1963. It was designated chiefly as a center for professional training and enrichment for high school teachers. Little by little, the institute expanded, until it became an independent university in 1972. At first, Henry Rosenfeld taught a few individual courses in anthropology there. In 1965 a program in sociology was started as part of the faculty of humanities and social sciences. This format persisted and, when the university achieved its independent status, the number of anthropologists in the department doubled: Michael Saltman, Nira Reiss, and Jonathan Oppenheimer joined the existing lecturers. Michael Saltman came to Israel after obtaining his first degrees in England and writing his doctorate about an African society in the United States. Nira Reiss (a native of Israel who grew up in the United States) was a disciple of American anthropology and specialized in linguistic anthropology. Jonathan Oppenheimer focused on Druze society. From that time onward, the program in anthropology has kept to a more or less set quota of about four or five lecturers.

With its expansion, Haifa anthropology proposed a unique format in the context of Israeli academia. It adopted the model of American holistic anthropology—the four-field approach that included sociocultural anthropology, linguistic anthropology, physical anthropology, and archeology. Its hallmark today is its preference for a regional anthropology outside of Israel, as opposed to "anthropology at home." However, it too is combined with sociology from an organizational perspective. The multidisciplinary approach required expertise in a number of realms of knowledge, and the department hired specialists according to specialization. The faculty members included archeologists, physical anthropologists, specialists in pre-history, and linguists. In 1973, a master's program specialization in anthropology was approved, and two years later it already boasted twelve students. The four-field approach was maintained at Haifa for some fifteen years, but due to difficulties with the different methodologies required for each specialization, and the existence of their equivalents in the university's other faculties, it did not draw students. The department subsequently reorganized so that instead of multiple sub-disciplines, it expanded the research fields in the territorial sense. New anthropologists recruited to the department had a regional expertise, and thus a broad regional coverage was achieved. Each different region of the world demanded mastery of a theoretical expertise and conceptual system unique to it. As a result, anthropology at Haifa has a larger representation of anthropology abroad than any other department at an Israeli university.

Henry Rosenfeld, the founding father of anthropology at Haifa, began his life in Israel as a kibbutz member (which also was an object of his research interest, but not of publication). (See the biographical article in the festschrift in his honor: Al Haj et al. 2005.) Later, the Arab village was for many years at the center of his interests, and he observed it from a variety of perspectives—chiefly in terms of economy and class division, and villages' relations with the state (Carmi and Rosenfeld 2010).

Michael Saltman, a native of London, studied anthropology at Cambridge, stayed in Israel for a number of years, and then went on for a graduate degree at Brandeis University. His fieldwork in Kenya dealt with conflict resolution (Saltman 1977) and led to a focus and expertise in the anthropology of law and traditional law (e.g., Saltman 1991, 2002). He carried out another significant field study in the Caribbean. When appointed a position at Haifa, he supported developing an anthropology that was not practiced "at home," and favored recruiting anthropologists who had ethnographic ties in different regions of the world.

Yoram Carmeli conducted fieldwork on a traveling circus in England (Carmeli 1987) and later dealt with issues of the state, family, and fertility (Birenbaum-Carmeli and Carmeli 2010); sport; and more.

Nurit Bird-David began her anthropological research in a hunter-gatherer society in India, as part of her graduate training at Cambridge (Bird 1982), and continued to pursue her interest in these societies (Bird-David 1994), and in other aspects of the environment and economy (Bird-David and Darr 2009).

In the early 2000s, the department was strengthened by the appointment of more anthropologists. Amalia Saar (2001, 2009) has studied issues of women, family, and employment among Palestinian women in Israel. Tsipy Ivry carried out fieldwork in Japan on issues of fertility and childbirth, and continues to pursue these interests through a comparative lens (Ivry 2006, 2010). Carol Kidron studies personal and collective memory, commemorative sites and practices, and psychological anthropology (Kidron 2009).

Anthropology at Haifa has presented an international model: Japan, the Caribbean, Africa, Europe, the Middle East and Israel. In addition to their regional and theoretical expertise, the faculty members are also diverse in terms of their research interests. Henry Rosenfeld was interested in questions of economy and class; Yoram Carmeli focused on play (1987), the economy (Carmeli and Appelbaum 2004), and family; Nurit Bird-David specialized in economic anthropology; Michael Saltman delved into anthropology of the law; Amalia Saar studied the anthropology of gender; Tsipy Ivry specialized in medical anthropology; and Carol Kidron researched psychological anthropology. The combination of regional and theoretical expertise as well as topical specializations creates a diverse anthropology that covers a variety of issues. The demand for anthropology abroad is also manifest in the way that students are encouraged to carry out studies overseas, beginning at the master's level, and even far away from Europe and America (Simhai 2000). Anthropology at Haifa offers a variety of topics that involve a diverse typology of societies, from tribal to post-industrial societies. The department's students are pursuing research on hunter-gatherer societies in southern India, on terminally ill patients, on the food culture of Russian immigrants in Germany and in Israel, on pubs in Ireland, on New Age religions, and on belief in UFOs in Israel.

Another function of the anthropology department is as a center for the training of anthropologists, who would later be dispersed among other disciplines and departments—education, communications, economics, political science, Middle Eastern studies, and medicine. This strategy would allow an expansion of the anthropological approach and method into diverse fields, just as a historical or sociological approach might extend into these fields. This could be implemented only if the training process is concentrated at one site—within a department that specializes in anthropology. This process takes place, in practice, at all Israeli universities; however, in Haifa this role was explicitly articulated as such.

It is not surprising that Haifa University's anthropologists are actively engaged outside the department of sociology and anthropology, especially in the faculty of education. Rivka Eisikovits (1983, 2008) and Debbie Golden (2006) teach topics that are at the nexus of the two fields, such as intercultural encounters and the anthropology of educational systems. From among a few dozen doctoral students, some implement qualitative methods. Tamar Katriel, an anthropologist specializing in linguistic representations of culture and in the study of contemporary Israeli society, is a member of the department of communications (Katriel 2004, 1985). Joseph Ginat taught at the department of land of Israel studies and in the Jewish-Arab Institute, which was devoted to the study of Arabs in Israel and in the Middle East, and taught courses in Jewish–Arab relations (Ginat 1982, 2009).

Alongside the diversification of areas included under the rubric of "anthropology" at Haifa, the anthropologists have cooperated with their sociologist colleagues both in research projects and other academic activity. Some of the department members published a joint critical journal named *Mahbarot Lemehkar Ulebikoret* (Notebooks on Research and Criticism), which appeared from October 1978 through December 1981. Mahbarot published, among other things, articles on Israeli society (Bernstein 1978), critiques of the education system (Swirski 1978), and articles on Arab and Druze society (Oppenheimer 1979; Carmi and Rosenfeld 1979).

In recent years, the department of sociology and anthropology established the "Anthropological Forum," which provides an opportunity for an intellectual exchange between the departments' lectures and guest lecturers and participants. The forum's sessions deal, from a variety of angles, with issues that have theoretical implications.

Haifa anthropology's uniqueness as supporting a holistic, interdisciplinary anthropology—in the sense of "the science of man"—was constructed along the prevalent model of American anthropology. As the discipline broadened, it naturally splintered and developed specializations. The combination of different specializations within one framework demanded special conditions that proved burdensome, both in the United States and in Israel. The demand for diversity becomes a double-edged sword because of the difficulty of developing a profound understanding of parallel knowledge fields, which are governed by different methodologies. Under the current organizational structure of Israeli universities, linguistics and archeology belong to the faculty of the humanities, and the program in human evolution belongs to the department of biology. In addition, anthropology in Israel was tied, even from the days of Buber and Eisenstadt, to the social sciences and the humanities—philosophy and humanism—and the disciplinary link to the natural sciences is unpalatable to some. Two years after the four-field approach was adopted at Haifa, doubts were already being voiced: "To be somewhat self-critical, we are not quite sure at this stage whether we are merely paying lip-service to the holistic ideal, or whether a genuine basis for a holistic anthropology is being established at Haifa."[17]

Concerns about the implementation of the four-field approach is shared even by its founders. A critique of the possibility of integrating the fields has been articulated by Borofsky (2002); he put the myth of holistic American anthropology to the test and argued that, in fact, it never was comprehensive in that way. According to him, anthropology in the United States gives emphasis to the cultural aspect.

In addition to the uniqueness of Haifa's four-field and regional approaches, the department of sociology and anthropology is noteworthy in its interpersonal relationships. Among the interviewees from Haifa University, of both the older and the younger generation, there is a shared feeling that the department is characterized by supportive and warm personal relations between the anthropologists (mostly females), as evidenced in the socializing that takes place outside the department. Similar relations exist between graduate students and faculty members.

Anthropology at Ben Gurion University: Behavioral Science

In its early phase, the University of the Negev (currently Ben Gurion University) operated under the aegis of the Hebrew University. In 1968, an interdisciplinary teaching framework was created within the social sciences by combining the departments of sociology, economics, and psychology. In 1970, the department of behavioral sciences was founded—at the time, the only department of its kind in the country. The department of behavioral sciences included a number of social science disciplines, but only in 1974 was the department joined by the anthropologist Shmuel Ben Dor. Ben Dor, who had a degree in anthropology and psychology from the United States, was an expert in psychological anthropology and had carried out fieldwork among the Inuit. For many years, he taught an introductory course in anthropology, as well as courses in methodology, culture and personality, and comparative cultural anthropology.

During the same time period, Alex Weingrod joined the department and was appointed its chair in 1974. Weingrod, who had carried out fieldwork in the Negev area in the past, was also acquainted with the region in his capacity as head of social research at the Jewish Agency Settlement Department (see the section "The Jewish Agency Settlement Department and Moshavim Study"). To strengthen anthropology at the department, a number of anthropologists were invited to spend a brief time at the department: Jillian Hundt, who researched medical anthropology among the Bedouin—a topic that would become very popular twenty years later; Yael Katzir, who studied a moshav of Yemenite immigrants in the Jerusalem area, and later became a member of the teaching faculty at the Levinski College for Education; and

Michael Ashkenazi, an Israeli who had studied at Yale, carried out fieldwork in Japan, and went on to England.

The conception of the behavioral sciences department was basically interdisciplinary, and it stressed connections of anthropology with sociology and psychology. However, the majority of the department's students were attracted to it because of its offerings in psychology and were less interested in anthropology or sociology. From the beginning of the 1990s, the department grew gradually as the university expanded and invested resources, and, with the generous donations that were received, the department became a drawing stone for scientists and students. The anthropology program within the department received a push and began an intensive process of recruiting lecturers, thus significantly growing the department faculty. New programs were opened and a master's and subsequently a doctoral degree program were authorized (in 1984 and 1995, respectively). The graduate programs have a disciplinary focus on anthropology, as opposed to the general course of study offered to undergraduate students.

The department was later joined by Fran Markowitz and André Levy. Markowitz, a native of the United States, wrote her doctoral dissertation on Jewish Russian immigrants to the United States (Markowitz 1993). At the end of the 1980s, she spent time as a post-doctoral fellow in Jerusalem, and remained in the country. Her work focuses on gender, race, and immigrants, and she recently published a book on Bosnia (Markowitz 2010). André Levy, a graduate of the Hebrew University, studied the Jewish community in Casablanca (with the exceptional support and encouragement of his department), and this became the focus of his dissertation. He studies various aspects of migration, of North African Jewry, and especially Morocco (Levy 2010; Levy and Weingrod 2005).

The anthropologists in the department never concealed their ambition to develop anthropology independently from sociology and psychology—if possible, as a multifaceted anthropology. However, this aspiration faced two obstacles. The first was the fact that anthropology had never extricated itself from its symbiosis with sociology in any of the other universities in the Israel. The second was that there were periods in which anthropology did not attract advanced students and the faculty was smaller. Parallel to anthropology's aspiring to independence, attempts were made to integrate it with other disciplines. At some point, there was a tendency to adopt part of the four-field model and to marry the behavioral sciences to aspects of physical anthropology, but this did not succeed. On the other hand, an effort had been made to interest students in archeology, because the university's archeology department had a decided cultural bent. Over time, the number of students seeking degrees in both of these departments declined, and these attempts were infelicitous.

In the mid-1990s, an understanding began to emerge in the social sciences in the Israeli academy that graduates would need to be integrated into the job market, and therefore training in applied programs ought to be offered. The "applied" orientation developed chiefly in psychology and sociology promoted programs in organizational psychology, organizational sociology, and so on. In anthropology, this applied orientation was developed based on the assumption that fieldwork would encourage social sensitivity and improve human services in the caring and paramedical professions such as social work, education, and nursing. A number of anthropologists proposed training programs in applied anthropology; however, this specialization did not generate demand—neither at Ben Gurion University nor at any of Israel's other universities.

The teaching faculty in the department also includes two researchers from the Blaustein Institute for Desert Research—the anthropologists Gideon Kressel and Pnina Motzafi-Haller. Gideon Kressel studied in the United States and in Israel, and joined the Desert Research Institute in the early 1980s. Kressel specialized in two topics early in his career: the anthropology of the Bedouin (urban and nomadic) and kibbutz and moshavim societies. In recent years, he has also began to take an interest in the society and economy of the Balkan states, and in India and China (Kressel 1992, 2010). Pnina Motzafi-Haller studied for her undergraduate degree in Jerusalem, went on to study in the United States, and carried out her dissertation work in Botswana (Motzafi-Haller 1994). In the late 1990s, she returned to Israel and has since turned her attention to women, gender, ethnicity, labor, and Mizrahi identity (Motzafi-Haller 2012).

The ranks of the department at Ben Gurion University were strengthened in recent years by the addition of new lecturers, such as Jackie Feldman, who completed his Ph.D. at the Hebrew University in the late 1990s, on the topic of youth pilgrimage from Israel to Poland (Feldman 2008). In the late 2000s, the department hired several other anthropologists—Nir Avieli (2011), Julia Lerner (2008), and Esmail Nashif (2008). The first two studied at the Hebrew University, while Nashif trained in the United States. The university also has anthropologists outside of the department of behavioral sciences: Aref Abu-Rabia in the department of Middle Eastern studies researches various aspects of Bedouin society in the Negev (from education through folk medicine) and also teaches at the medical school (Abu-Rabia 2009).

The intellectual ferment at the university and its expansion in recent years have turned it into a drawing point for many researchers. Formerly a marginal university, it has since become a coveted place of learning in and of itself. The departments of humanities and social sciences are characterized by an innovative, critical, and self-assured spirit, and, as such, they have been successful at recruiting suitable faculty members. At the same time, because of the university's location in the city of Be'er-Sheva, the institution is expected to promote a social agenda and develop and maintain relationships with the social milieu in which it operates. As a large city with a large immigrant population and many social problems, Be'er-Sheva has little attraction for academics, and a large number of the faculty members live in the exclusive suburban communities that border the metropolis. And despite the university's declared social commitments and the fact that the city's academic community is vibrant, dynamic, innovative, and ideologically and socially engaged, the community has not achieved a critical mass that might influence the city in terms of program development and unique directions.

The a priori interdisciplinary nature of the behavioral sciences—in which sociologists, psychologists, and anthropologists are bound together by ties that are not self-evident—creates an inherently problematic situation. When one of the "heads" of this many-headed Hydra forges connections with other disciplines, this threatens its internal cohesiveness even more. The department is therefore characterized by dynamics of cleaving together and splitting apart. During the early years, as the department of behavioral sciences was expanding, voices skeptical of the interdisciplinary marriage were heard.

The process of generational change also left its mark: the founding generation that had flown the banner of cross-disciplinary integration retired. And indeed, in 2007, a significant organizational change took place in the department of behavioral sciences. The split transformed the balance of power between the different disciplines represented in the department, and, in my opinion, empowered anthropology. The uniqueness of anthropology at Ben Gurion University is its authorization to grant an M.A. specializing in anthropology and not only in sociology combined with anthropology, as in other universities. This feature has created a draw for anthropologists who wish to train and specialize in anthropology alone.

ANTHROPOLOGISTS AT MUSEUMS

In American anthropology, from its very beginnings, anthropologists played a crucial role in museums, which was in keeping with the spirit of four-field multidisciplinary anthropology. At these institutions, anthropologists contributed to ethnography, archeology, and even to specific areas of the natural sciences that are represented both in the central and backwater museums throughout North America.

As opposed to the United States, the connection between anthropology and museum exhibition in Israel is marginal, to say the least. The Israel Museum in Jerusalem currently employs in the department of Jewish ethnography a number of ethnographers trained in the field of folklore, as well as Debbie Hirshman, who integrates knowledge from the fields of anthropology and archeology .However, during the late 1980s, museums themselves became a field of anthropological research, which produced at least three studies: Maya Melzer-Geva's on intercultural learning in an exhibition (Melzer-Geva 2012), Shelly Shenhav-Keller on the display of memory at the Beth Ha-Tefutsot (Diaspora Museum) (Shenhav-Keller 2005), and on settlement museums (Katriel 1997). The appeal of the topic of museums was related to the general interest at the time in the issues of collective memory, invention of tradition, and imagined communities.

ANTHROPOLOGY AT COLLEGES OF EDUCATION

Three types of colleges exist in Israel: multidisciplinary regional colleges (both private and public) colleges of education, and university-sponsored regional colleges (e.g., branches of Ben Gurion University or Bar Ilan University). The multidisciplinary colleges do not offer studies in anthropology as a field of knowledge in its own right. A few colleges that are not university sponsored have departments of sociology and anthropology (e.g., Yezreel Valley College or Kinneret College) and employ anthropologists as lecturers in the fields of social science and education. Those that are university sponsored teach anthropology in the format of the patron universities.

Anthropology is not taught as a subject in its own right at Israeli high schools, so the teaching colleges do not train teachers of anthropology. In colleges of education, such as Beit Berl College and Oranim College, the students of the social sciences are trained to teach a curriculum that includes anthropology. In addition, Beit Berl College for some years supported a program in anthropology in the framework of multidisciplinary studies in the social sciences, which led to a B.A. from the Open University, but that program was an exception. At the other colleges, anthropologists teach courses that service the education curriculum, or qualitative methodologies course, or electives in areas of the lecturer's expertise (economic anthropology for economy majors, etc.).

APPLIED ANTHROPOLOGISTS

In contrast to the vision of anthropology in its incipient stages, applied anthropology never established itself within either the public or private sectors. In the fields of health and mental health, anthropology received some recognition in the 1980s and 1990s as a result of the convergence of a few factors. First was the contribution of the anthropologist Phyllis Palgi in the field of mental health, and her success at convincing others of the importance of involving anthropologists. Second was the relatively prominent representation of psychiatrists of Latin American (and especially Argentinian) origin in the mental health sphere in Israel—professionals who had been trained in a tradition of incorporating anthropologists into psychiatric practice, especially in hospital settings. Third was the popularity of the field of medical anthropology in North America in the 1980s. Applied anthropology in the late twentieth century and the beginning of the current millennium made its presence in a small number of appointments of applied anthropologists in the health field; a number of anthropologists who are involved in evaluation projects in the fields of education, immigration, and in social entrepreneurship; and a few others in private research institute. Anthropologists who are recruited into such projects contribute both their expertise in qualitative methodology and their personal expertise in the fields of health and immigration (see Shabtai and Mizrahi 2004; Kalifon 1997).

Anthropology carried out in foreign fields can potentially ignore the reality in which the researcher lives and teaches. In the Israeli circumstances of "anthropology at home," the connection between the outside (events in society) and the inside (events in the academy) is almost immediate. Some respond quickly, and some more belatedly; some develop applied research projects and others academic research. The "applied" practitioners attempt to deal with a problem presented by the decision-making apparatus (usually public institutions) and expect the research to produce results. In the obverse, the "theoretical" response is manifest in the choice of research fields and the research questions. The question of whether to respond to a request from an outside institution that wishes to become involved in applied research is a complex one. Some anthropologists take this position from the outset: Phyllis Palgi, whose work in the Health Ministry defined her research subjects; Anita

Nudelman, who works for the Youth Aliyah sections (an organization charged with the absorption of young immigrants to Israel); or Malka Shabtai, who served in the Israel Defense Forces and made her research skills available to the military. Others responded to appeals from outside institutions when a problem arose that an anthropologist was capable of solving. Harvey Goldberg, for example, researched modes of addressing the problems of "Disadvantaged Youth" in a development town (Goldberg 1984) or food consumption patterns for a medical study, and Haim Hazan devoted a study to urban renewal projects. Since the 1970s, research produced has more commonly taken a critical perspective—for example, in the mental health field (Basker et al. 1982), in the framework of absorption and welfare policy (Hertzog 1999), and in other human services.

THE NATIONAL AGENDA SHAPES THE ACADEMIC AGENDA

The factors that shape the arena of knowledge production and dissemination are translated into issues, such as the topics to be researched, research priorities, emphases, theories and schools that characterize an era, and so on. The research and course topics in the academic sphere are largely affected by anthropologists' personalities and personal preferences. (For example, some lecturers' restless temperament leads them to change their course topics or bibliography every year, whereas the more stable lecturers teach the same course for years.) Of equal weight, however, are external forces such as funding and academic trends.

In Israeli anthropology, as in other national anthropologies, the research agenda is created through interactions between the national agenda, the global anthropological network, and the micro-politics in the university and in the field. Processes within Israeli society and the image of anthropological knowledge at different phases of Israeli history determined, to a great extent, the demand for anthropology.

In the 1930s and 1940s, the expectancies and image of anthropological knowledge were formulated in terms of salvaging and preserving the treasures of the past. The study of Oriental Jews was meant to document their culture just as it was about to be lost in a mélange of other cultures, moments before it was expected to disappear and be swallowed by the new society that was being constructed on the basis of European culture. In the 1950s and 1960s, new tasks were at stake; the anthropologist wore the cap of the social problem solver, addressing problems that had emerged out of mass immigration and the intercultural encounter of different immigrant groups. This was formulated in terms of acculturation or assimilation, which ultimately meant the absorption of the immigrants into the dominant society. Handelman (1975) argued that American cultural anthropology and psychological anthropology would have made a good fit at that time with that research agenda and the questions it engendered. It is quite possible that had representatives of the British school been dominant at that time, a different set of questions might have been asked. The scientific agenda was dictated by the way in which one's intellectual vantage point dovetailed with what were defined at the time the burning issues of Israeli nation building. Later, the local anthropology arena became populated with disciples of the Jerusalem school of sociology who were employed in the Jewish Agency Settlement Department. They advised the settling institutions on urgent practical issues. The work of the anthropologists was a true reflection of the issues that preoccupied the public agenda, both in terms of topics and the manner in which they were formulated. In the early state years, social scientists were perceived as purveyors of the knowledge necessary for fulfilling public jobs, tending to address social problems and deal with issues concerning governmental decision making. At the Hebrew University and Tel Aviv University, there was an explicit declaration of the purpose for which the faculties of social sciences had been established: the cultivation of a generation of technocrats that would comprise the bureaucratic human infrastructure for the government and its agencies in the emerging state (Gross 2001). This was the reason for the creation of the departments of economics, sociology, political science, and the Asian and African institutes in the 1960s—when ties with developing countries were being forged and Israel sent aid missions and held ongoing contacts with countries in those regions. The development of social science disciplines that are not defined as professions was preceded by the development of the faculties and schools of law, medicine, and education. The universities were therefore perceived, in addition to being research institutions, as a system for the professional training of cadres of experts who would formulate policy and manage the state and government affairs. Within the faculties of social sciences, the public image of the sociologists and anthropologists was of experts on immigrants, the "Others" (chiefly those immigrants of Mizrahi origin). They were enlisted to the national project in order to solve problems that cropped up in the moshavim or in the development towns, in order to help advance "weak" or "underprivileged" populations. The national agenda overwhelmed the research and teaching agendas.

With the development of anthropology within the universities and the specializations within each, unique links to societal processes and phenomena came into being. In Jerusalem, the problem-solving approach persisted. Yitzhak Eilam, for example, advised the Absorption Ministry on the subject of the absorption of Georgian immigrants, Eric Cohen conducted a survey on ethnic groups and minorities in Israel (Cohen 1988), and Don Handelman contributed a study to the Welfare Ministry. As an anthropology practiced at a conservative university, at least until the 1980s, the discipline was characterized by its treatment of theoretical issues that were a response to social processes in the areas of ethnicity, Jewish–Arab relations, bureaucratic relations and the state, pilgrimages, and saint worship. Beginning in the 1990s, the emphasis shifted from ethnicity to topics that had not been at the forefront of research earlier on: the army and militarism; religiosity and politics; return to religion and leaving the religious fold; and anthropology of the body, health, and disease. Research opened itself up to new horizons: the "we/us" became an object of research—the middle class, secular Israeli, Jews, Ashkenazim. The questions asked were different ones—no longer the historicization of the immigrant and ethnic groups, but rather the study of their contact with other groups and the nature of their identity construction. At the same time, research "away from home" was also represented—especially in Asia and Africa.

EURO-ANGLO-AMERICAN ANTHROPOLOGY SHAPES ISRAELI ANTHROPOLOGY

The links between local and world anthropology are manifest in two contextual spheres: in the institutional/funding sphere and in the sphere of content. In the institutional contexts, the influence and input of world anthropology centers (North America, and Europe to some extent) are quite crucial. In the sphere of content, the intellectual developments and the new trends engage in dialogue with Israeli anthropology and receive their local character, which takes shape as a result of the combined tendencies of worldwide trends and of local social processes.

The triad of society-power-knowledge is translated into the academic reality via a full spectrum of interpretations. The image of the anthropologist's knowledge and our expectations from the anthropologists—as a problem solver but also as someone removed from the "burning" and immediate issues—will have implications for anthropological practices in the academy. Even if the anthropologist does not appear to have been the mouthpiece of the establishment who is mobilized to national causes, he or she is still expected to respond to unfolding social processes.

The anthropological research projects at the universities and elsewhere were supported at first by local funders (such as the Jewish Agency) or by international funders (such as the American Foundation, the U.S. Department of Agriculture, or Unesco). For example, some of the sociological studies of immigrants and their settlement were written as reports for the United Nations or for the U.S. Department of Agriculture (Ben David 1963). Another source of funding was a private media corporation (the British "Granada" channel), which supported the Bernstein Project. Over the years, the involvement of international bodies continued, and the Americans and the Europeans indirectly supported research in Israel by means of public, bilateral academic research foundations. For example, the anthropological projects that Rosenfeld initiated were supported by U.S. foundations: the anthropological center he created and, later, his activities promoting peace, which were generously supported by a foundation grant. Goldberg received funding for research on Middle Eastern Jewry from an Italian Jewish foundation (provided by a Libyan Jewish businessman living in Italy), from the Jewish Theological Seminary to conduct research on the history of that institution, and also from the Jewish millionaire Leon Tamman. In addition, the "Manchester School" of British Anthropology, was supported with funding from Lord Bernstein in the 1970s; this school's disciples continued to maintain links with England, and the school sent their students to train in England.

In the mid-1980s, the effects of American anthropology began to pervade Israel by way of the anthropologists who were active in Israel, and this trend was reinforced by those students who returned after a period of training in America. Little by little, American anthropology acquired a position of dominance in setting the intellectual agenda. Similar to the other social sciences and humanities, the connection to America was considered then, and still is, an indispensable landmark on the path of any anthropologist pursuing a scientific career in Israel. The United States is the destination for postdoctoral students and for attending conferences. To advance in one's career, one had better have a letter of recommendation from someone in America. Many Israeli anthropologists have lived in the United States—for durations of a few months to a few years—and they make a yearly pilgrimage for the annual meetings of the American Anthropological Association, membership in which signal identification with international anthropology. American anthropologists are regularly invited to lectures and conferences in Israel or take sabbatical leaves in Israel.

Although each university in Israel has forged a unique program, they have all focused mostly on the study of Israeli society. The tension between wanting to be relevant to the international community and the desire to be relevant to the community of colleagues and to daily life has produced an academic anthropology that combines the two: international criteria and an orientation toward the center, by means of studying the local.

THREE

the ISRAELI ANTHROPOLOGICAL ASSOCIATION *as a* SITE *of* ANTHROPOLOGICAL PRACTICE

The Israeli Anthropological Association (IAA) is a voluntary association that overlaps with other (chiefly academic) systems; the ties between these systems shape a number of the association's characteristics. The identities of its members and its identity as an organization are constructed in relation to professional and national identity, political and intellectual activity, and to informal socializing. My acquaintance with IAA was gained during my own tenure as the first secretary of the association (a short time after its establishment and until the mid-1980s), later as a board member between 1998 and 2002, and as president during the years 2007–2010. I have first-hand experience with its decision-making process and the way in which its activities are organized. I have also made use of the IAA newsletters, which have appeared consistently since its establishment, as well as its other publications. I have personally participated in all of its thirty-seven meetings[1] and have conducted fieldwork observations on them. Additional information can be found in an autobiographical work by the IAA's founder, Marcus Goldstein (1995), and in books by Moshe Shokeid (2002, 2012).

THE HISTORY AND NATURE OF PROFESSIONAL ASSOCIATIONS

Professional associations had developed already in the mid-sixteenth century, formed as trade guilds or bureaus that were intended to protect their members and the profession itself from the interference and intervention of outside bodies, such as competing guilds, or public stakeholders attempting to meddle in the definition of the profession and its activity. The guilds were determined to obtain a monopoly over professional training and the prerogative of defining the entry threshold into the profession, in order to prevent laypersons from practicing their trades. This was particularly the case in respect to guilds of lawyers, dentists, and physicians.

Following the challenge to the altruistic and liberal image of the professions that emerged in the 1960s and 1970s, critical social scientists developed an understanding that professional associations were part of a structure of prestige and power within a society's system of social stratification. When the foundational concepts in the field of the sociology of knowledge began to be elaborated, the discussion shifted from the organizational aspect (Collins 1990) to an analysis of the interrelationships of knowledge and power.

In regard to anthropology, the field's presentation as a profession and the image of the anthropologist as a professional are not matters that can be taken for granted. It therefore should be asked whether, and to what degree, the IAA is a professional association, observing the practices of professional identity constructed via the association. In the history of anthropology, evidence points to the phase of professionalization as utterly critical to its development (Darnell 1998, 2001; Stocking 1974). It is therefore important to identify the crucial point at which anthropology becomes identified as a profession and as a discipline, when its practitioners are regarded as exclusively licensed to practice it, and amateurs lacking the "proper" training according to the newly determined criteria are excluded.

Over the course of the discipline's lifetime, the discussion of professions and processes of professionalization was a central concern of sociology. According to Durkheim (1958), professional associations offered their members the production of collective sentiments and the pleasure derived from the professional's association with others of his own ilk. Associations allow their members opportunities to conduct their life courses according to similar moral goals. That sense of fellowship and professional awareness develop during the process of professional training and are preserved and enhanced due to the fact that members take upon themselves a commitment and collective responsibility toward their fellow professionals. The community of association members, to a large degree, determines the image of the profession and its goals, and enables an exchange of knowledge between themselves and the public.

In many senses, the professional association is an arena for domination and the exercise of power, but also for professional empowerment. Its activity provides a framework, a time, and a place for professional encounters, information updates, and the coalescence of a professional identity. At the same time, it is an additional social arena in which power struggles, processes of exclusion and inclusion, and a manner of domination and dependency take place. The intellectual and scientific activities of an association are accompanied by ritual aspects; these rituals are most visible at the yearly meetings. Such events play an important role in the shaping, unpacking, and reinforcing of professional identity, and in the generation of academic activity that contributes to scientific discourse. Discussion of common topics of interest at the meeting sessions may stimulate new ideas and breed cross-fertilization, and conversational circles might blossom into new joint publications. At a meeting, members meet, converse, hear and share innovations and personal and professional gossip, search for and offer jobs, give advice, and invest in renewing contacts or severing them. The value of corridor talk is sometimes greater than that of activity at the central podium. The preparatory activity for the meetings, as well as decisions regarding the format and contact, is saturated with personal contact that includes elements of rapprochement and distancing, confirmation and support, criticism and hostility, the realization of momentary interests, fulfillment of past commitments, creation of future commitments, and the development of supportive milieu around key personages. The interpersonal encounter at the meetings is crucial in the current era, which is characterized by a multiplicity of available and rapid channels of communication, such as telephones and Internet. To a great extent, it serves as a substitute for routine face-to-face interactions, which were the means for immediate connections in the not so remote past.

ORGANIZATIONAL, PROFESSIONAL, SCIENTIFIC, NATIONAL, AND SOCIAL CHARACTERISTICS OF THE IAA

The founder of the IAA, Marcus Goldstein (1906–1997), among the last students of Franz Boas, was an uncompromising empiricist. He was interested in many fields, including human evolution, public health, and Judaism. He arrived in Israel in 1971, after a career at several American universities and medical organizations in the United States. During the years 1972–1995, he served as an associate professor at the department of anatomy and anthropology at Tel Aviv University's medical school. The model he envisioned was that of four-field anthropology, which was familiar to his colleagues, Israeli anthropologists trained in the United States. However, it was at odds with the leading organizational model for anthropology at Israeli universities, in which the rigid departmentalization and organizational separation between faculties prevailed: humanities (archeology and linguistics), medicine (anatomy and physical anthropology), and social sciences (social and cultural anthropology). It was also at cross purposes with the tradition of social anthropology to which the greater part of the British-educated Israeli anthropologists belonged.

Of the early days of the IAA, Goldstein writes in his autobiography:

> When we came to Israel in November of '71, I was astonished to find that the cultural/social anthropologists, the archeologists, and the few physical anthropologists, were each in their own separate department in the universities, totally unlike the situation in the U.S. . . . In fact, there was no, and is no, department of anthropology as such in Israel. . . . Why not, I asked, have an Israel Anthropological Association which could include, bring together, faculty members of all the major branches of anthropology? Meetings would be held at least once a year where members of all branches of anthropology in the several universities could become acquainted, present result of their research, and discover how not infrequently there were aspects of significant interest to all. (Goldstein 1995, 77)

The initial reactions to Goldstein's proposal to establish the IAA wavered between apprehension and utter opposition. The opponents, mostly those who had trained in Britain, claimed that there was no place for an independent anthropological professional entity, and that "it would not work here." For some, the combination of physical anthropology with social and cultural anthropology was both foreign and bizarre. And yet, the response to the founding convention of the IAA in Jerusalem was impressive, and apart from the department of sociology and anthropology at Tel Aviv University, members from all the other universities arrived and expressed interest in establishing the association. The IAA was officially established in 1973. Goldstein was elected as chairperson, assisted by a board of representatives of the various branches, and the bylaws were formulated and sent to members for ratification.

The IAA was established as an "Ottoman" (voluntary) association, and registered with the non-profit registrar as soon as it was established. As a membership-based organization, it defined external criteria for membership at first, but currently only a desire to join the association is required. Anyone who identifies him- or herself as an anthropologist and pays membership dues can be a member of the IAA. In the past, there was a distinction between students, who lacked voting rights, and full members. Currently, membership grants full voting rights in the general assembly and the right to be elected for any of the association's offices, including president. In the past, this right was reserved only for those holding a master's degree or a higher degree (irrespective of the area of the degree or the department that conferred it). In recent years, the criterion for full membership (and voting rights) has changed, and it is based solely on the payment of membership dues twenty-four hours before the annual meeting.

The IAA's budget relies on membership fees and the support of external entities. For many years, the following organizations and bodies supported the IAA: the Jerusalem Institute for Anthropological Research, the departments of sociology and anthropology at the various universities, the Public Trustee (Custodian of Absentee or Inherited Funds), the Ebert Foundation, the Center for Canadian Studies, and more. The municipality of Ashdod, the Van Leer Institute, and various colleges and universities supported the IAA by allowing it to hold meetings in their facilities free of charge. The universities also assisted in the funding of the secretary salary, mail and phone expenses, and the allocation of meeting halls for the various ongoing activities. Additional support came in the form of covering the costs of hosting overseas guest lecturers and printing the meeting proceedings or program. In exceptional cases, the university or college underwrote the costs of holding the meeting outside its own premises. For example, during the Second (Al-Aqsa) Intifada in the early 2000s, due to the reluctance of members and guests to stay in Jerusalem, a number of meetings backed by the Hebrew University were held outside the city, in its surrounding hill country, which was "annexed" to the city in order to authorize the financial support. Another monetary source was private foundations created by IAA members, such as Marcus Goldstein, who contributed a prize for an outstanding M.A. thesis.

THE IAA AND THE BOUNDARIES OF ANTHROPOLOGY

The term "Israeli anthropology," as subsumed in the IAA's title, invites consideration of its meaning, which was redefined from time to time by the contents and modes of the association's activity. Even if during some periods there was a consensus among members about the boundaries of the discipline, the definitions of anthropology as held by the IAA and as conceived within the academy did not always overlap. From the very beginning, the IAA deliberated over the question of anthropology's boundaries, and the possibility of combining its various sub-fields. The vision of the IAA founders and early members—to develop Israeli anthropology according to the American four-field model—survived for only a few years. American influences on Israeli anthropology have been crucial, throughout the many years of the latter's existence, and have even been intensified recently. The founders of the IAA, however, most of whom were educated in the United States, did not succeed at applying the American model to Israeli anthropology. Goldstein combated to the best of his ability the attempts to evade the imposed marriage of the four fields. He warned over and over again that members needed to close ranks, and also made sure that folklorists and physical anthropologists highlighted their appearances at meetings and in newsletters. Goldstein, together with the IAA board, insisted that the role of chairperson would rotate among representatives of different specialization—although, in fact, a folklore specialist never served in the office of chairperson, and from among more than ten past chairs, only Marcus Goldstein and Pat Smith were physical anthropologists. In order to persuade his colleagues to support the four-field approach, Goldstein quoted an interview in which Walter Goldschmidt, then the president of the American Anthropological Association (AAA), claimed that a diverse anthropology had greater value than the sum of its parts.

Developments within the IAA were a miniaturized reflection of developments in American anthropology—the main source of inspiration for Goldstein and his future colleagues. The AAA had adopted the four-field model from the time of its foundation until today. On the occasion of the AAA's centenary year, however, Borofsky (2002) argued in a paper he published in the association's journal, *American Anthropologist*, that the four-field structure is a narrative anthropologists have constructed about themselves. A statistical survey of the content of the articles appearing in the journal during its 100 years of existence showed that only ten percent reflected any kind of cooperation between anthropologists of the different specializations. Borofsky identified the roots of the cooperation in what he called the "Golden Age," during the lifetime of Franz Boas. Over time, these forms of cooperation evaporated, leaving behind only a relic of a myth, enforced by resistance to change, but by no means reflecting a reality. But, despite the influences of the theoretical trends holding sway overseas, the organization underwent processes that are typical of many professional organizations, chief of which has been the splintering into specializations. Bucher and Strauss (1951/1966) had addressed the problematic nature of the discipline's subdivision, in describing the splintering that has occurred in other professional associations. As with dynamic processes in other fields, the splintering is instigated by the rise of a new perspective on several aspects of professional identity, which deviates from the conventional view. These analyses clarify that the dilemmas concerning the co-existence of the four fields was not unique to Israel, but rose to the surface even in the crucible of that idea.

The efforts of the founders at the IAA to unify the specializations were maintained until 1977, when this artificial framework began to erode and come apart at the seams. The physical anthropologists who attended the 1977 meeting were already concentrated within a single panel session. In a conversation held a few years after the event, one participant stated that the panel speakers were talking among themselves only, and there was no point holding this insider dialogue within a broader framework. Five years later, there was an attempt to revive the four-field approach at a meeting in which sessions in folklore, social and cultural anthropology, physical anthropology, and archeology were held together, in addition to applied anthropology. Some twenty years after their disappearance, the sister fields appeared together again in a meeting in 1995 in a session labeled "biological anthropology," which included presentations from the field of physical anthropology. Again, in 2002, a meeting themed "the Body" invited a discussion of physical anthropology. But the physical anthropologists did not respond to this call, even though the IAA's board encouraged them to participate.

Along with the trend toward sub-specialization and the IAA's circumscribed focus on social and cultural anthropology, in recent years, an attempt to develop a dialogue with the humanities has been under way. This change can be attributed to the tendency of local anthropology to emphasize the narrative aspect of social life and the connection to history. The narrative turn invited scholars of literature, history, Jewish studies and psychology (life narrative), writers and artists, law and media professionals, and historians to participate in the meeting. These connections were most apparent at the 2000 meeting, titled "Anthropology and Its Neighbors." Nevertheless, the new and developing field of cultural studies, which might have been a natural ally to anthropology in this endeavor, remained on the outside. The exclusion was in no way unmotivated; cultural studies is too close for comfort to anthropology, as both regard "culture" as their object of study, from different and opposing points of view. The sense of competition between the two and their disparate methodologies has prevented an alliance.[2]

Shrinking or expansion of disciplinary territory was also a direct outcome of the policy of the acting chair at any given moment. Some chairs viewed it as their task to increase the scale of involvement of the association's activity, and they therefore invited, or allowed, representatives of different disciplines to participate in meeting panels. It follows that the IAA not only accepted a broad definition of a multifaceted anthropology, but also drew in presenters and audiences wielding other disciplinary identities, as well as researchers who had trouble finding a platform from which to present their ideas.

THE IAA AS AN ISRAELI ASSOCIATION

The Language Wars

In the question of whether the IAA, as a national association, is indeed Israeli, I begin by addressing an issue that I view as having symbolic import in relation to the IAA's activity in the Israeli context—the IAA's struggle over the use of Hebrew, or the "language wars" between Hebrew and English. Language wars in the Israeli academy are of old vintage. In the early twentieth century, when the first Israeli academic institutions—the Technion and the Hebrew University—were established in Palestine/Eretz Israel, a battle was waged over the language of instruction: should it be Hebrew or German? In the Technion, the battle took place during its first years, before World War I. The academic instructors, most of whom were immigrants from German-speaking countries, preferred to conduct their academic activity in their native tongue. They were confronted by defenders of the Hebrew language, who viewed this preference as a slap in the face of Zionist nationalism. The temporary victory of the proponents of German led to the resignation of the Zionist members of the Technion's board of directors.

German was pushed aside for understandable reasons. Hebrew had been adopted as the language of the Israeli academy. However, in the mid-1970s, the struggle took place between English and Hebrew. During the IAA's initial phases, English was the language of discourse and of publications. The founder, Marcus Goldstein, was not fluent in Hebrew and rarely used it, and other members of the board were new immigrants from English-speaking countries who found it convenient to use their native tongue. The first issues of the newsletter appeared in a bilingual edition, but from 1977 onward, it appeared only in Hebrew. Since 1979, once every few years the IAA has made an effort to publish a special English edition of the newsletter devoted to overseas members, as part of the IAA's marketing efforts to interest audiences abroad. Since the IAA's creation of its own website at the beginning of the 2000s, the call for papers for the annual meeting has also been published in English.

The decision about the language of the newsletter was the outcome of tacit agreement: no public debates on the issue ever took place. By way of contrast, the language of the annual meeting was a topic of formal debate and controversy, which from time to time was explicitly addressed in the general members' assembly. In 1981, a decision was taken to Hebraize the meetings and to allow lectures to be presented in English only when the presenter was not a native speaker of Hebrew. This decision was honored until the end of the 1980s, but from that point onward, meetings presentations fell almost equally to the sides of Hebrew and English, with slight fluctuations from meeting to meeting. The justifications for holding lectures in English were technical: the presence of the overseas guest speaker required a universal etiquette of hospitable communication, and, importantly, such speakers could not otherwise participate. However, beyond these aspects of communication and etiquette, the linguistic practices and the surrounding conflicts had a more complex significance. During the early years of anthropology in Israel, English was the language in which most anthropologists had the greater facility, due to their countries of origins. Later on, as the field became more established, English became the language of professional discourse within the Israeli social sciences generally. Publications by academics—books and articles, overseas meetings presentations, correspondence with colleagues, as well as the general contribution to scientific knowledge—were mostly performed and executed in English. Knowledge of English was, and still is, perceived within the educational system as an entrance ticket into the intellectual and academic world—a means of connecting the scientist/researcher/intellectual to the centers of anthropology. As the use of electronic mail expanded, English became the language of communication even in day-to-day communication among Israeli colleagues, at first due to the technical contingencies of the inter-institutional email services, and later as a matter of choice. Some years ago, at the height of the academic boycott of Israel following events of the Intifada, Tamar El-Or expressed her chagrin (in an email written in English, of course) concerning the fact that virtual discussions (by emails) about political issue among members of the Hebrew University department were taking place in English. She asked: when will we discuss the painful issues of our daily lives in Hebrew?

This linguistic duality also manifested itself in a discussion held at the IAA discussions on the topic of publishing an anthropological journal. One of the major reasons for initiating such a publication was the possibility of conducting discourse on Israeli issues in Hebrew on an Israeli, locally published platform. This initiative was never realized. (However, the journal *Sotziologia*

Israelit [*Israeli Sociology*], which is in Hebrew, includes anthropologists on its editorial board and features anthropological articles.)

The language issue, therefore, is a symptom of the tensions between the international and the local, between cosmopolitanism and Israeliness. Confronting the proponents of keeping Hebrew the IAA's dominant language, others support a policy of linguistic latitude. Students for whom English is not a native language are encouraged to write in English, based on the argument that they will be better off becoming accustomed to the language in which they will continue to pursue their academic careers.

Structure and Activity

Another way of appraising the Israeliness of the IAA is to examine its structure and the contents of its activity. Adoption of the AAA's model as a guide to structuring the IAA, as proposed by its founder during the IAA's early years, was met with opposition rooted in a belief about the essence of anthropology and its local sociocultural emphasis. However, over the years, the organizational structure of the IAA's activity was adapted to parallel that of the AAA: the organization of a yearly meeting that travels from one site to another, the publication of a newsletter, and the leadership structure comprising a chairperson accompanied by board members who represent the various sections of anthropology (recently the title was also changed from chairperson to president). The features of the annual meeting are also reminiscent of the AAA: multiple parallel panel sessions; the discussion of association affairs by the general assembly, publication of public statements, and more.

Israeli Versus American Topics

Another dimension of the IAA's Israeliness concerns the degree to which it has given voice to research in Israel, discussed Israeli issues, and provided a platform for Israeli anthropologists. The centrality of the discussion of Israeli society at the IAA is reflected in the large number of lecture topics focused on Israel, and plenty of discussions devoted to "home" affairs. It reflects the prevalent practice of "research at home" characteristic of Israeli anthropologists. The view from home is joined by a view from the outside—that of researchers from overseas who have studied Israel and present their findings at the meeting. For example, Herbert Lewis lectured in 1977 on a community of Yemeni Jewish immigrants in an Israeli town, Larry Loeb lectured on Habban and Habad in 1978, Lisa Gilad presented her study of Yemeni immigrants in 1981, Don Seeman reported about his work on Ethiopian Jewry in 1994, and Yoel

Bauman presented a paper on national parks and national memory in 1995. In this respect, the IAA was and still is Israeli.

Even if the topics of panel sessions at the meeting are defined by the organizers as general ones—such as ethnicity, medicine, the military, the body, gender, religion—the presentations generally approach these issues via their manifestations in the Israeli field. The proportion of research not centered on Israel at the first meetings in the early 1970s was about one third of all presentations, while from 1977 onward the panel sessions began to take on an almost exclusively Israeli color. Even though some Israeli researchers have studied non-Israeli topics, they have preferred to contribute their research and insights on Israeli society at IAA meetings.

Despite the prevalence of Israeli society as a research object, the inspiration for Israeli anthropology has come from research centers in the United States and Europe. At the same time, the choice of meeting topics reveals the profound influence of American anthropological academic discourse. In the 1980s there was a two- to three-year lag before American topics entered Israeli discourse; in recent years, however, ideas are diffused much more quickly, for reasons that are institutional, ideological, as well as theoretical.

For most of its existence, the IAA was supported by external foundations, mostly the Jerusalem Center of Anthropological Research, directed by Edgar Siskin. Siskin was a cultural anthropological from the United States who was a specialist on the native American Washoo tribe (Siskin 1983) and a Reform rabbi in a suburban Chicago community. He decided to make his home in Jerusalem after his retirement and created the foundation out of personal resources, along with funds donated by members of his congregation, for the purpose of advancing Israeli anthropology. His assistance was realized in the funding of a yearly visit to Israel of a distinguished guest anthropologist from abroad at the annual meeting. The Jerusalem Center for Anthropological Research supported the IAA from the end of the 1970s until the mid-1990s.

The IAA continued the tradition of inviting a guest speaker to the meeting, despite the great effort involved in raising the requisite funds. The guest was the keynote speaker at the meeting, and his or her presentation related to the central theme of the meeting. The rationale for inviting a guest speaker was to bring to anthropologists on the periphery (Israel) information and scientific knowledge emanating from the center (usually the United States and Europe). During the first years of Israel's existence, Israelis did not often participate in international projects abroad, and therefore Israeli anthropology made an effort to remain connected to the center in whatever way possible. It was Siskin's interest to invite speakers of world renown in order to justify the activity of the Jerusalem Center for Anthropological Research to the foundation's donors (also from the American Jewish community). For the IAA members, the guest speaker was a hook for networking within world anthropological networks. His or her academic evaluation could be sought, and his or her interest in local research could be elicited, while also obtaining updates about activity overseas. After making the guest's personal acquaintance during his or her stay in Israel, he or she could be asked for recommendations in the process of a job search or graduate and post-graduate education abroad, as well as for sabbatical engagements. The guest committed to presenting the keynote talk at the meeting and taking an active role in at least one of the panel sessions. In addition, he or she was asked to make the rounds of the leading universities to present a lecture or meet with faculty and advanced students. The meetings at the universities were sometime accompanied by informal social encounters in the homes of colleagues. Siskin usually gave the IAA the freedom to choose the guest, but his relationship with the IAA came to an end due to his criticism of the IAA's leftist political leanings.

The guest was chosen by the IAA board, but the opinion of the chairperson held considerable weight in the choice. More often than not, the guest was selected on the basis of personal acquaintance with the association chair, their being on the same "professional wavelength," or their sharing of similar theoretical or topical interests. Usually, the choice of guest was a compromise between several alternatives when no consensus emerged.[3] Some of the guests (especially Jewish ones) had visited Israel in the past and had ties in Israel or with Israeli anthropologists. Others visited Israel for the first time on the occasion of the meeting, and were unfamiliar or unknown to most of the Israeli anthropologists. The dilemma of whom to choose as guest wavered between inviting a reputed anthropologist, whose work and ideas were already well known, and inviting promising and charismatic figures who had just launched their careers.

The central guests at the meeting had a large impact on the local community. For example, the inspiring visit by Victor Turner in the early 1980s led to some studies of pilgrimages and saint worship/burial sites (see Bilu and Ben-Ari 1997; Weingrod 1998a), as well as the investigation of Judaism as culture (Goldberg 1987). The guests' visits contributed to anthropology's emergence from isolation to take part in a more central anthropological agendas. In addition, they served as a channel of bi-directional communication, creating a reputation for Israeli anthropology in the world arena.[4]

The Association's Name

Another aspect of defining the boundaries of Israeli identity at the association is the dispute that has taken place in recent years over its title. Uri Davis, one of the IAA's members, has consistently requested to devote an agenda item to discussing a change of name—from the Israeli Anthropological Association to "The Anthropological Association in Israel." According to him, the concept of Israeli anthropology excludes the membership of potential Palestinian anthropologists, because the meaning attributed to "Israelis" does not include Arabs or Palestinians. Davis's proposal has been rejected by majority vote at a number of general assemblies, and the proposal of a name change has now been removed from the agenda.

Political Activity

The IAA's Israeli character may also be assessed in light of its relationship to issues that occupy the agenda of Israeli society. Throughout its years of activity, the IAA has responded to current political and social issues by publishing public statements in the Israeli press. This activity is a channel for exploring issues of professional identity, ethics, and Israeliness. For most IAA members, as Israeli citizens, this is their sole political activity, and is therefore of significance in forming their identities.

THE IAA AS A PROFESSIONAL ORGANIZATION

The issue of the IAA's identity as a professional organization can be examined from two different angles: (1) the IAA as an organization that cultivates its members' professional interests, and (2) the IAA's modes of promoting the professionalization of its members. For the purpose of the analysis, I shall address each of these aspects separately, although it is clear that they are connected.

Following Foucauldian concepts, the distinction Jan Goldstein (1984) draws between a "discipline" and a "profession" may illuminate the differences between the two. A profession is a body of knowledge that maintains a monopoly, as well as autonomy and a concept of service, as an integral part of the profession. When discussing the concepts of profession, Foucault had psychiatry chiefly in mind, but his definition may also be apt in respect to anthropology.

The IAA was founded as an association of professional anthropologists—that is, those holding an academic degree in physical or social anthropology, folklore, or archeology, most of whom were university employees. Over time, the stringent criteria determining membership eligibility in the IAA has loosened, and the sole criterion for membership became the payment of membership dues. This change implies the tacit distinction made between membership in a professional association and recognition of a professional identity. Not all IAA members identified themselves as anthropologists. When the American and British anthropological associations were formed, they also included members who were amateur ethnographers or anthropologists, lacking formal training. In Israel, anthropology is not formally defined as a profession (e.g., in the roster of professions), but, informally, it still makes membership contingent on proof of knowledge earned within the academy. As opposed to other professions, such as law, psychology, medicine, and social work, it enjoys none of the monopolistic and autonomous possibilities for setting criteria for an "entry ticket" into the profession. Most anthropologists are not service providers, with the exception of some applied anthropologists who make their knowledge available to their clients. Nevertheless, the IAA attempted to work toward the creation and preservation of Foucauldian professional attributes: a body of knowledge, monopoly, and autonomy.

THE IAA AS A GUILD

Many professional associations, especially those belonging to the applied academic professions, regard it as their role to represent the professional interests of their members, and to act as gatekeeper, keeping out those who don't have possess strict qualifications. In principle, the IAA attempted to promote the professional interests of its members along three different axes: (1) setting rates and fees for employment, (2) marketing the anthropological profession among potential employers and finding employment for its members, and (3) attempting to create a formal definition for the anthropological profession in order to receive recognition by the state as one of the caring/therapeutic professions.

Some five years after the IAA was founded, it formulated a price list for anthropological services, consultation, and lecturing fees. The goal was equipping members—especially those employed outside the universities—with a document that would define their conditions of employment. The price list was updated two years later, after the board asked members to report about its effectiveness in their contacts with employer organizations. In practice, the usefulness of this price list was negligible. The conditions of employment within the universities are governed by the labor relations between university employees and management; the IAA did not attempt to influence those, understanding that these power centers were beyond its operational reach. Even strong professional associations, such as the Israeli psychologists' and social workers' associations, take steps now and again to affect the conditions of employment of their members, by means of a long strike. However, it is well known that the conditions of employment of those employed in the caring/social science professions—such as psychologists and social workers in the public sector—are among the worst in the Israeli white collar professions.

Another sphere of the IAA's professional activity, the inclusion of anthropology in the roster of recognized professions compiled by the Hadassah Career Counseling Institute, was the outcome of a regulation process targeting the caring professions, in wake of the parallel attempt of the psychologists' association to legislate a Psychologists Law in 1980. These associations attempted to place their professions on a par with those of physicians and lawyers. The psychologists formulated entry requirements for the profession in order to prevent therapists who were not academically trained from practicing, and to safeguard the exclusive status of clinical psychologists for financial reasons. The Hadassah Institute, one of whose functions is also to provide a definition of the various professions, approached the IAA and proposed examining the issue. The IAA board held a discussion about whether anthropology should or ought to be defined as a caring/therapeutic profession, but no binding decision was reached, nor was any further action taken to promote the issue. The question arises—what is the rationale of including anthropology within the category of caring/therapeutic professions? The reason is historical: Phyllis Palgi, who was the chief anthropologist at the Ministry of Health and worked mainly in the field of mental health, opened the door to the employment of anthropologists in medical and mental health institutions. Anthropologists worked at Talbiyah Psychiatric Hospital, at public mental health clinics, and also in the Youth Aliyah institutions from the mid-1970s until the end of the 1980s. I myself worked for about a year as an anthropologist at the Lod mental health center. Anthropologists were perceived by their employers, and in their own eyes, as experts skilled in intercultural mediations. As such, they wished to engage in unmediated interaction with therapeutic clients, to have access to their medical records, and to be present in therapeutic sessions in order to provide the proper institutional and personal counseling. However, because they were not defined as professionals, they were prevented direct access to clients (although these rules were not always strictly observed). A number of cases in which health institutions used anthropologists as providers of therapeutic services are known. In the late 1970s I was a witness (concealed behind a one-way screen) to a therapy session held by an anthropologist who was treating an Ethiopian youth at a psychiatric hospital.

Cottrell and Sheldon (1964) discuss the problematic nature of collaboration between social scientists and therapeutic professions (medicine, social work, and psychology). They found three reasons why it is difficult to join forces and collaborate: the different organizational cultures, the immediate social context in which the social sciences operate, and the vague expectations as well as contested nature of these expectations. This threefold problem is reflected in the relations between anthropologists and therapists in the institutional health systems. (For more on this problematic issue, see Palgi 1993.)

In general, anthropologists and therapists were not much in demand in the extra-academic world of employment. A few opportunities existed in the public sector, including government ministries and agencies devoted to providing social services and social advancement, such as the Ministry of Absorption and the Ministry of Health, or municipalities and local organizations. In addition, a handful of anthropologists were recruited into research institutions and extra-governmental enterprises such as the Brookdale Institute, the Jewish Agency, the Youth Aliyah organization, or the Joint Distribution Committee (JDC). A certain change took place with the immigration waves of the early 1990s, due to the capital that governmental bodies and external foundations invested in research, some of which was carried out by anthropologists, as anthropologists took part in the research projects of NGOs and non-profit organizations. (For research on this topic, see, e.g., Salamon and Kaplan 1998. For a general review of the activity of applied anthropologists in Israel, see Shabtai and Mizrahi 2004; Kalifon 1997.)

The IAA assists in helping anthropologists find employment by various channels. In 1977, a position for an anthropologist at Bar Ilan University was posted, and in 1983 an employment committee was formed at the IAA in order to create demand for positions for anthropologists as well as for publishing available positions, but these initiatives were unfruitful. The search for candidates for academic positions—then and today—bypasses the IAA and follows both formal and informal routes, through postings on departmental websites and on the American Anthropological Association website. The building of the IAA's website in the early 2000s enabled a new venue for advertising job vacancies; yet, despite the availability of this platform as another channel for job searches, hardly any use has been made of it at all.

In addition to the activities mentioned, the IAA has also published its list of members, which provides information both for the purpose of professional activity, and as a way of informally strengthening ties among members. The first list was created and distributed close to the establishment of the IAA in the mid-1970s, the second appeared in the mid-1980s, and, lastly, the third appeared in the mid-1990s. An additional initiative to create a database of anthropologists and their activities was undertaken a number of years ago, when a large survey was conducted by the IAA using advanced Internet technology—a survey to which most IAA members responded.

In 1985, the IAA made an all-out effort to market its members and published an English-language directory, detailing the names of anthropologists and classifying them according to various criteria: affiliations with the universities (even outside the departments of sociology and anthropology) and colleges; affiliations with institutions such as museums, government ministries, or the Jewish Agency; names of IAA members outside Israel; and names of graduate students. In addition to names and addresses, the directory also included degrees and titles, as well as research interests. The directory was intended for internal use in Israel and also as a calling card for Israeli anthropology in international contexts. The publication of the members list, and especially the directory including fields of activity and central publications, could have represented the anthropological community's attempt to display its worth to others and also to itself. When the IAA's website was created, it was expected that members would construct their own personal pages on it; however, to date, most members have not taken advantage of this feature to present their work and qualifications.

THE PUBLICATION OF AN ANTHROPOLOGICAL JOURNAL

As a professional association seeking to promote its members professionally, every so often the IAA proposes the creation of a designated Israeli anthropological journal. The initiative, the discussion in the member's assembly, the inevitable agreement about the importance of the issue, as well as the inaction in implementing the idea, have become a permanent ritual that repeats itself at IAA board meetings. The idea was first promoted by Goldstein, who viewed the founding of a journal as indispensable for the professional development and nourishing of Israeli anthropology, and he struggled to carry it out. The goals formulated were social-ideological ones—relating to the idea of the promotion of knowledge and understanding and tolerance between Jews deriving from different cultures, as well as between Jews and Arabs—in addition to the goal of publishing research on Israeli society (Goldstein 1995, 79). Goldstein requested the support of Cyril

Belshaw, then the editor-in-chief of *Current Anthropology*, and expressed his willingness to devote himself to the task. The proposal was brought up at the IAA board meeting, but was rejected on the grounds that those interested in publication could do so within other journals published in Israel. In 1981, the journal initiative was raised again, and was voted down due to the argument that it was become the "waste bin" for below-par articles that were rejected by major journals abroad. Another argument was the practicality of the venture: much effort would be required to edit such a journal, and no volunteers came forth. In 1984, the IAA appointed an editorial board for the creation of an anthropological journal, but it did not accomplish anything. Paradoxically, it is possible that the absence of an Israeli anthropology journal has actually contributed to the prestige of Israeli anthropology, because researchers had no choice but to publish in international journals. Publishing in Hebrew would have only exacerbated Israeli anthropology's marginality.

The decision to establish a journal at one of the general members' assemblies in the early 2000s suffered a similar fate. The reintroduction of the proposal was the result of a sense that the IAA had gained in strength and was capable of raising funds and finding resources to finance its activities. This proposal was also rejected on the grounds that no one could be found who was single minded enough to take on the mission of founding and editing a scholarly journal. In 2002, the idea came up again in a slightly different version—the publication of a journal that would serve as a platform for student publications, like the journal *HAGAR*, which is put out by the department of Middle Eastern studies at Ben Gurion University. Again, no one could be found to push the initiative through.

A comparison with other professional associations in the Israeli social sciences reveals that many of them do put out their own publications. A journal titled *Israeli Sociology*, which has been published by the department of sociology and anthropology at Tel Aviv University since 1998, is not, admittedly, directly connected to the Israeli Sociological Association, but it does serve as a platform on which this association's members (along with anthropologists) frequently publish. The Israel psychologists' association has been publishing a journal since 1986. The economists put out a journal with the prestigious publisher *Am Oved*. The associations of social workers, criminologists, and geographers all have their own journals. This wealth of journals published by Israeli social scientific professional associations raises the question of why the sociologists and anthropologists don't have one of their own. A number of possible reasons come to mind:

1. In his autobiographical book, Moshe Shokeid describes the quest for promotion in the Israeli social sciences, arguing that researchers are expected to perform double duty by proving that they can publish in international forums, especially in English, while their everyday reality is circumscribed by the framework of a national university in which Hebrew is the dominant language. Insofar as academic appointments and promotion are concerned, publication in Hebrew repays significantly less in terms of status and overall weight, and usually researchers with original work will attempt first to publish in an international language (Shokeid 2000). Taking on the task of founding and editing a journal would require time and energy that would otherwise be spent on advancing one's personal promotion track within the universities, which do not value publications in Hebrew. This being the case, participants in the race for promotion forgo local publication venues. More senior scholars, who have already established their academic reputations and careers, are left with more time to publish in Hebrew, but the prestige involved in publishing in an international journal, even one that is not of the first rank, is greater.

2. Behind the scenes of anthropological practice, there is wariness about publishing studies focused on Israeli society in Hebrew. Practicing anthropology at home, and writing about research subjects in their native language, presents researchers with the possibility of exposing their research to its subjects. Writing in Hebrew increases the chances that the subjects will become acquainted with the research performed on them. Methodological and ethical preferences are considered within the delicate and complicate relationships between the researcher and his subjects.

3. The professional associations that consistently put out Hebrew-language journals are strong associations with large numbers of members. They enjoy a valued status in Israeli society and anchor the academic knowledge acquired in the field in publications of an applied orientation targeting a variety of different audiences. Israeli anthropology and the IAA, its public representative, have still not yet attained this status; for now, professional knowledge is passed on through presentation in academic meetings, informal networks, and the anthropological English-language journals.

MEMBERSHIP IN THE IAA AS A SIGNIFIER OF IDENTITY

Membership in a professional association can serve as a signifier of its members' identity. Israeli anthropologists usually belong to several associations simultaneously (e.g., the American and European anthropological associations and the Israeli associations in adjacent fields in the social sciences). The activity of the prestigious international associations, which includes meetings and journals, draws Israelis to join these associations. Membership in the international associations serves various interests: aspiring to a cosmopolitan identity, affiliation with supranational frameworks, and, especially, avoiding exclusive affiliation with a professional association in a marginal locale—in other words, combating fear of provincialism. Israeli anthropologists' membership in competing Israeli associations, such as the Israeli Sociological Association, enhances the obscurity of boundaries between sociology and anthropology in Israel. When Israeli anthropologists who had participated in IAA meetings were asked why they do not join as members, some presented cost as the reason, because of the burden of paying double and sometimes triple membership fees. The decision of where to invest one's membership fees is tied to considerations of professional identity and scientific prestige. When it is necessary to choose, many will choose the international associations or the larger Israeli associations. Although the participation of Israelis in international meetings is large relative to its population size, and relative to the general level of academic activity, most nevertheless do pay membership dues to the IAA. It might be a ritual activity that has little academic or professional payoff, but whose chief virtue lies rather in promoting the connection to the local national community as a symbolic act of defining the national component of one's personal identity.

POLITICAL ACTIVITY AND SOCIAL ENGAGEMENT

The IAA identifies itself as a socially and politically engaged association, following the model of the AAA. The ethos of its members, who regard themselves as "culture" professionals, includes a commitment to react to events or phenomena in Israeli society that constitute human rights abuses or offenses to the cultural rights of various groups. The actions through which the IAA puts this ethos into practice are the publication of public statements, declarations, and calls for papers on current Israeli issues. (The IAA's first public statement, regarding the protection of the rights of an anthropologist from Paraguay, was an exception.) The reasoning for such initiative is the belief that anthropologists' voices must be heard, and that their personal and professional commitments urge them to be outspoken and make an impact.

The process of formulating a public statement begins with the initiative of one of the association's members, which he or she then presents to the other members at the annual meeting. After the assembly discusses and votes on a draft statement, the IAA passes it on to the press. The draft itself usually includes, as an integral part of the statement, justifications for the involvement of anthropologists in the issue. An alternate path is when the initiative is taken by the IAA board and chair; thus, recently, a public statement opposing the closure of a department at Ben Gurion University has been distributed to various websites—it is also signed by past chairpersons of the IAA.

The following are the public statements and respective issues published by the IAA throughout all its years of activity:

1. The first public statement was published in 1976, supporting the human rights of an anthropologist from Paraguay who had been incarcerated by the regime. The IAA appealed to the Foreign Ministry to act on behalf of his release from detention. This was the first and last time the IAA attempted to defend an anthropologist from the international anthropological community.

2. In 1978, a public statement was addressed to the Israeli government on the issue of assistance to Ethiopian Jews in their country of origin and in Israel.

3. In 1980, the IAA appealed for the protection of the rights of Bedouin in the Negev.

4. In 1982, a public statement was issued regarding the Antiquities Law. It was initiated by archeologists and was intended to defend the academic rights to conduct archeological excavations wherever deemed fit.

5. In 1983, a public statement was issued on the topic of the Lebanon war. At the same time, a discussion about the Israeli–Palestinian conflict was taking place in the AAA newsletter, a discussion whose echoes reached Israel and affected relations among IAA members in Israel.

6. In 1988 there was a proposal to issue a public statement about the Intifada. The assembly decided to publish an open letter in the newspaper, and the cost was covered by donations of the members who supported the statement.

Since 1988, no public statements have been issued (apart from the letter mentioned in the last item). At the 2008 meeting, a discussion took place on the ethical question of whether the IAA ought to make a political statement, following a discussion of the political/security situation after the "Cast Lead" operation and war in Gaza. The speakers called up examples from the past to prove that political statements had always been a part of the IAA's activity, but no such statement was formulated at the general assembly. The upshot was a decision to create a committee that would discuss the issue and formulate a draft to be voted on.

Public statements and announcement on current issues in Israeli society are a standard practice of professional associations in Israel and of anthropological associations abroad. In Israel, the sociologists, psychologists, and the social workers all issue public statements. The members of the AAA also publish statement on topics related to the Israeli–Palestinian issues—as for example, at the November 1982 AAA meeting, in which a number of members initiated a condemnation of the "Israeli occupation in Lebanon" and requested that the assembly ratify it. Despite the objections of a number of Jewish and Israeli anthropologists, the resolution was passed and the condemnation was published. In response, Israeli anthropologist Shlomo Deshen wrote a letter to the AAA newsletter, requesting to condemn the condemnation. A few months later, at the 1983 IAA meeting, the issue was brought up both at a panel session and at the members' assembly. After a stormy debate, a response was formulated, condemning the condemnations, and was sent to the British Anthropological Associations newsletter (RAIN). The public statement evoked the "destruction of Palestinian culture" and called on the United States to quit supplying Israel with American weaponry, which assists the occupation of Lebanon and the destruction of its culture. In response, Israeli anthropologist Henry Rosenfeld wrote a letter in the IAA newsletter, taking sides with the condemnation and its initiators. The AAA became an arena for conflicts between Israeli and world anthropologists and among Israelis as well.

The public image of the profession and the discipline helps construct the identity of anthropologists as committed experts who should not be permitted the luxury of secluding themselves inside the ivory tower. Anthropologists are perceived by themselves and by society as authorities on the culture of other people, whose rights require protection. Historically, the Bedouin and the Palestinian were "Others" who required protection; to them were joined other underprivileged groups, such as Ethiopian immigrants. The expression of the anthropological commitment to weakened groups was reflected, for example, in the formulation of the 1980 public statement that called for the defense of the Bedouin land rights "[b]ecause the right of every cultural group to live according to its traditions in a pluralist society must be defended."

Marta Topel, who carried out a study on Israeli anthropology in the mid-1990s, made use of the key concept of "moral capital" (inspired by Bourdieu's "cultural capital"), to describe the struggles of Israeli anthropologists in international journals (Topel 1998). She shows how these struggles enhance the moral capital of the participants, through which they increase their academic prestige. Topel surveyed three conflictual interchanges that took place between Israeli anthropologists and their colleagues within the pages of international scholarly journals: between Moshe Shokeid and Stanley Diamond (Shokeid 1992b), between Moshe Shokeid and Ted Swedenberg (Swedenberg 1993), and between Harvey Goldberg and Jonathan Boyarin (Goldberg 1992). Publication of political-moral debate in professional publications in journals and in newspapers highlights the anthropologist's moral capital.

Political statements by IAA members, whether through the public statement channel or through other communication channels, have had their own price tag: Edgar Siskin, the director of the Jerusalem Center for Anthropological Research, who supported the IAA during its early years, removed his support due to the "left-wing" orientation of its members. At the same time, the IAA as a professional association did not channel its social involvement to any real action on the ground. Even the personal involvement of IAA members in radical activist groups, such as the Coalition Against (Palestinian) House Demolition, movement against military service, or Shin (an organization for the promotion of women's rights), did not lead the IAA to take any proactive steps to promote social causes.

In periods of political crisis and the undermining of Israel's international standing, the political identification of IAA members is problematic. The revival of the issues of occupation, terror, settlements, and the Israeli–Palestinian conflict in 2000, along with the terror campaign against Israeli civilians, led to a critique of the government's actions on the one hand, and to a sense of insecurity on the other. At the IAA's May 2002 meeting, a session was held on "anthropology and the situation" (meaning the security and political situation). The IAA chairperson deemed it necessary to raise questions regarding the role of anthropologists in interpreting the events, reacting, and taking action. Within the Israeli scientific community, a debate was raging at the time regarding the international boycott on scientific cooperation with Israel. In this case, an internal front against the boycott began to form, even though opposition to the government did not abate in insider discussions. The 2008 IAA meeting took place just after the IDF's incursion into Gaza. The meeting's key speaker, Michael Lambek, who at first hesitated to accept the invitation, finally agreed, and initiated a discussion about the political situation at the meeting's general assembly. His presence and initiative forced IAA members to voice their views; perhaps without Lambek's intervention, these topics, which are controversial, would have remained under wraps without being openly broached.

This phenomenon merits viewing through a comparative lens, especially by examining the American model. In an article published at the centenary issue of the AAA, Susan Trencher (2002) surveyed the AAA's practice of publishing statements, from the 1930s through the 1970s; her findings point to the existence of two central controversies in respect to this practice. The first is a debate over the very legitimacy of publishing statements that are relevant to the public sphere, based as they are on data collected on civic issues and not on academic research. The second is the debate over the image projected by the publication of statements—as if all anthropologists were cut of the same cloth. The Israeli case reveals intense involvement of a number of anthropologists in social causes as well as the use of academic prestige and of academic tools to analyze political situations that require taking a stand. Alongside these outspoken members is a silent majority of anthropologists who hold opinions—ranging from moderate left-wing to the radical left—who are not politically active, as is typical of the social scientist community in general in Israel.

Another way to view the activity and political involvement of the IAA is to ask to what extent it entertains a vision of contribution to the community as a goal unto itself. The IAA is more likely to make such decisions when it feels it is not dependent for its survival on external resources and has the freedom to define its goals autonomously. The association's declared goals, as reflected in various texts, do not address the direct contribution to Israeli society, but, in practice, a number of actions have been taken that can be characterized (although not explicitly so) as community involvement. From the mid-1990s on, the annual meeting has included an excursion in the area where the meeting was hosted. This was preceded, in the early 1980s, at the Jerusalem meeting, by a first excursion into the field, which took participants out of the meeting precincts to a central session held at the Israel Museum. The Ein Gedi in 1995 was a turning point: it was the first meeting held outside a university, and the participants were invited to tour Masada. The visit to Masada was directly tied to the meeting theme, and its prominent discussions were devoted to collective memory. Following this meeting, the practice became a habitual one. At Zikhron Ya'akov, participants were offered a tour of the prehistoric caves on Mount Carmel and of historical sites in the town itself. The Jerusalem meeting in 2000 offered a visit to the tunnels excavated beneath the Western Wall and to the Old City of Jerusalem. The planners were doubtful about the degree of participation because of the political implications of such an excursion. The Tel Aviv meeting of 2001 included a dinner event at a Bukharan restaurant in one of the city's southern neighborhoods. In 1999, the meeting took place at a hotel in Upper (Jewish) Nazareth, but the activities were held mostly in Arab part of the city. The 2006 meeting in Ashdod was the first to be held in an urban center considered to be a "new city" settled mostly by immigrants from North Africa in the 1960s and Russia in the 1990s. Michael Feige (1998) made a pointed comparison of this activity with that of the Israel Exploration Society (archeological association) in the "development towns," new immigrants' cities. He pointed to the role both associations played in defining the place of the development towns in the national narrative. Feige analyzed the links between academic research and sociopolitical processes in both cases.

The Israel Exploration Society used to hold popular archeological meetings in selected development towns in which archeological sites were found. Its goal was both to convey a social message and to relate to the local archeological site. In recent years, however, the anthropologists have only evinced an interest in these towns in regard to the emerging ritual practices and pilgrimages connected to their saintly shrines.

Feige is correct in that holding an annual meeting in a development town was never considered an option in the IAA during the years in which I served as secretary, and later as a board member in the years 1999–2002. But it has come to my attention that the possibility of holding the meeting in Kiryat Gat, during Eyal Ben-Ari's tenure as chairperson, did come up, although it was not realized. In 2008, when I served as chair of the IAA, we looked into the possibility of holding the meeting in Acre; however, the municipality's meager financial support was not sufficient to make this possible. In later years, meetings were held in academic institutions in the center and periphery of the country, but the practice of offering local excursions was abandoned.

Although archeology was a field that excited the imaginations of both layperson and experts, anthropology was not successful at drawing public attention. The large number of participants at the Israeli Exploration Society's meetings, which hosted politicians and many public figures, contrasts starkly with the small number of non-anthropologists from the public at large at the IAA meetings. The connection between the IAA and the community was one of an academic and declarative nature, without any concrete attempts to materialize such a connection. Many anthropologists studied development towns or immigrant settlements but preferred to hold their annual ritual at hotels or at kibbutz guest houses. Beginning the middle of the 2000s, however, this trend was altered, and the meetings now take place in peripheral locations, despite the lack of direct engagement with the hosting environment during the meeting.

THE IAA AS A LEVER FOR PERSONAL AND SCIENTIFIC DEVELOPMENT AND ADVANCEMENT

Scientific activity is based on values imbued with the rhetoric of voluntarism: the notion is that the scientist "contributes" his or her knowledge for the benefit of an abstract entity named "science." By means of this contribution, the scientist promotes him- or herself and society. Scientific activity takes place within a the formal and hierarchical space of academic organizations and institutions, but also within a democratic space, in which peer review and the right for academic freedom are the order of the day. At the same time, one cannot ignore the fact that alongside the contribution to the collective, research and publication advance the careers of individuals who take part in these activities.

The justifications for the activity of scientific associations, including the IAA, are in keeping with the aforementioned objectives. The association is presented as a contribution and commitment to the advancement of knowledge, of the profession, and of the discipline. At the same time, it provides the platform and opportunity for the self-promotion of its members via its activities. The IAA founders' appeal during the association's early years—"come, learn, exchange opinions with your colleagues"—was a declaration of intent and a justification for the annual meeting, and it took place both within the formal context of the lectures and within the informal context of corridor talk. The IAA newsletter (in the past) and the IAA website (in the present) include lists of members' select publications, announcement of meetings abroad and in Israel, reports on participation in meetings, the presentation of new curricular programs at the universities, announcements about the activity of local anthropological forums (Tel Aviv, Jerusalem), personal announcements (congratulations, obituaries, foundations in memoriam of deceased anthropologists), job vacancies, warnings about a fraudulent dissertation, a price list, and fellowship announcements.

The IAA's activity is indeed also an opportunity for personal and professional advancement. The annual meetings were defined as knowledge promoting and as a mechanism for presenting new ideas for peer review, for discussion of topics on the scientific agenda, and as a venue for exposure to younger colleagues. Participation in the meeting is an economic activity, because with the insubstantial investment of one or two days, one can quickly be updated on what is "cooking" in one's colleagues "kitchens." For those enjoying job security at their institutions, usually senior employees, the cost of participation in the meeting is reimbursed through personal research funds or by the institution itself, and the time away from regular work duties is also supported by academic institutions. Catching up is accomplished due to the immediacy of reporting on research, the summaries of findings, and the informal discourse among colleagues. In recent years, the yearly meetings have had the character of an interdisciplinary encounter, inviting participants to display an interest in adjacent fields, such as history, psychology, art, geography, literature, and even genetics. The inclusion of colleagues from other disciplines was an outcome of the personal initiative of session organizers and of the policy outlined by the meeting's program committee. The meeting topic occasions dialogue and enables discourse among participants who normally would not meet randomly on academic turf. Intense activity surrounds the visit by an overseas scholar. As a small and isolated academic community whose contact with overseas colleagues was for many years limited, experiencing a new refreshing, up-to-date, and challenging encounter at the meeting became a necessity, not a luxury. The visitor's contribution was not limited to his or her keynote presentation, but was also evident in the personal conversations with members, responses to their lectures, encounters with students, and presentations at academic institutions. The visits even helped stimulate local initiatives. For example, the visits by Victor Turner, and later by Barbara Myerhoff in the early 1980s, were a catalyst for panel sessions on their research topics and later for a book that proceeded from these sessions (Goldberg 1987).

Because of its special character, anthropological research, more than other kinds, is in need of this kind of encounter in order to develop. Whereas in the exact sciences and the life sciences collaborative work in the lab and at research institutes is the norm, and dialogue and conversation are part and parcel of the process of scientific knowledge production, anthropologists are alone in their fieldwork, and the meeting is the one venue that enables interaction among colleagues. A by-product of the meeting, the collection of paper abstracts, is another tool for academic cross-fertilization. Since the mid-1990s, the collections of abstracts have appeared regularly as part of the institutionalization and enrichment of the IAA, which was facilitated by digital printing technologies and the use of the IAA's website.

The IAA also provided an overarching framework for the activity of the Jerusalem and Tel Aviv anthropological forums, which were active on and off during the 1980s and 1990s. The announcements about the forums' meetings were distributed via the IAA newsletter. The IAA's website and email communications have facilitated the dissemination of information about the anthropological forum at the Haifa department.

Every so often, the IAA has initiated an additional activity between the meetings. For example, in 1993 a series of workshops and day seminars were held. There was also a series of meetings on the theme of visual anthropology. In the last two years, Bar Ilan University with IAA conducted mini-meetings on professional anthropological topics.

Personal development within the academy occurs chiefly in the university channels; and yet, the contribution of the IAA should not be underestimated, particularly the way in recent years (since the mid-1990s) it has benefited the advancement of young researchers. For most of its existence, and as part of the association's democratic outlook, the IAA's policy has been to encourage students (even those who had not yet completed their master's degrees) to present their work, providing a platform for the initial exposure of student work at the meetings, with the encouragement and patronage of the student's supervisors. This exposure has several objectives: a public claim to a particular research territory or field of expertise (in a small scientific community such as Israel, it is commonly felt that competition over research fields should be avoided); the gaining of experience in presenting a lecture at a local meetings, as part of training and a as general rehearsal for presenting overseas; and peer review by senior and junior scholars. The student presentations have taken place both in invited sessions, initiated by the master's thesis supervisors, on the topic of a seminar or research workshop that they were conducting (e.g., life narratives at the 1996 meeting), and by the initiative of the presenter. In addition to the debut of young researchers, such sessions provide a platform for the supervisor to make his or her research activity known. The element of marketing oneself at a meeting presentation has become so elaborate that the young presenters often come more to make themselves heard than to listen to others. They thus forfeit the opportunity to be enriched by colleagues' knowledge, which could be of great avail to them precisely at this point in their careers. The problem has become more acute because of the multiple parallel sessions at the meetings—so much so that some panel sessions have been attended only by the presenters, without an audience. And indeed, as a response to this state of affairs, during the past three years, the IAA has tended to limit student presentations and to allow only students with a master's degree, subject to the recommendation of their supervisors, to present at the meeting. Another route for the advancement of young researchers is the M.A. thesis competition, which was instituted at the 1995 annual meeting. Participation in the contest depends on the supervisor and the student's initiative, as well as awareness that the competition exists. Hence, apart from scientific excellence, it also reflects the centrality and concern of its supervisor. An IAA board member approaches external readers from among the local anthropological community to rank the theses. The chosen thesis is awarded a special session, and, in some instances, the winner has received a modest monetary prize. (It should be noted that in the Israeli academy, an M.A. thesis is expected to present a significant contribution to empirical research, and typically is based a substantive period of ethnographic fieldwork, rather than merely a literature survey or theoretical disquisition, and is valued accordingly.) A number of meetings in the mid-1990s included sessions devoted to student encounters, which were facilitated by a board member and raised shared research issues, such as fieldwork dilemmas (at the 1996 meeting). This practice stopped after 1998, but the students' place in the IAA board is guaranteed by the existence of a special slot for students presentations.

All presenters—junior as well as senior—initiate and organize sessions on their respective research fields. Sessions are organized in various venues: the session initiators create a closed session; the organizers post a call for papers to the entire membership and then select a topic. The initiative for a session on a specific topic unintentionally creates a stimulus to write on it; this encourages the development of a practice of knowledge production among young researchers and senior researchers alike on the session topic.

Another venue for public exposure is the book celebration, first instituted at the 1996 meeting. The event is used to launch books published in the past year. The presentation includes sometimes the offerings of the books for sale. This opportunity has been taken advantage of by a number of anthropologists since its institution, but it is not clear whether or to what extent it has enhanced interest in the books or increased sales in numerical terms. It seems that the financial motive of the book launch, as of any other academic publication, is underplayed to focus on the image of the contributing, rather than the profit-making, scientist.

At the same time, since the end of the 1990s, publishers of books on social issues have set up sales points at IAA meeting—for example, Tcherikover Press, which has occasionally published books by Israeli anthropologists and sociologists. It was involved in publishing anthropology titles in the 1980s, but went out of business in the 1990s. The relationship of the IAA with Resling Publishing House has become especially close. In addition to placing a sales point at the IAA meeting, for a number of years IAA members received two books of their choice from the Resling series as part of their membership fee. Resling was very active in publishing a selection of anthropology classics in Hebrew. Since the beginning of the 2000s, the publisher has put out translations of books by Victor Turner, Mary Douglas, Claude Lévi-Strauss, Marcel Mauss, and Clifford Geertz (see Abuhav and Shilo 2011). The current work was also published as a book in Hebrew by Resling (Abuhav 2010). Resling views the meeting's participants as commercial potential, and will certainly use the opportunity to promote sales, particularly when some of its titles are authored by meeting participants.

THE IAA'S AUTONOMY

The IAA's autonomy (or lack thereof), can be examined from a number of points of view. From the financial angle, the existence of a voluntary organization such as a professional association is dependent on the amount of academic and financial support it can muster for its activities. The rhetoric and ethos of "contribution" to science enlist participants to donate money through membership dues and the annual meeting fees. The membership dues are fixed according to the status of the members: seniors (Ph.D.s and upward) pay the full prices, and students and senior citizens (recently) pay a reduced fee. However, the membership dues do not cover the expenses of the IAA. The IAA is sustained by additional monetary sources: the universities, external foundations, and colleges that indirectly support the activity. During its early years, the IAA was dependent on the Hebrew University, its main supporter, which paid the secretary's salary and assisted with postage fees and office supplies. Later, the support came from the university with which the acting chair was affiliated or the institute (universities, colleges, cities, and others such as Van Leer Institute) that hosted the yearly meeting. In its early days, the IAA's activity was limited, and costs were not particularly high. Later, the IAA assumed the costs of the secretary's salary and the website maintenance using its own funds. The support received from Israeli universities ever since its founding, and also from colleges in recent years, indicates an increase in the legitimacy of anthropology in the academy and—even more so—the attractiveness, drawing power, and reputation of anthropological pursuits.

Other sources of financing the heavy expenses of hosting the key speakers from overseas are the Jerusalem Center for Anthropological Research (headed by Siskin) and the German Ebert Foundation, which supported a meeting on Palestinians in 1999. In the 1980s, there was an unsuccessful attempt to raise government funds from the Interior Ministry's Public Trustee (Custodian of Absentee or Inherited Funds).

During the years 2005, 2007, 2012, 2008, and 2009, IAA meetings were held in the Sapir, Achva, Beit Berl, Kinneret, and Yezreel Valley colleges, respectively, and were supported by these institutions. The funding of the visit by the guest lecturer was supported in exchange for having the guest present a lecture at these other institutions. Before the 2005 meeting, the possibility of holding it at the Beit Berl College was considered. There was a disagreement between the college and the IAA over the overseas visitor selected, and the meeting took place at Achva College instead. This case is a sign of the IAA's insistence that it remain autonomous, among others, in respect to the choice of guest speaker, even at the cost of the withdrawal of support of external bodies.

Some meetings were held at isolated sites that were unaffiliated with an academic institution. The annual meeting has taken place at the guesthouses of kibbutzim (Ein Gedi and Ma'ale Ha'akhamisha) and in hotels in urban centers (Zikhron Ya'akov, Nazareth, and Jerusalem). Another site was the Sde Boker Research Center, which hosted the annual meeting in 1993 and 2003. In 2006, the Ashdod municipality supported the meeting. Holding the meeting at an isolated site as opposed to having an intramural activity under university auspices has some advantages, such as the forced retreat of the participants from their daily work routines, which would promote more sharing among members, especially participation in the evening.

THE EVOLUTION OF THE IAA

A historical view of the IAA reveals three periods in its development: (1) the formative stage, 1974–1979; (2) a period of institutionalization during the years 1980–1995 (including a relative reduction of the scope of activity); and (3) growth and expansion since 1995.

In 1993, after some twenty years of activity, the associations' goals were revamped as follows: the renovation and expansion of anthropological activity, the development of a feeling of belonging and partnership, enabling communication services among members, increasing public awareness to anthropological activity, and distribution of knowledge.

Observing the development of the IAA points to the advancement and accumulation of knowledge and experience, which well suit the standard view of the development of science as a project of the modern (Rabinow 1991). At the same time, the generational changes create a sense of lack of continuity. The decreasing presence of the founding generations and their abstaining from IAA activity point to a change in the character of the IAA, and perhaps of Israeli anthropology in general. The autonomy of the IAA, stemming from its formal status as a voluntary association, enables a gradual changing of the guard to take place. There is only a minimal sense of renewal in the annual discussions at the meeting, but seen from a thirty-year perspective, the change is noticeable. The change is evolutionary not revolutionary.

FOUR

LIFE COURSES *of* ISRAELI ANTHROPOLOGISTS

What leads a person to become an anthropologist? "Anthropology allowed me to dream." "Under the umbrella of science, anthropology let my imagination roam." "We were young, enthusiastic, and up for a challenge, and we wanted to do a new kind of non-institutionalized anthropology that would have its own contribution." "Research doesn't belong in a drawer—anthropological research is meant to advance distressed populations." "Anthropology is a mother tongue." "Everywhere, I was always an outsider, observing things from my own corner." This selection of responses by anthropologists to the question why they chose this vocation reflects a variety of motivations, drives, interests, and images.

In examining the realm of anthropologists' life paths, I focus on the individual and on the way in which an individual's career was woven together to produce a professional anthropologist, researcher, author, lecturer, and breadwinner. By examining the impulses and motivations of the anthropologist in directing his or her career, as well as the dilemmas confronting him or her at different intersections, while also considering forces that had an impact, I seek to learn about anthropology from a fresh angle, applying an innovative methodological approach to enrich and diversify the overall picture.

The discussion of anthropologist's life courses will go in three directions: a methodological survey; the presentation of the interview material relating to the Israeli anthropologist's image of his or her life course; and a discussion of the motivations, images, and life courses of anthropologists in Israel, within a broader context.

(MY) INTRODUCTION TO ANTHROPOLOGY

Before presenting the life courses of my anthropologist colleagues, I would like to present my route to anthropology and invite the reader to join me and interpret its meanings.

As a student of anthropology in the early 1970s, and later as an active anthropologist in the Israeli academy, I was witness to the crises, high and low points, and the upheavals and efforts of Israeli anthropology to pave a legitimate path for itself within the Israeli academy. Through the prism of identity politics, I am seen as belonging to the very heart of the Israeli hegemony: I am Ashkenazi, a descendant of an ancient forbear who arrived in Jerusalem eight generations ago, with 15,000 of his descendants, some of them now occupying key positions in Israeli society. On my maternal side, I am the third generation of Russian Zionists pioneers who founded Kiryat Anavim, one of the flagship kibbutzim of the Third Aliyah. My parents were members of the Palmah (Elitist military units during the British Mandate and later in the 1948 war).

I grew up in the center of the country in a middle class residential suburb planned for families of army professionals, attended a good high school, and was a member of a socialist youth movement, until I was conscripted to military service as an IDF officer. My family's financial standing was similar to that of other middle class families, not higher, and I never suffered from any kind of oppression or discrimination due to my ethnicity or for any other reason. At the same time, I was taught social awareness and moral sensitivity, which have to a great degree directed my political and ideological stances in relation to the challenges of racialized and ethnicized life in Israel.

Well, why become an anthropologist? As a child, I was not particularly moved by adventure books or stories of journeys (because I was a girl?), but at a very young age I knew the names of many capital cities around the world. My grandfather was responsible for my familiarity with the globe. When he visited, I would cuddle in my bathrobe, and we would amuse ourselves with trivia tests about the world. This experience intertwined love and warmth with knowledge and learning, a connection that was never severed as I matured. Wandering over the globe with my fingertips and leafing through black-and-white photography books were my only exposure to representations of the world outside of the provincial suburb where I grew up. Until after my military service, my world was largely limited by the borders of the neighborhood. The neighborhood residents—middle-class employees of the security establishment who, despite their discrete military ranks, were indistinguishable in terms of lifestyle and wealth—were Ashkenazim (or at least blind to other ethnicities), secular, mostly natives of Israel, or immigrants who had arrived at a very young age. Although the neighborhood had been built near an immigrant transit encampment (ma'abara), which later was turned into public housing projects (shikunim), Neve Magen did not interact or engage in relations of any kind with the residents of those projects. There was nothing in common with the Mizrahi immigrants. Even during my time in the military, which is purported to be a melting pot or at least provide encounters with people who had lived and grown up in entirely different social worlds, no such encounters took place in practice because of the conscious or unconscious filtering of friends to include only those who were familiar and similar.

Memories of my grandfather and a charismatic school teacher had inspired me to seek a geography degree at the university, but while attending a random lecture in a course on Indian culture I was captivated by the lecturer and her topic. As a result, I ended up enrolling in the behavioral sciences department at Be'er Sheva University (now Ben Gurion University) in 1969. By the middle of my freshman year at the department, I realized I was in the wrong place: where were the Indian culture, myths, and gods? Instead, I was instructed in introductory statistics, the language of bees in Hilgard's psychology textbooks, and the production-possibility frontier in my Introduction to Economics class. I wasn't drawn to the sociology classes or to the lecturers, but I was prepared for a second try at the sociology department of the Hebrew University. After migrating from the desert to the hills, I found my place in the lively atmosphere of post-1967 and pre-1973 Jerusalem (this is how we periodize our lives: between wars). I was stimulated both by sociology lectures devoted to the grand theories, from Marx through Weber and Durkheim, which aspired to unlock the rules underlying the everyday interactions that had always intrigued me. I was even more fascinated by courses in anthropology, the most enthralling of which was the introductory course taught by the late Itzhak Eilam. Eilam was a master anthropologist, an eloquent adventurer who had conducted fieldwork among the Hima people of Uganda. In his introductory class, once a week, a gateway opened and I entered into the life-world of these pastoralists, made up of cows, flies, blood, milk, women, men, and spears. The modest visual aids at the lecturer's disposal were a bunch of photos and a milk jug he had brought back from the field. From week to week we were enriched by knowledge of the Hima, and with it grew our curiosity about this strange society in which married women were allowed to have sexual intercourse with many men, and not exclusively with their husbands. How could this be explained? What are the effects on society? What are the effects on women? And on men? Eilam evoked the basic anthropological questions, supplying answers in the form of a tightly wrought functionalist system, which included everything: climate, food, familial and intergeneration role distribution, sibling relations, parent–child relations, marital relations, paternal households, and so forth. Eilam was a master of his craft, and again I experienced the magic I had encountered during the single lecture on Indian culture.

During our second and third years of undergraduate study, additional courses in anthropology were introduced into the curriculum, acquainting us with lecturers with a different style who had studied other regions of the world, including Israel. Harvey Goldberg, an immigrant from the United States, joined the department's faculty and introduced us to the world of North African and Libyan Jewry. If Eilam had opened a window onto anthropology, Goldberg led me confidently through its meandering pathways, up to the completion of my Ph.D. (and to the present as well, wherever the path turns). Eric Cohen opened the gateway to Thailand and its tourism and was one of the pioneers and founders of the anthropology of tourism. Don Handelman was interested in entirely different ethnography: closely observing the day-to-day interactions in an elderly care center, or in the bureaucratic labyrinth of the Welfare Ministry, which we came to know through the grueling odyssey of his protagonist, Saadiya. Handelman expanded the range of theoretical approaches available to us. Uri Almagor added French structuralism and millenarian movements to our baggage of knowledge. Henry Rosenfeld integrated his Marxist analysis and insights with a profound knowledge of the Arab villages and Israel's Arab population.

Toward the end of my graduate studies, anthropology received formal recognition as part of the sociology department (which now added the title "Anthropology" to its name), and, with time, it became bigger and stronger. Alongside classic classes on rites of passage, millenarian movements, and kinship, new topics related to contemporary Israel began to appear: the absorption of Georgian immigrants, immigrant communities from India, folk healing in Moroccan moshavim, and so on. Worldwide winds began to blow in our isolated and marginal corner of the world, brought in with visits by guest lecturers and scholars who presented their most cutting-edge studies.

For a native-born Israeli, at a time when obstacles to crossing boundaries were as real as the boundaries themselves, traveling abroad to conferences on an intellectual quest or to pursue studies were possibilities that were much less taken for granted than they are today. My trip as a master's student to an international conference in India was therefore a constitutive event. This experience included encounters with anthropologists from all over the world, hearing varieties of English accents; a visit to a factory that manufactured Ayurvedic medicines; music and dance performances in Mumbai, Pune, and Delhi; and especially the sense of being a foreigner and a stranger when exploring rural paths and city streets. The visit to India in the late 1970s—then unknown territory to most Israelis—whetted my appetite for the "exotic" and for the adventurous spirit required for research in a foreign and distant field. Since then I have visited many places in the world and participated and presented at a number of international conferences, but nothing compares to the initiation of that first visit to India.

My work as a research and teaching assistant in anthropology and sociology exposed me to different aspects of life in Israel. As a graduate student, I read autobiographies of Armenian refugees who escaped Turkey and arrived in Jerusalem or the United States (as part of a study on the Armenian community in Jerusalem); I prepared an index for a sociological work on the history of the Yishuv; I interviewed Israelis who served as experts in new nation states in Africa (as part of a big research project on Israeli aid to Africa); I conducted fieldwork in one of the neighborhoods of Kiryat Shmona (as part of a research project on detached youth in that town); I interviewed Libyan Jews living in different parts of Israel about their life in their country of origin and about their ties with Italy and Italians, about marriages and livelihoods, and their foods and modes of preparing them (as part of a medical study); for a few months, I worked as an anthropologist at the Health Ministry in the town of Ramle; I served as a teaching assistant for course in anthropology; outside the university, I taught an introduction to medical anthropology for nurses in hospitals; and I wrote entries on anthropology for the general Israeli encyclopedia.

In 1980, I had the privilege of joining Harvey Goldberg and the late Eileen Basker in writing the first introductory textbook to anthropology, in Hebrew, entitled *Adam, Hevra, Tarbut (Man, Society, Culture)*, published by Tcherikover Press (Goldberg et al. 1980).

The consecutive birth of my two elder children in the early 1980s held up my professional activity, until they grew older and my career as a senior staff at Beit Berl College became established. As in the case of many students in the

Israeli social sciences, studies progressed in fits and starts. I applied myself to finishing up the remaining requirements for my M.A. and resumed student status, hoping to reincarnate the experiences I had had twenty years earlier. But I had changed, the studies had changed, and anthropology had changed; yet my belief in its ability to say a few meaningful things about reality never faltered. In research I conducted about wedding gifts in Israel, I applied insights about the contemporary "us" in the here and now. An article I wrote on this topic was published in the late 1990s in a collection of anthropological papers on Israeli society, which I edited with my colleagues Esther Hertzog, Harvey Goldberg, and Emanuel Marx (Abuhav et al. 1998, and in English, Hertzog et al. 2010). Collaboration on these two books increased my involvement in the anthropological scene in Israel and gave me the opportunity to take a broader look at the current state of the art. My appointment as representative of the academic colleges to the IAA also added a new dimension to my relationship with the discipline. My enmeshment in the anthropological community in Israel materialized in my election as chair of the IAA for 2007–2009. Over time, I specialized in the anthropology of Israeli society and taught this subject at Beit Berl College. Serendipity, which is a strong force in the shaping of our lives, also played a part in my choice of a dissertation topic for my Ph.D.—although, in retrospect, I know that the passion to invest myself in such a demanding undertaking had always been there. Chance conversations with friends gave birth to my Ph.D. topic: a historical view of the development of anthropology in Israel. The combination of my interest in the subject, my insider's view of it, and its affinity with local history—a recently developing field—alerted me that I was positioned in the right time and place. My doctoral dissertation was the basis for a book in Hebrew (Abuhav 2010b) and for the current book. My attraction to history, and local history in particular, was combined in the dissertation with attention to the pioneers of Israeli anthropology. As a result of intensive study of their endeavors, I wrote an article on the contribution of a couple of the first anthropologists of the Yishuv period: Erich Brauer and Raphael Patai (Abuhav 2003) and was invited to write the entry "Raphael Patai" in the *Encyclopedia of Modern Jewish Cultures* (Abuhav 2005c). Erich Brauer, whose biography and career I researched for several years in archives and libraries, was the protagonist of my film Erich's Suitcase, produced by Beit Berl College and directed by the filmmaker Yael Katzir. An interest in translations of anthropological texts into Hebrew inspired writing an article together with a colleague who had done a linguistic analysis on anthropological texts translated to Hebrew (Abuhav and Shilo 2011).

I came to anthropology because of curiosity and an attraction to the exotic. I stayed because of my attraction to people and my interest in the ways they live their lives. I identify with the anthropological perspective because it offers, to my mind, the most valuable and appropriate method for profoundly observing human reality. I am proud to say that I have enjoyed every moment of it, and I am fortunate to belong to those who have the privilege of loving what they do.

METHODS FOR STUDYING THE IMAGES AND LIFE PATHS OF ANTHROPOLOGISTS

The interpretation of life paths is a multilayered and multifaceted enterprise. In recounting their lives, narrators represent reality as it was experienced by them in the past—an experience that is at once consciousness, emotion, and feeling, expressed in a story. Bruner (1986), who wrote about the anthropology of experience, explains that there is a tension between experience and the story told about that experience—a tension which is sometime conscious and sometime unconscious. The ethnography, the story addressed to the self, and the story addressed to the other (the interviewer) create a complex picture comprised of multiple representations. Watson, one of the founders of the interpretive method (Watson 1976), addressed the tension between the description of a life as experienced by the individual phenomenologically and represented by motivations, personality, and conflict, and the external structures and categories that are imposed on the story by its interpreter. Watson proposes an approach that combines hermeneutics and phenomenology—an approach that can provide an adequate theoretical framework for bridging the gap between experience, narrative, and the interpretation of both. In both interpretive movements, that of the research and that of the research subject, there is use of metaphors and images that are accessible to the world of the interpreter. Both my anthropologist research subjects and I drew our key concepts and metaphors from the world of anthropological knowledge, from a repertoire of concepts with which we were accustomed to think and which serve as tools for the interpretation and description of social phenomena, especially from the anthropological world. By way of contrast, one can imagine that psychologists would use metaphors derived from their own disciplinary world to describe their professional motivations, ideology, and theories.

In this study, as in my other ethnographic work, I confronted a dilemma that is characteristic of interpretive work: to what degree is the interviewees' interpretation of their life courses mine or theirs? To what extent am I committed to an emic point of view, representing the subjects' view of reality, and to what extent do I privilege the researcher's understanding and the point of view that is external to the subjects' interpretations? Or, in other words, what is the relationship between an analysis of the first order, which is based on the establishment of categories of knowledge collected from the informant and which is mostly descriptive, and an analysis of a second order, which is based on the researcher's theoretical conceptual scheme and analysis of categories? (See Shkedi 2003, chapters 9 and 11.) Until recently, writing about Israeli anthropology had been based on an interpretive strategy that represented the researcher's point of view. This strategy bypassed the dimension of the first order, beginning directly with the second order, and therefore the picture it produced is both partial and dichotomous. For example, Loss (2001) examined the motives of anthropologists who studied Mizrahim in Israel; he based his study on limited interviews with his research subjects and chiefly on his own interpretations of their texts. In my own interviews, on the other hand, I allowed the subjects to present their "professional ID" and to shape their own interpretive outlook about the motivations and drives behind their anthropological activity. My strategy allows both perspectives—the external and internal—to be combined: the subjects' interpretation is juxtaposed with that of the researcher, and both may be overlaid by the reader's interpretation.

The analysis of life-course materials through an anthropological prism is based on the method of "grounded theory," which emphasizes listening to what interviewees are saying and using the subjects' interpretations as theoretical building blocks (see Shkedi 2003, 9, 11). The notion of grounded theory was developed by Glaser and Strauss (Glaser and Strauss 1967; see also Gibton 2001) and was elaborated especially in the field of education by Hutchinson (1988). In this method, the first stage of my work is to look for general types of professional life courses among Israeli anthropologists. The second stage is to identify the major categories, which I formulated as the main *motives* for his or her anthropological activity. Categories might include a multicultural environment, marginality, or commitment to social struggles. The next stage in the process was to emphasize the differentiation between the categories, and the fifth and the final stage was to link these categories with categories identified in my other research arenas and in studies by others.

The standard methodology (but not the one I chose) for examining anthropological activity is the analysis of anthropological publications in order to answer questions that pertain to the question of life courses. This method draws on the tradition of the history of ideas and on an epistemological analysis of anthropological theories. Its components are theoretical, and it analyzes the philosophy of anthropological knowledge and the ways in which it is produced. All these are subordinated, according to this method, to motivations and ideological drives shaped by power relations—between researchers and subjects, between occupiers and those occupied, between the First World and the Third World, between developed and developing countries—in the context of which relations anthropological research takes place and produces knowledge. This approach resonates within current Israeli anthropology, which is quick to assimilate central discourse to the language of local anthropology and voices arguments regarding the national, Zionist, colonialist, and Orientalist impulses of social scientists, including anthropologists.

In contrast to this research strategy, the alternative methodology that I am proposing may contribute to this discourse, sometimes by supporting it and at other times by contradicting it. If the Foucauldian discourse that describes scientific activity in terms of knowledge/power suffers from the liability of reducing and simplifying the overall picture, the methodology I propose can thicken the description and help complexify it. The use of knowledge/power concepts for any body of knowledge, especially in the context of power relations, eradicates any notion of the individual or of agency. Because this discourse constitutes a complex of opinions, images, implicit premises, and conjectures, arising at the intersection of varied social arenas, it ignores intellectual biography and the power of individuals to shape their own lives. Israeli anthropologists have different biographies, possess different types of resources, and are motivated by diverse drives. From the point of view of the main social players, the construction of one's personal career is not adequately reflected in the interpretation of the content of their publications, as legitimate as that effort might be. There is a biography behind the article, as well as power in the micro-relations within the academia, and motives and impulses that cannot be accounted for by reading and analyzing the published books and articles. In conversations with me, the anthropologists constructed a more complex personal and professional story along with their own interpretation.

Another methodology used for asking "What makes scientists [including anthropologists] tick?" is the examination of motivations as revealed by psychological personality tests. This methodology was ascendant in the 1950s and was used for the comparative research of a variety of scientists from various disciplines.

Beyond these two methodologies—textual analysis and personality tests—I propose a third, which is based on in-depth interviews with anthropologists about their professional careers. In addition to supplementing the weaknesses of other methodologies, this approach also has theoretical implications. When it comes to studying researchers who worked long ago—the early British or American anthropologists, for example—one has no choice but to rely on ethnographic texts and, when possible, on other personal documentation, correspondence, or memoirs. (On British anthropology, see, for example, Kuklick 1991; Kuper 1973, 1996. On U.S. anthropology, see Darnell 1971; Stocking 1991.) The professional representations of the research are his or her publications: articles, books, research reports, reports on applied work, introductions to books. Even if numerous, these publications do not sufficiently expose the impulses, motivations, temptations, interests, and calculations of their writers, leaving the readers to assume that the common discourse adequately expresses interpersonal variety. In contrast to Malinowski, Evans-Pritchard, or Boas, the anthropologists at the center of my discussion are not figures from the past—they are active and preeminent in the academic field, and gave me the opportunity to discuss and construct a thick and richly detailed picture based on their own words. Moreover, I complied with the basic rule that anthropologists of all theoretical orientations adhere to, allowing the interviewees (in my case—Israeli anthropologists) to define and voice him- or herself.

I should note that a recounting of a life course is a retrospective telling that interprets the past from the vantage point of the present. Despite such drawbacks, the interviewees' interpretations of their lives are valuable because most were aware of the process of reversal and read their life stories with heightened awareness, while conscious of the contemporary political and academic implication of their accounts.

Ethnographic Encounters in Israel, a new edited book by Fran Markowitz (2013) is a significant addition to the current discussion. It is about the Poetics and Ethics of Fieldwork, as mentioned in its subtitle. Some of the dozen contributors to this book are outsiders, some are halfies, and some are insiders. "Yet not one of is a complete insider or outsider to the ongoing issues that percolate in Israeli society" (Markowitz 2013, 5). The authors expose, challenge, argue, and explain her or his motives and identities and the difficulties and fun of carrying out fieldwork in Israel.

The categories that I identified while analyzing the interview materials dovetailed with the narrative of the development of anthropology in the institutional arena and in the arena of the Israel Anthropological Association, adding up to a history of the discipline that combines institutional development with the history of ideas. Thus emerged a general argument that ties together the personal stories of anthropologist, with a macroscopic view that looks at the place of anthropologist in the processes of nation building in Israeli society, and later at the development and shaping of Israeli society after the establishment of the state.

THE MATERIALS: TEXTS, PSYCHOLOGICAL TESTS, AND LIFE-COURSE NARRATIVES

To examine the life courses of anthropologists in Israel, I conducted in-depth interviews with some fifty anthropologists, who exhibited different characteristics, and I asked myself how these anthropologists developed a distinctive and coherent professional identity. In my conversations with my subjects, the point of departure was the question "How did you become an anthropologist?" and they were asked to describe landmarks in the story of their life course. They presented their childhood backgrounds, the social environment in which they were raised, their early education, their family histories, the processes of academic training they underwent, and the decisions they took at different crossroads in their lives.

In analyzing life courses I examined three axes:

1. The axis of constructing a personal career: where the anthropologist grew up, where he or she studied, why he or she chose anthropology, how his or her career took shape, and what developments paved his or her particular path within the discipline (the plot line of the personal career was shaped by conscious and intentional decisions on the one hand and by external, uncontrollable, or fortuitous events on the other)
2. The anthropologist and the discipline: theoretical orientation, relationship to a school of thought, an interest in people and an engagement with others, the establishment of research interests, interpersonal relationships in academia, and the social processes that accompany scientific activity

3. The anthropologist in the midst of tumultuous social events: nation building, Zionism and post-Zionism, Judaism, colonialism, nationalism, war, peace, human rights

The presentation of stories, ideas, and musings about Israeli anthropologists who were interviewed about their life courses presented a complex and multidimensional picture of the anthropological drive and its actualization. The narrative constructed along a diachronic plot line outlined the professional biography of an anthropologist, from which I reconstructed the context of the professional practice. The axis of individual career building also addressed pre-professional or extra-professional socialization and links to communities such as youth movements or political movements that influenced the adult anthropologist. This axis also touched upon relationships within the nuclear or extended family, reports about relocation to other cities or continents, and significant figures who influenced one's career. Most of the interviewees mentioned their theoretical contributions to Israeli anthropology as well as their fulfillment of their formal roles, academic activity, training of students, and professional advancement. A number pointed to their involvement in broader social processes. It was my task to search for the links between the personal and public stories—between the biographical facts and the central themes they presented.

Biographies and autobiographies are valuable sources for life courses of Israeli anthropologists. The middle of the 1990s saw the beginning of a publication trend of autobiographical works by anthropologists, which present parts of the story of the development of Israeli anthropology from a personal point of view. First mention should be reserved for the autobiographical work of Marcus Goldstein, who was the founder of the Israeli Anthropological Association (Goldstein 1995). Although a physical anthropologist, he nevertheless contributed through this activity to sociocultural anthropology. Goldstein's book traces the development of physical anthropology in Israel and, in so doing, illuminates several chapters in the history of the IAA. After Goldstein, the founding mother of applied anthropology in Israel, Phyllis Palgi, sketched out the creation myth of applied anthropology and the medical anthropology of medical systems in an article titled "A Personal Story . . . How It All Began" (Palgi 1993). Pnina Motzafi-Haller, who studied in Jerusalem and later received her Ph.D. from Brandeis University, described how she constructed her identity as an anthropologist, a Mizrahi Jew, and a woman (Motzafi-Haller 1997). At the turn of the third millennium, the stream of autobiographical works increased. Shokeid (2002, 2012) and Rabinowitz (Rabinowitz and Abu Baker 2002), opened for readers a window onto their personal and professional lives, in books that emerged out of their own individual motives. They wove the stories of their personal career paths as ones intertwined with their other identities, as children, parents, partners, citizens, and intellectuals committed to a social and political agenda. The common denominators of these two works are the desire to illuminate dimensions of the general and public, of the Israeli and the international, via the personal dimensions, and the need to foreground the unique contribution of each of these dimensions to the settings in which they were active—academic, intellectual, or ideological. By providing a personal angle, Shokeid, in a way, represents his contemporaries. Rabinowitz, an anthropologist of the generation after Shokeid, presents his story differently. He conducted a dialogue with the book's co-author, Khawla Abu Baker—a personal dialogue, but one that represents a dialogue between two ethnic entities within the Israeli space, rendering it therefore also a national dialogue. The main thrust of the book is its comparison of the Zionist and Palestinian narratives, an exercise that also sheds light on Israeli anthropology during the phases in which the author was involved.

Two books that have appeared in the past two years are *Ethnographic Encounters in Israel: Poetics and Ethics of Fieldwork*, edited by Markowitz (2013), and *Serendipity in Anthropological Research: The Nomadic Turn*, edited by Hazan and Hertzog (2012). The books discuss the experience of carrying out fieldwork in Israel, as experienced by researchers—Israeli and non-Israel—at different time periods. Markowitz also exposes her readers to her unique experiences in personal and ethnographic encounters she has had since her entry into Israeli society and a researcher of this society.

In analyzing the material, several possible focuses became apparent. I followed the guidelines of the interpretive method by allowing "the material to speak for itself." The common theme given salience by the interviewees—and which also stood out to me—were the pull and push factors when it came to the choice of anthropology as vocation.

The focus on the professional career of anthropologists can be tied to the literature dealing with questions of career formation of scientists and academics more generally. In the 1950s an attempt was made to address the topic of "the making of a scientist" from a psychological perspective, with attention to the personality structure and personal and family history of scientists and academics. The most famous study was conduct by Anne Roe, a clinical psychologist who had researched various psychological topics before embarking upon major studies of creativity and occupational psychology (1952). One of her two major publications was *The Making of a Scientist* (1953), a study of sixty-four eminent male scientists in biology, physics, and the social sciences. Roe asked whether a connection could be found between life histories, intellectual functioning, or personality traits and the choice of a particular profession or career. Roe's method included clinical research, psychological testing, and in-depth interviews. The study was carried out in the context of the culture and personality school, which assumed the existence of a standard or average personality within each culture and assumed that the links between culture and personality are reciprocal and that macro features of personality may be identified through psychological testing, such as the Rorschach and other projective tests. Roe looked for scientists who were considered preeminent in their fields and turned to thirteen of the most famous American anthropologists. Eight responded, including anthropologist from the fields of physical anthropology, archeology, and social and cultural anthropology—all white American men under the age of sixty.

In her findings, Roe identified a number of generalizations that characterize the anthropologists questioned. In their families, education was esteemed as having intrinsic value, regardless of the profession of the head of the household. Most of the anthropologists in the study reported a sense of difference from their social environment, sometime accompanied by a sense of superiority. They emphasized their need for independence, together with a difficulty in breaking away from their parents. Most were characterized as achievement oriented and ambitious, a fact that emerged from their having become outstanding scientists who "made it." In considering the question of why anthropologists had chosen anthropology in particular, Roe assumed that social scientists are interested in people. She discovered that both psychologists and anthropologists experience a tension between an unconscious lack of self-confidence and a sense of superiority to others. According to her logic, people engaged in social psychology and anthropology have a sense of superiority, even if this is unaccompanied by status symbols: A view from above enables psychological or anthropological research.

Roe's premises and her simplistic research approach lay it open to criticism. She herself was aware of some weaknesses of her own methodology. Her sample was unrepresentative because of its focus on famous scientists, the sample for the psychological tests was too small, and the complexity of human situations did not allow conclusions of a causal nature to be drawn. In addition, the anthropologists included in the study represented all fields of anthropology, which follow different traditions and research methods, and therefore any attempt to generalize her data in terms of "the anthropologist" is problematic.

The research strategy that Roe introduced was transformed about a decade later by Dennison Nash (1963) into an outline of the portrait of the "anthropologist as stranger." In Roe's study, anthropologists were depicted as people who liked people; favored "exoticism"; were intelligent, capable of a sense of distance, flexible, and tolerant of ambiguity; and usually possessed a non-authoritarian but autonomous personality. To Roe's findings, according to which anthropologists derive satisfaction from the very act of doing research, Nash added that the experience of fieldwork challenges them and allows them to be exposed to stimuli. An anthropologist who lives among strangers most of the time aspires to belong to a community of similars: in the company of his or her fellow anthropologists. Nash's conclusions supported Roe's hypothesis that certain basic personality features are shared by anthropologists, whose work typically involves the study of the unfamiliar.

Some thirty years after Nash, Michael Agar (1996) reexamined the question of the connection between the metaphor of the anthropologist as a "professional stranger" and his actual work in the field. Agar found similarities between anthropologists: they find intellectual stimulation in spending time in an environment that is different from the one they are accustomed to, they enjoy the aesthetics of structural and taxonomic analysis, and they derive satisfaction from their unique fieldwork methodologies. According to him, an outstanding feature of anthropologists is intense curiosity about the diversity of human life, but not all enjoy doing ethnography.

In summary, two methodologies have been used to ask why anthropologists have become what they are: one imposes external, theoretical, deductive categories at the macro level by analyzing the motives and ideological positions of anthropologists, usually from a critical point of view, while the other reductively examines personal and psychological dimension at the micro level. The middle ground that I propose is similar to the meso level (a term coined by Faist [1997] in a discussion of immigration). It explains the choices of people who are faced with a variety of possibilities—often leading to a choice that is positioned between the expected norms and the individual and unique act of agency. Professional choices are made the same way—by navigating between the general normative expectations and individual proclivities.

THE INTERVIEWED ANTHROPOLOGISTS

The interviews with Israeli anthropologists took place during 1996–2002. Some fifty anthropologists were interviewed, about a third of the number of self-identified anthropologists in Israel. A few Israeli anthropologists have kept their distance from the IAA and never participated in the meetings or in other activities.

The interviewees were chosen according to the following criteria: First, I interviewed some fifteen anthropologists who could be said to belong to the founding generation. I wanted to learn about the development of anthropology in Israel as they had witnessed and experienced it, and also about their personal-professional biographies. In addition, I interviewed another thirty-five anthropologists representing various characteristics of the community, according to the parameters of age, place of training (United States/Europe/Israel), institutional affiliation, and place of employment (within or outside a university).

Although the study deals with "Israeli anthropology," it does not include physical anthropologists because of the structure of Israeli anthropology, as outlined in the introduction. Over the years, I developed contacts with many anthropologists, as an undergraduate and a graduate student at the Hebrew University, as secretary of the IAA, as a board member and chair of the IAA, as a participant in IAA meetings, and as editor of two books with collected papers of Israeli anthropologists. The colleagues I met opened their doors to me and gave generously of their time, and, in most cases, I was spared the need to overcome any hurdles in entering the field. At the same time, I deliberately chose to interview anthropologists with whom I had no prior acquaintance, in order to balance the picture and avoid errors of omission that can occur when relying on methodology based on social networks.

The characteristics of the pool of interviewees are described in the following tables:

INTERVIEWEES ACCORDING TO INSTITUTIONAL AFFILIATION	
Hebrew University	13
Tel Aviv University	10
Haifa University	8
Ben Gurion University	6
Bar Ilan University	3
Colleges	6
Applied	4

INTERVIEWEES BY GENDER

Women	Men
24	26

INTERVIEWEES ACCORDING TO COUNTRY IN WHICH PH.D. WAS AWARDED

North America	Israel	England and Europe
20	15	15

INTERVIEWEES ACCORDING TO ACADEMIC DEGREE/ TITLE

Professor	Doctor	Doctoral candidate
20	28	2

GENERATIONAL BREAKDOWN OF INTERVIEWEES

Born between the mid-1920s and the early 1940s	Born between 1940s and early 1960s	Born in the early 1960s
28	16	6

THE INTERVIEWS: CONTEXT AND METHODOLOGY

The life courses of the anthropologists interviewed for this study were elicited through open, in-depth interviews, each session lasting 1.5–2 hours. Most of the interviews were held during a single sitting, but some were spread out over two sessions; a smaller number used three sessions. The longer interviews were held chiefly with members of the older generation, who provided information both about themselves and about the development of anthropology generally. I met with a number of key interviewees several times during the research period to obtain feedback about sections of my draft, especially those sections concerned with conflicting narratives, which were deemed sensitive.

At the beginning of the meeting, the interviewee was asked to speak about his or her life as an anthropologist, and to begin the story from whatever point in time and space that appeared to him or her as the launching point. The interviewees presented their own life stories intertwined with the stories of the "supporting characters" in their own personal anthropological life plot: teachers, colleagues, students, and family members. These personal accounts were enriched by other sources that served as support and validation: reflexive prefaces to books, first-person accounts in scientific publications, and information from other interviewees. The dynamics with interviewees—some of whom had been my teachers, some my colleagues, some my students, and some with whom I had had no previous contact—developed differently in each case, in accordance with the nature of the dialogue. But I did not once encounter resistance to being interviewed, or even as much as a hesitant consent. In one case, after approaching a person with whom I had no prior acquaintance, I learned that he "had looked into me" before agreeing to the interview.

The interviews usually took place at the home or office of the interviewee, or at a neutral public venue (café or restaurant). The venue was usually chosen by the interviewee so that his or her definition of the interaction—as well as the nature of our relationship, beyond the interviewer–interview situation—could come into play. When there was a prior acquaintance or friendship with the interviewee, I was often invited to his or her home, where, in his or her own territory, the interviewee could master the situation more easily on one hand, but could also express generosity on the other. The familiar tone of such home interviews was also affected by the engagement of family members, usually spouses. Interviews that took places at the workplace lent a bureaucratic and goal-oriented air to the encounter. Most of the interviews in office spaces took place at a room on campus, in the interviewee's own intimate professional space, allowing access to his or her bookshelf to pull out an article for a relevant quote or to proudly present his or her latest book. Most importantly, the interviewee could here exhibit his or her professional self, as constructed by the professional space. One interview, with an anthropologist who is also a clinical psychologist, took place within an untypical setting: in his clinic. He seated me in the client's chair, near a small table, with a box of tissues separating us. The conversation was patterned after a therapist–client encounter. In retrospect, this unique situation underscored the duality of the roles that we filled. As in a mirror image, I was the one asking questions, and the subject, normally the listener, laid out his biography before me. Although this was an exceptional occurrence, it highlighted the complexity involved in a researcher becoming the object of research.

Placing a mirror in front of anthropologists whose own craft is the interviewing of their subjects presented a unique challenge. My position as an anthropologist studying anthropologists raised a number of dilemmas: the problematic nature of studying up, the challenges presented by research on researchers, and the mode of presentation of the findings. In a number of cases, I asked the interviewee for his or her general view concerning the masking of the research subjects' identities: was this desirable or not, and, if so, how it should be done. I also asked interviewees whether they had any reservations about being explicitly quoted in print. A number of anthropologists requested, without any prompting, to be shown the materials pertaining to them prior to publication. For nearly all of those interviewed, the opportunity to present their professional accomplishments and contribution to Israeli anthropology was both important and meaningful, and the interview provided them with a platform for this.

Status reversal was an especially conspicuous issue in my work, not least due to the fact that Harvey Goldberg and Eyal Ben-Ari, my supervisors, were also interviewees, while another central interviewee was a member of the academic doctoral committee (Vaada Melava). Alex Weingrod's agreement to join the committee was accompanied by some hesitation. In response to the supervisor's request to join, he confessed his dilemma: "Regarding the Vaada, I have a prior and interesting question: The topic of the dissertation is the history of anthropology in Israel . . . and Orit . . . interviewed me as part of her research—I am an informant in her study—and I believe that she wishes to interview me again. Now, can I be an informant and a member in the 'scientific committee,' both subject and (maybe) object?"[1]

This correspondence reflects the complexity of the relations between a researcher and her subject, while pointing to the multiple roles involved in research-related interaction: a student who studies teachers who both evaluate and direct the quality of her work.

As an example of "studying up," my research conspicuously and radically exposes the dilemmas arising from researcher–subject relations, thus engaging actively with the studying up trend of the last decades. This trend has at once influenced and been influenced by the crisis of representation and authority of the 1980s, which called for a redefinition of the "native," of the "field," or of the "Other." (For a description of the power relations between a researcher and subjects in the colonial and other contexts, see Geertz 2002.) Many anthropologists, and social scientists generally, have taken a critical and reflexive look at power relations and hierarchies of knowledge (Swidler and Arditi 1994). Consequently, communities of intellectuals and other elite groups such as economic elites, laboratory scientists (Rabinow 1999), and women academics (Mizrahi 1995) have become an object of study. The view from below reorganizes the parameters of the relations between the researcher and his or her subject, allowing the emergence of new kinds of ethnographies, in which the subjects share authority and become partners in the research, more than was formerly the case.

Research literature dealing with the methodological challenges of "studying up" is relatively sparse. Laura Nader's well-known article advocates this approach and elaborates a number of its advantages (Nader 1974). Studying up yields insights about the division of power and responsibility in the researcher's own society, and about the democratization of scientific activity; it contributes to a fuller understanding of society at large by adding the point of view of the elites.

Elizabeth Sheehan (1993a, 1993b) offers her treatment of this theme in a study of intellectuals and academics that has affinities with mine. She conducted fieldwork on Irish academics, as a graduate student, and presented the difficulties she encountered in carrying out anthropological research on university intellectuals. Due to the great similarity with my own work, a comparison of the two studies is instructive and contributes to the appreciation of the dilemmas and challenges I faced in my own fieldwork. Sheehan confronted two challenges regarding her identity: first, she was an American ethnographer in Ireland; second, her status in the academic hierarchy was below that of her interviewees. The resistance of the Irish to the entry of American ethnographers was a product of centuries in which the Irish had been negatively represented by research, because they were regarded by American researchers as guinea pigs for studies on cultural themes. The work of Nancy Scheper-Hughes (1979, 257) is mentioned in this context. Being cut of the same cloth as my interviewees, I was never suspected of any such attitudes.

More relevant is Sheehan's discussion of the complexity of her relations as a doctoral candidate with the Ph.D.s and professors she studied. She argues that the politics of research and academic culture are premised, a priori, on the exclusion of academics as objects of research: "There is some suggestion of bad taste in elaborate professional codes of academic culture to consider such colleagues subjects to study" (Sheehan 1993a, 255). Therefore, when she entered the field prepared to write about people whose intellectual prestige and status were greater than her own, the subjects sometimes treated her as a student, sometimes as a colleague, and sometimes even as an intruder, although they were all part of the same professional environment. In my own case, the construction of the research setting was marked by the dualities of my status as a colleague, a student, and a researcher—an issue that came up on a number of occasions. The researcher's confidence in having more control of the research situation than do the subjects (in respect to methodology or the academic modus operandi outside the field) is undermined when these subjects are academics of repute who are experts in their field.

Differences in formal academic status or academic degree were not the only factors that augmented the distance between the researcher and her subjects. In Sheehan's experience, the esteemed status that most of her subjects held within Irish society at large, their frequent media appearances, and their deep familiarity with Irish society and politics allowed them to position her as inferior. When an anthropologist studies her own anthropologist colleagues, the subjects are highly skilled at her craft, and they can evaluate her performance. One eye is cast on the interviewee's own performing role, while the other eye expertly scrutinizes the interviewer's professional ability. For example, in one of my first interviews, I did not bring a tape recorder to the session. The interviewee, a younger anthropologist, wondered how one could carry out an interview without recording it, and expressed some dissatisfaction at this. (She may have been concerned that loose documentation of the interview, without a recording device, might lead to inaccuracies that could damage her somehow.) It did not occur to her that in the "past" (in the 1970s and 1980s), interviews were frequently recorded in handwriting. Recording equipment was both expensive and unwieldy; interviewees were leery of recording devices because they had not been exposed to communication technologies that are common today. Thus, researchers were obliged to develop shorthand skills for documenting interviews, which they could later flesh out.

The experience of entering the field, which for Sheehan was beset with fears about closed doors, was in my case generally smooth because I had already been firmly planted within the research field for many years. My personal address book was my main tool for establishing contact with my research subjects, and I was not at the mercy of arbitrary decisions of gatekeepers of the academic system, whose role it is to prevent direct access to lecturers. Recommendations from previous interviewees or from academic acquaintances opened doors and hearts for Sheehan, and her fears that the interviews would be refused proved false. Once she began her series of interviews, not only did they respond favorably, but, "In a few cases, my delay in contacting individuals may even have been viewed by some of them as a minor slight, a failure to recognize their academic status and potential contribution to my study" (Sheehan 1993a, 256).

Although I myself received encouragement from most of the anthropologists with whom I consulted during the early phases of the research, a handful of non-anthropologists expressed doubts. Chiefly, I was warned that it would difficult to conduct historical research on living people, and that my being an Israeli anthropologist would not allow me to skillfully and objectively observe other Israeli anthropologists. Happily, the interviewees did not raise objections about the very legitimacy of the ethnographic research method, although it is not unlikely that a number of my interviewees took issue with the tactic I chose. Many remarked, even at the very early stages of the interview, that I was doing "an anthropology of anthropologists." Thirty years of involvement in Israeli anthropology spared me the excruciating legwork that Sheehan undertook to "soften" the interviewees and the work of reading the interviewees' publications before the interview. Sheehan also encountered difficulties at the end of her study: close to her departure from Ireland, one of her interviewees admonished, in friendly tones, that she beware of publishing anything unpleasant about him or his colleagues. I, on the other, hand did not have the option of escaping the field, which is my home. Therein lay one of the crucial and central ethical/methodological dilemmas of my work. How could I write critically of my interviewees, when they would be evaluating and grading my academic work? As members of a small community who enjoy academic stature, they had the power to take measures that might obstruct my career. I was aware that critiquing individuals or groups of anthropologist could be problematic: critiquing those who were to evaluate my work could be infinitely more complicated.

As in other social contexts, the relationship between a researcher and his subjects can be regarded as exchange relations. The goods that I received as a researcher were the resources of professional advancement and prestige, increased potential to advance within the discipline, and the opportunity for meaningful employment. The interviewees received the experience of playing the other side in the transaction (some even noted their enjoyment of this aspect), the incentive to tell their own story to themselves, and the most important reward—a platform. The interview gave them the opportunity to be recorded in the annals of the creators of Israeli anthropology, while highlighting their personal story and individual contribution. For deeply committed professionals, such a reward was not a trivial thing. The intelligentsia's willingness to participate in academic research supports the ethos of "contribution to science" and bolsters the principle of academic freedom of expression and the freedom of—or even the need for—criticism.

The dilemma of whether to disguise the interviewees' identities presented a challenge. Seeking to draw on their own dilemmas as researchers, I asked my interviewees whether I should code their identities. More than an abstract question, this was a way of sharing responsibility with them. Responses varied. Some argued that the community's small size and the intimate acquaintance among its members, as well as the accessibility of the material, prevented any possibility of masking identities. Complete exposure—along with its benefits—was therefore to be preferred: "You have no choice—it's a small community anyway. What cannot be hidden, you ought to consider not writing at all. If the analysis of the interviews is thematic, and you break them up, then identification is less of a problem."

Others thought that "you will no doubt require some kind of meta-language." It did occur to me at some point to allegorically use well-known characters from literature and mythology to describe the life course of anthropologists. One anthropologist with whom I shared this thought said: "The collective associations tied to such characters are liable to overwhelm the fresh and personal worlds of meaning that you endow them with." Any type of coding that translates one system into another meant to represent it diminishes the authenticity of the voice. The use of codes was susceptible to contamination by related worlds of interpretation and associations. After weighing the trade-offs of both approaches, I decided to reveal the identities of the interviewees.

The interviewees certainly took the fact that their identities would be disclosed into consideration, and I suppose that they trusted me not to betray one of the basic principles in anthropological ethics—discretion. If not for their belief that I would adhere to this principle, no relationship of trust could have been forged. Almost every anthropologist has experienced a blunder or an embarrassment due to a failure to uphold the scientific tradition and position that places a value on the accuracy of information. In colonial anthropology, when the subjects did not read what we write, such errors had scarcely any effect on the research field. But anthropology at home ("when they read what we write" [Brettell 1993]) is first and foremost a discreet anthropology. I attempted to tread carefully in this delicate field.

IMAGES IN THE LIFE COURSES OF ANTHROPOLOGISTS IN ISRAEL

The images I employ to describe the life courses of Israeli anthropologists were selected from a repertoire of images in my own anthropological vocabulary, but they are mostly similar to the formulations of the interviewees themselves. The central analytical categories and concepts cross the continuum of a life course, in which some of these images overlap: "curiosity in regard to others" is similar to a great extent to "multiculturalism," for example. Some life courses are best described by more than one metaphor—for example, those of "wandering" and "immigration."

The following are the metaphors and images that emerged from the life courses of the anthropologists:

- The anthropologist as immigrant: nomadism, marginality, multiculturalism
- The anthropologist as committed: engagement, identification with others, formation of personal identity
- The anthropologist as curious toward others

I shall now present these images, and the way in which they are exemplified in the life courses of anthropologists, by dividing each image into sub-patterns.

The Anthropologist as Immigrant

The metaphor of the immigrant combines a number of sub-images: wandering, marginality, and multiculturalism—all different dimensions of the general metaphor of immigration. In the stories of life courses, these images were woven together, but one image sometimes was given more salience than others. What these images of immigration within one's life course have in common is the granting of meaning to various stations in one's biographical path.

The background of Israeli anthropologists will clarify why this image is so significant. The founding generation of Israeli anthropology, in the period between the beginning of the 1950s and the early 1970s, was comprised of a small number of anthropologists, most of whom came from North America. Of the thirteen anthropologists who established themselves in Israel, only three were native-born Israelis. In the generation of the early 1970s to the mid-1980s, the proportion of native-born Israelis rose significantly, from 16 to 25. As professional anthropology became established, other immigrants joined them after having already developed professional careers overseas. The third generation includes Ph.D.s and doctoral candidates who studied and trained in Israel. However, in my research population, native-born Israelis in Israeli universities comprise only half of the total.

Every anthropologist may be seen as a kind of migrant nomad who ventures out to carry out fieldwork, even if the distance between "home" and "the field" is shorter today than it was in the past. The experience of immigration permits the anthropologist to maintain a dual point of view in which pictures from the past are embedded in the present; it creates a perspective that allows an understanding of a culture and society that is different from his or her own. An anthropologist who has already experienced living in more than one culture and was an immigrant himself or herself is likely to better understand the lives of other immigrants.

Nomadism as an existential metaphor implies movement and transit—between continents, territories, cultures, disciplines, and research topics. This basic metaphor was the main inspiration behind Haim Hazan and Esther Hertzog's initiative to create a collections of works on the occasion of octogenarian celebration of Emanuel Marx, "a mentor of Nomadism with an anthropological home" (Hazan and Hertzog 2012, cover page). Although nomadism is a pattern of movement and temporariness, it may also contain elements of permanence or cyclic patterns. Many anthropologists experienced their personal and professional lives as a nomadic lifestyle that included movement between different spaces, and they use their experiences as nomads as a key to understanding the lives of others. Anthropologists move between home and field, between field experience and the text they create on the computer. The anthropologist leaves the secure location of home to take risks of uncertainty in the field and to cope with self-examination during fieldwork. Lévi-Strauss (1955) made use of the image of the immigrant to describe his anthropological activity. He likened himself to a Neolithic nomad who travels through the forest with his band and cultivates the land and, after exhausting its fertility, moves on to a new plot of land.

The anthropologist is an immigrant of a special kind: the essence of his work is migration toward the "Other" in the research field, even if the research field is close by. Indeed, every anthropologist migrates at least once in his or her lifetime—a migration that is characterized by temporariness, a planned entry and exit, and a long professional preparation that is perceived as an important part of the research. In the Israeli example, anthropologists migrated to Israel for the dual purpose of research and aliyah. Academic careers and anthropological careers also include periods of temporary migration for sabbaticals or long-term internships, such as post-doctoral studies abroad, in which the academic has the status of a temporary migrant worker.

As in the study of any profession, anthropological training demands the acquisition of a new language. The anthropologist is required to display primary literacy in an unfamiliar academic environment and later in a new anthropological field; in this sense, he or she is no different from a psychologist, economist, or historian. At the same time, as Nurit Bird-David says, "anthropology is a mother tongue," which is acquired after mastering the mother tongue with which one has grown up. Now a new professional language must be learned, which is more than just an intellectual jargon, but is closer in its depth to one's mother tongue. Some of the anthropologists/immigrants to Israel undergo an experience of double and triple linguistic migration, with the need to learn Hebrew before, during, or after the acquisition of the anthropological tongue. Studying a group outside the anthropologist's own culture requires learning the language of the researched group. Chambers (1994), who conducted fieldwork in Naples, Italy, compared the features of fieldwork to those of immigration: the gradual entry into a new landscape and new environment; the impossibility of translation from one language to the next, which always changes its meaning and is never sufficiently precise; writing as a journey between the lines of the text; the beginning of dialogue with the research subjects or the destination country, and its continuation; and the abandonment of old stereotypes and the adoption of new ones.

Immigration takes on an additional central meaning in Israeli society, which is an immigrant society: in the 1960s, most of Israeli anthropology focused on the huge waves of immigrants who arrived from the Middle East and North Africa and as refugees from Europe after World War II. Anthropologists of this generation studied the processes of the immigrants' absorption and settlement. In the beginning of the 1970s, new waves of immigration arrived from the Soviet Union and the United States, earning the attention of social scientists. Some of these scientists were anthropologists, but most were sociologists. In the early 1990s, additional waves of immigration from Ethiopia and CIS provided new research fields for many anthropologists.

The practice of the anthropologist is presented as that of an outside observer, a temporary guest in social situations—one who is not a permanent dweller (in the research field), but who rather adopts nomadism as a way of life. Although the image of the nomad implies that a person is not rooted in one place and that he or she lacks commitment to a place, the work of the Israeli anthropologist is characterized by concern and active engagement in events at home. The images of the immigrant and the committed person are therefore not mutually exclusive, although at times they are inherently in tension with one another due to the dual vantage point of insider and outside.

Deshen has argued (Deshen 1979) that Israeli anthropologists have tended to seek research fields that will fit in with their romantic outlook. In a discussion of anthropologists working in Israel he has written: "The study of a colorful group . . . is an anthropological challenge that the reality of immigration in Israel has presented to researchers (1979, 78). For example, S. D. Goitein and Erich Brauer worked with immigrants shortly after their arrival in the country and "were formidably impressed by their exotic uniqueness" (Deshen 1979, 79; Tzur 2003). Deshen notes that the insistence on finding romanticism within colorful, remote, traditional groups has prevented anthropologists from dealing with the study of urban Mizrahi Jews, abroad or in Israel. But the increasing rarity of communal and traditional field sites has forced anthropologists to "investigate human realities that are characteristic of cities and modern urban society, realities of disintegrating relationships, loneliness, and of superficiality of cultural devotion and human relations."[2] Deshen dedicates his 1979 article to the memory of Yitzhak Eilam, presenting an example of

> academic anthropologists who sometime play the part of Sartre's "spoiled believer" type. They learn about the life-ways that are different from those they themselves practice. But, at the same

> time, they fulfill roles within their own society. Even if they are not entirely at peace with these roles, they do not undermine them. They deliberately hide the truth from themselves, a truth that have discovered by gazing through the inverted mirror of their own research (Deshen 1979, 82).

The inversion of which Deshen speaks is the positioning of the researcher—the Tel Aviv Sabra who grew up in the secular socialist atmosphere of the 1940s and 1950s, who served in the army within a kibbutz—vis-à-vis his research subjects who are his utter opposites. To Deshen, Eilam represents the researcher who travels between two cultures with which he identifies: "At the time of his death he was involved in the world of his research subjects, but stood in the world of his own society" (Deshen 1979).

The discussion of the anthropologist as immigrant dovetails with the discussion of the anthropologist as a "professional stranger" (Agar 1996) who embodies the essence of the ethnographic endeavor. The weakness of the metaphor of the "stranger" is that it is static, whereas the metaphor of "immigrant" is more dynamic, permitting movement and change.

Several sub-images may be identified in the image of the nomadic anthropologist: the backpacker, adventurer, cosmopolite, immigrant to Israel (*oleh*). The backpacker is the curious wanderer who seeks distant worlds, while anthropology provides an intellectual anchor to his or her wanderlust. This type tends to formulate his or her experiences as a world traveler in anthropological terms. Even when the motive for traveling is a personal search and not curiosity for world cultures, the encounter stimulates him to take an interest in anthropology. The adventurer sets out on his or her academic path, with a tendency for heroism, danger-seeking, and adventure. He or she is attracted to the kind of fieldwork that involves extreme situations, coping with physical hardship, and giving up creature comforts. The cosmopolitan feels at home in the world, wanders freely among cultures and society, and seeks a temporary place to put down his belongings. Tomorrow he or she will continue to a different place, liberated from the burden of nationality and from a commitment to a particular territory. The *oleh* is connected to his or her Zionist and Jewish identity through the research of other Jewish groups.

In the next section, I shall present the life course of a number of anthropologists who each, in his or her own way, represent a different type of wandering, a different generation, different theoretical orientations, and different connections to anthropology: Aref Abu-Rabia, Michael Saltman, Eric Cohen, Uri Almagor, Gideon Kressel, Nir Avieli, Anat Ariel De-vidas, Don Seeman, and Rivka Eisikovits.

The stereotype of the nomad—the Bedouin—is represented by Aref Abu-Rabia. When I asked him what brought him to anthropology, he answered: "I am 'Aref Abu-Rabia,' member of the Abu-Rabia tribe," as if this identification were a self-explanatory key to his professional identity. Being a member of a Bedouin tribe, the plot of his life story was presented by him as a series of wanderings between the significant stations of his life. "In principle, a person must take a turn in his life every ten years," he stated, and lived up to this statement. From a childhood with his tribe in the Negev, he moved to Nazareth for high school, after which he continued to England to pursue academic studies. He worked as a teacher and a supervisor in the Ministry of Education, and later changed direction and developed a career as an anthropologist. Despite his wanderings, the most stable element of his career remains his research field—the Bedouins—which for him means doing research at home.

Michael Saltman of Haifa University embodies the connection between the different elements of the image of anthropologist as immigrant. Saltman immigrated from London to Israel, went back to study in England and later in the United States, returned to Israel, and then left to do fieldwork in Africa and the Caribbean. He chose a position of marginality within the established community of local anthropologists. Born in London in 1937, he received his education and grew up in a Jewish environment. He studied anthropology, geography, and history as an undergraduate. Later, during a brief visit to Israel in 1956, he participated in an archeological excavation in Hazor, an experience that affected his decision to immigrate to Israel. Of his military service in the Israel Defense Forces, he says, "I learned Hebrew in the army; there were many French-speaking soldiers in my cohort, and I was the interpreter. I acclimatized to Israel because of the army." The experience of military served as an intercultural encounter. Saltman returned to England for a master's degree and, after a year of studying, returned to Israel and found a position in the foreign ministry as an expert in training envoys to Africa. Some years later, he left for the United States to pursue doctoral studies at Brandeis University. In the context of his research, he carried out fieldwork for two years in the "bush," a day and half drive from Nairobi Kenya, with his wife and child, who was only a few months old. After his return, he joined Haifa University, conducted another field study in the Caribbean, and visited there a few times. Saltman's life course fits in with his basic theoretical position that in Israel anthropology should not only focused on research at home: "Anthropology at home closes theoretical thought rather than enlarges it; each region has a theory proper to it, and thus many theoretical possibilities open up." One can see in Saltman the model of the nomad, migrant, and marginal anthropologist, in the sense that he avoided being active in the Israel anthropological community.

Eric Cohen is an anthropologist whose life course contains all the images of nomadism: backpacking, adventure, travel, and immigration. He is an intercontinental, interdisciplinary, interfield and intertopic nomad, if one may say so. Cohen moves between identities of sociologist and anthropologist, between West and East Asia (Israel and Thailand, respectively): "I always searched for the way to combine being outdoors with intellectual work." As a child, he grew up in Yugoslavia, where he had already become interested in remote parts of the word. He immigrated with his family to Israel and began academic studies in Jerusalem, and when his sociological identity had solidified, he decided to change direction and move closer to anthropology. As a patrolman in the army, he felt that "this was a personal identity even more than a professional one." In mid-career, tourism became the central topic of his research: "when I went on a trip to Thailand and visited a temple in the northern part of the city, I saw tourists and guides negotiating with one another." In addition to a focus on a topic, Cohen feels that "jumping around has advantages. It keeps one alert and prevents unnecessary repetition." Cohen resisted the "tendency of anthropologists in the past to see traditional communities and subjects. I went for new topics. I had no program in life; my studies were occasioned by opportunities." In the middle of the 1990s, he began to take an interest in migrant workers in Israel as nomads of a different kind. Cohen created a link between an academic interest in foreignness (tourism) and nomadism as a way of life (for years, he divided his time between Israel and Thailand, with residence in both countries).

Gideon Kressel and Uri Almagor came to anthropology after adventurous journeys in the world. Almagor noted that his motivation to wander arose from contact with other cultures, which had begun even in his parents' home. His father, whose family had been exiled to Egypt during the World War I, collected books about the British Empire. His father's work brought many British visitors into his childhood home—people who, for him, were "representatives of the wide world." His mother, a native of Europe, also had command of several languages. "I grew up in a home," he says, "that was internationally oriented." He attributes his attraction to travel to this background—an attraction that he pursued by working for two years as a sailor on a merchant liner to Africa. From there, he wrote articles about Africa for popular news publications. He was able to fulfill his nomadic desire to travel inland on the continent when a commercial company hired him to be their representative and to report about local's everyday habits for the purposes of marketing. "It was after this that I decided to become an anthropologist. I didn't know exactly what anthropology was, but I wanted to give my adventuring spirit an academic character." From this point, he continued on the clear path that he had designed, to study at the Hebrew University (sociology and comparative religion) and in England (a Ph.D. in anthropology). His choice of field site in East Africa was motivated by a search for a "place that was not impacted by Christianity or Islam—a pagan society." He presents his arrival among the Dassanech as a heroic and adventurous act: "I took the Land Rover down from Eilat to Ethiopia, where I crossed the desert of Danakil by myself." Almagor declared that he and Yitzhak Eilam, both of whom were disciples of the British Manchester school, were the "last heroic generation of anthropology (in Israel)," after which the "interest in the anthropology of the Third World came to an end."

Gideon Kressel also came to anthropology after an adventurous journey around the world. After a grueling military service that had led to a severe injury, he went to travel in Africa for four months. "As a child I had read about Livingstone and Wingate, and wanted to fulfill childhood dreams." After completing a bachelor's degree in Jerusalem in sociology and Middle Eastern studies, he began a journey to the East, in which he traversed Asia, continued to the Philippines, and finally ended up in North America, where he continued his studies. "I wanted to explore worlds, like Phileas Fogg or Hesse's Siddhartha." The field site for his doctorate at Tel University was at home, the Ju'arish Bedouin of Ramle. He continued to study the Bedouin of the Negev, where he lives, but did not give up on studying remote fields: in recent years, he has conducted research in Bulgaria and China.

Nir Avieli is, in a way, a representative of a younger generation of anthropologists who came to the discipline after having seen the world as backpackers. A student of Eric Cohen and Uri Almagor, Avieli had spent time abroad as a child, but mostly wandered with his family within the borders of Israel. As a child, "I read the entire *Am Oved* adult series of books [mostly translated world literature].” He encountered the anthropologist Margaret Mead through literature too: “My mother bought me Mead’s book deliberately” was the opening sentence of his own life course report. These books were a vehicle for travel to other times and cultures. After completing his military service, he began a journey from North to South America, and later to East Asia. Backpacking, he taught me, is “the general state of living somewhere else: for example, working for four months and then traveling for four months. It is a planned journey around the world with regular stations at given times.” Although Avieli did not experience backpacking “by the book,” because at times he made long stops to pursue studies, “I developed anthropologist talents due to my travels, spatial abilities, and ability to figure out a place’s layout within a few minutes and orient myself.” The transition from one place to another seemed trivial and commonplace to him—the entire world is basically similar; people are similar to one another: “I find the trivia of being human, and that is what moves me—and this is to be found at the end of the world.” Avieli embarked on his wanderings from a very “local” place, from his membership in a small-town community, extended family, and membership in a youth movement. As a professional traveler today, he combines his academic career with work as a tour guide for Israeli travelers to Eastern Asia.

I asked a number of anthropologists to what extent the taken-for-granted backpacking experience of young Israelis and their adventurous exposure to foreign cultures might have been a reason for their attraction to academic anthropology studies. Cohen pointed to the fact that only a small proportion of those who turn to anthropology are former backpackers: “there is a huge gap between the backpacking experience and the study experience.” When backpackers come to study after their big trip, they search for the exoticism and the experience that they had when they were on the road, but do not find this among the library shelves. The conclusion of my interview subjects was that those who ultimately choose an anthropological career are not mere backpackers: beyond the wanderlust, there is an intense intellectual preoccupation and a need for academic knowledge. But the backpacking phenomenon in and of itself provides fertile ground for research. In recent years, many studies have been written about backpackers, all deriving from personal experience, which was later translated into an intellectual one.[3] The genre of writing about backpackers seems to have replaced the genre of the Africanist anthropologists and the researchers of the Third World. It is “softer,” less adventurous, and somewhat reflexive, and it ties the enchanting aspects of travel with local and global social, psychological, and political processes.

Anat Ariel De-Widas, who was a member of Haifa University's faculty and later moved to France, had wandered as a child in Europe because of her parents' work. When they settled in Israel, she wandered between Israel (home), South America (the travel and research destination), and France (the place of study and the intellectual center): "I felt at home nowhere and everywhere. When there is an emotional home, you know you can return and begin everything from scratch." Her emotional home is family in Israel. For her, wandering is movement in the world, for a variety of reasons, in different human formations, which all end with a return to home. Her wanderings are a mixture of travel, temporary unfocused and non-committal migration (in terms of career), chance arrival in a place, and the establishment of a base for the sake of work that would finance the next career chapter, as well as stopping at stations for research purposes (whether pre-planned research, or the collection of raw data for the purpose of future, uncharted research).

Don Seeman experiences wandering of a different nature, in his dual career as an anthropologist and yeshiva student. Seeman had first chosen to study marine biology and zoology, which exposed him to the fields of physical and social anthropology. At a number of significant points during his life, while searching for his own path, he needed a break to make decisions about his future. He turned to an ultra-Orthodox yeshiva before his doctorate. After the first Gulf War, he also spent time at the yeshiva: "I wanted to grasp the stick by both ends." The physical shifts between the university and yeshiva were an expression of his desire to combine anthropology and Judaism. The existential compulsion toward anthropological nomad was articulated by Seeman as follows: "The anthropologist is a hybrid creature; he needs to prove that he understands the desire and the territory of the Other." Seeman's life course exhibits three central components of migration: wandering, marginality, and multiculturalism. He represents a life course of movement between worlds that do not, on the surface, appear to bear any connection—anthropology, biology, and Judaism—as well as movement between actual places: Israel (university, yeshiva), Ethiopia, and America. During the years in which he belonged to the academic community of the Hebrew University, he was an exception in terms of his level of religious observance, and due to his political views, which were further to the right than those of most of his colleagues. After the final interview I conducted with him, he announced his intention to leave the Hebrew University and move to the United States, but he later returned to Israel.

The anthropologists interviewed for my study perceive the images of transitions and wandering in the sense of a personal migration or in the sense of movement between worlds—an explanation of what would later lead them to a professional engagement with anthropology. Those who had the sense of being strangers while wandering have the potential to better understand "strangeness," and examine it with an informed eye. The personal experience is interwoven with the academic and intellectual pursuits, contributing deep insights thereto. Although the experiences of wandering are not identical to those of migration, they share much in common. The articulation of the personal experience into one's life course, through the metaphor of wandering, was usually just one angle within a broader perspective presented by the interviewees, as most of them associated wandering with marginality and multiculturalism.

The Anthropologist as Marginal

Marginality in one's life course was one of the factors that the interviewees presented as having influenced their choice of anthropology. Marginality could have been social, personal, or cultural. At the field site, marginality accords one a unique perspective as a sideline observer looking from the outside inward. In a marginal position, anthropologists develop a keen set of inherently professional senses. The ability to maintain flexibility and observe things both from within and without is an important and unique tool in the anthropologist's toolkit.

Among the anthropologists that I interviewed, I identified a number of patterns of marginality: social marginality due to life circumstances, marginality arising from the condition of immigration, political or ideological marginality (which is not always marginality, but rather a position of "Otherness" and uniqueness), and marginality within the context of Israel's academic community. In this section, I will present the life course of a number of anthropologists who emphasized their marginal starting point as a motivation to engage with anthropology, whether this was the prime motivation or whether this was a leitmotif within the central narrative. Even the anthropologists who defined themselves as marginal were not marginal in every aspect of their lives, and for some of them marginality was more of a stance they adopted toward reality, and less of an emotional and social experience.

Some of the interviewees migrated between countries in their childhood or youth, and the experience of having lived in different places was interpreted by them as a source of attraction to anthropology. Rivka Eisikovits sees herself as a "classic case of the way to become an anthropologist." Having grown up in Transylvania, an intercultural region, and having spoken a different language at home from the langue of instruction and speech at school, she had experienced discontinuity already in her experiences abroad. The move to Israel was, to her,

> . . . my personal laboratory as a child. Until today, I can remember my excitement and the difficulty of speaking out loud in classes. I even had difficulty finding my own house according to the local system of numbering homes. I was preoccupied with the difficulties of the transition, with questions of identity, with an adolescent's sense of belonging and lack of belonging, with acceptance and rejection. The new immigrants in my class were kept at arm's length by the Sabras. The Sabras went to youth movements—the immigrants were the urbane crowd.

When she first encountered anthropology as part of her academic studies, she recalled, "I was able to connect to my biography, to existing simultaneously in several languages, to the comparative view, to voluntary marginality. The skills I had acquired led me to anthropology."

Anita Nudelman also emphasized the fact that she came from "split worlds." Nudelman's biography began in childhood in Argentina, with a North American mother and an Argentinian father. Later, she moved between the secular and orthodox religious worlds. These experiences enhanced her curiosity about people, which led her to the study of human relations at the university and from there to anthropology. The accounts of Eisikovits and Nudelman portray both as people of split identities, as "hybrids" who felt difference, marginality, and separation.

Eyal Ben-Ari grew up as a child on a kibbutz, the son of parents of South African origin who spoke Hebrew in the United States and English when in Israel. His parents' employment led the family to move to a development town (Kiryat Gat), and later to New York, and finally to settle in Jerusalem. In New York, he studied at a Jewish school where he "didn't connect," and in Jerusalem he attended a prestigious school in an elitist neighborhood: "I felt like an outsider and didn't fit in. My path to social acceptance was through basketball, but I belonged to the 'wrong group'—to the 'Beitar' club in a 'HaPoel' neighborhood. So I developed an awareness of social sensitivity. I was an outsider in an elitist society, and knew what it meant to be a loser and socially rejected." Ben-Ari's marginality was anchored in personal experiences that led him to become interested in the social sciences. This was the primary drive that led him to the career of anthropologist/sociologist. Later, he assumed very central positions within Israeli anthropology as the head of a department, the head of an institute, and the chair of the Israel Anthropological Association.

Dan Rabinowitz describes the origins of his anthropological career thusly:

> There is something that is shared by all people, but which is more accentuated with anthropologists, and that is the feeling that you are an outsider everywhere, looking at things from a corner. This is something I felt from as far back as I can remember. Partial participation—that is the position of the anthropologist. This is something that becomes institutionalized and is given routine expression with anthropologists—there, but not entirely there.

Rather than speaking of a position of marginality and externality within science, Rabinowitz's personal and professional biography (as he explained to me, and as described in the book he co-authored with Khawla Abu Baker [Rabinowitz and Abu Baker 2002]) emphasizes the central position his family held. His father was a judge, and his mother was a music teacher; he himself was educated at a prestigious school in Haifa. Rabinowitz worked at an "outward bound" field-school in the Sinai desert for the Society for the Protection of Nature in Israel, and he wrote for the Haaretz daily—emblems of entry into established Israeli society and to the anthropological world. For Rabinowitz, like Ben-Ari, his solid socioeconomic position was combined with a sense of personal or social outsiderness.

André Levy, on the other hand, emphasizes his distance from the Israeli "center" in his own life story. He was born in Casablanca in Morocco, and grew up in the port town of Ashdod in the 1960s. His father immigrated to Israel for ideological (Zionist) reasons, although, according to Levy, he dared not admit this:

> My father appeared to have adjusted, but in fact he had given up. . . . Life in the neighborhood was community oriented, but cut off from the everyday life of the school, which had an enrolment of mostly Ashkenazi students. During my childhood, I was transferred from a good elementary school to an awful school, without being given any explanation for this. In high school the situation got even worse: it was decided that I would be tracked for training as a customs agent.

Levy refused to switch study tracks, and, aided by his history teacher, "who cultivated me—it was in her classes that I was first able to enjoy studying," he gained confidence. His entry into anthropology occurred by way of psychology, sociology, and education: "I did not understand the academic career track and was in no rush to go anywhere." In spite of an apparent indifference toward his anthropological studies, when he took a class that dealt with North Africa, he felt that "they were talking *about* me and *to* me," and his attitude toward anthropology then changed. Levy, Ben-Ari, and Rabinowitz all hold central positions in Israeli anthropology, irrespective of the sense of marginality they experienced throughout their lives, and which led them into their anthropological careers.

The Anthropologist as the Product of a Multicultural Society

Another central theme in anthropological life courses is the anthropologist's exposure to a multicultural society[4] before choosing an anthropological career. Many Israeli anthropologists pointed out the connection between exposure to a variety of cultures and their attraction to anthropology, and many found the roots of their attraction to understanding others already in childhood, because they had grown up in a multicultural society, community, or family. In this section, I shall cite a few short statements by diverse voices that spoke about the topic of multiculturalism.

Some of the research subjects had experienced a multicultural setting during childhood, and some had this experience as adults. Those who spent their childhood in a local, culturally homogeneous setting encountered cultural diversity in various new environments. For some it was the army, as backpackers, or through personal acquaintances that led to an intellectual interest in the "Other." A smaller number of native-born Israelis discovered their interest in anthropology following their encounter with others in Israel, or because of a culturally diverse living environment.

Henry Abramovitz, Gideon Kressel, and Jeff Halper spoke about the cultural diversity of the place in which they had grown up as a source of inspiration that engendered their later cross-cultural interests. According to Abramovitz,

> I grew up in a multicultural city—Montreal, Canada. I already understood the importance of multiculturalism as a child. We lived in an area that was mostly Jewish and French, but there were also English, Italians, Portuguese, Blacks, Jamaicans, and others. My

> parents also had different cultural styles: we were Romanian on my mother's side—an extended but close family. My father's side was Ukrainian—a dispersed and reticent family.

The point of departure for Gideon Kressel's story was multicultural exposure: "As a native of a heterogeneous kibbutz—it was a melting pot, like any other place . . . my ear was exposed to German, Hebrew, French, Italian, Hungarian, Russian, and other languages, which aroused a great appetite to know how to distinguish among cultures."

Jeff Halper grew up in Hibbing, a steel miner community in Minnesota, U.S.A, a place that was "remote and cut off, but professional miners from all different parts of the world came to work there." When Halper grew up, he became interested in the social sciences for ideological and social reasons, but he attributed the birth of his anthropological vocation to his encounter with diverse nationalities in the small town where he grew up.

For some of the interviewees, the intercultural encounter occurred in the course of academic studies. Although the encounter may not have been the catalyst to study anthropology, it assisted the formation of their identities as adults who recognize the existence of other cultures, and even produced an intimate acquaintance with the "Other."

The encounter with remote cultures through exposure to literature also bred anthropological curiosity. During their childhoods, books were virtual sites of multicultural encounters, which in retrospect seem to have motivated these anthropologists' interest in culture. As a child, Don Handelman read widely from books he borrowed from the municipal library. "When I first had the experience of reading fiction, I was hooked. Literature had a great impact on me: I could imagine alternative worlds, and this is much like cultural difference. . . . Anthropology allow me to dream." Multiculturalism is not, therefore, limited to our world: it can expand into fictional worlds.

Haim Hazan, like Handelman, speaks of the imagination that develops with reading as a central instrument of scientific thought: "Anthropology is a scientific field, under the umbrella of science, which allows the anthropologist to view himself as an artist and let the imagination loose. This is the seduction of anthropology. Not only as an academic, but as a person, I cannot give up the possibility of allowing my imagination to roam freely." For Hazan, the anthropologist's identity is "beyond discipline and methodology. It is the ability to use oneself as an instrument of research, and thus it is closer to art and literature, which contain ideas, images and inner worlds."

Lisa Antebi and Anita Nudelman represent the anthropology that develops in conditions of cultural diversity within a family, and of multiple transitions during adulthood. Antebi was born in Paris to an American mother and a Czechoslovakian-born father who grew up in Egypt. She lived alternately in France, the United States, and Israel, "and it was clear to me that my professional vocation would have to do with multiculturalism."

The Image of the Committed and Engaged Anthropologist

Haim Hazan says:

> The uniqueness of Israeli anthropology is its central characteristic: directness. It has neither the cynicism or simplisticness of British and American anthropology. Even when an Israeli anthropologist writes about Japan or East Africa, he uses direct, clear, sometimes even somewhat crude expressions—you understand what the main message is. In addition, everyone cares and is compassionate—no one is indifferent. When an Israeli anthropologist writes about other places, he will draw on Israeli irony and cynicism. But when he writes about Israel, he displays forthrightness and even callousness. The Israeli anthropologist is concerned with questions of identity and research is a solution for him. The writing of Israeli anthropologists, even when writing about others, is about themselves. They do not succeed in compartmentalizing themselves, and their critical capacity fades. One's roots and identity become anthropological questions.

Hazan's statements were a point of departure into two different directions of inquiry: (1) the issue of Israeli anthropologists' commitment and engagement, and (2) the examination of the formation of personal identity, and the realization of personal interests through anthropological work. The committed anthropologist identifies with an ideology and draws his or her own personal contours in respect to it. In parallel, his or her personal identity—whether Jewish, Zionist, or national—takes form through the intellectual pursuit of anthropology.

In examining the central images of Israeli anthropological identities, one finding stands out: the intensity of the researchers' involvement in the developments of Israeli society. The concepts of "commitment" and "engagement" in this context require clarification. In the Israeli anthropological community, commitment is channeled to two paths: to social causes on the one hand, and to the national ideology on the other. These two targets of commitment would appear to be mutually exclusive. After all, national commitment is considered to be blind to power relations, whereas commitment to social causes turns its back on pan-national solidarity. I found, however, that my interviewees do not recognize a tension between these poles. Shokeid (1992b) proposes three distinct concepts: involvement, advocacy, and commitment. The first relates to the involvement in the lives of informants, which occurs especially in situations of research at home. The second relates to anthropologists who take the role of advocates for the community they study. The third is an ideological position that requires obedience to overarching, transcendent, humane, universal, or moral principles. Although the "involved" anthropologists and the "advocates" are committed primarily to their profession's research traditions, the "committed" anthropologists are liable, he argues, to be at odds with the professional norms of anthropology. Shokeid confronts loyalty to professional principles with loyalty to ideological principles, and thus alludes to the contemporary discourse around the conflict between these perspectives.

This contemporary debate in Israeli social science (the "new" versus the "old") has its roots in an article published by Israeli anthropologist Eric Cohen in the 1960s, in which he addresses the relationship between values and research (Cohen 1968). Cohen refers to the contribution of social scientists to policy-making in the area of immigrant absorption or in respect to Israel's Arab population. "Is the water here so cloudy that we cannot see through it?" he asks, arguing that a social scientist has no exceptional moral virtues, but is exceptional only in his or her ability to recognize the price paid for implementing ethical decisions. Immoral research is study that makes use of immoral means; however, the unethical applications of research findings cannot be regarded as a measure of its immorality. As a way out of these dilemmas, Cohen proposes a commitment to humanism and human values. This discussion alludes in no uncertain terms to the ethical deliberations of anthropologists who are committed to goals defined by the establishment, and who sometimes are positioned at the crux of decision making that could ultimately harm their research subjects.

Applied Anthropologists The specialized field of applied anthropology in Israel (see Shabtai and Mizrahi 2004) contributes an addition dimension to this discussion. This specialization encompasses various areas of interest in social and cultural anthropology and, by definition, makes use of anthropological knowledge to solve social and political problems. Applied anthropologists provide information, evaluate projects, formulate policy, and directly intervene on behalf of their clients. The clientele is diverse: governmental authorities, NGOs, business organizations, non-profits, community groups, and even individuals. Within the broad field of applied anthropology, there is a standard distinction between action anthropology, research and development anthropology, advocacy anthropology, and cultural brokerage; in Israel, however, no distinction is made between these concepts. Among my interviewees were a number who defined themselves as applied anthropologists; some of them gave voice to their particular professional identity in an issue of the journal *Practicing Anthropology* that was devoted to applied anthropology. The editors, Jeff Halper and Anita Nudelman (1993), claimed that Israeli anthropologists assisted governmental agencies, schools, health services, and other public bodies to understand the culture, aspirations, and problems of new immigrants (*olim*). They also proposed forms of residential settlements to provide solutions for the needs of the immigrants and for the state's needs.

The role of the applied anthropologist has been described as follows by Phyllis Palgi:

> I had the privilege of being the first applied anthropologist in the state of Israel. . . . The head of the department [of mental health in the Ministry of Health] attempted to develop a nationwide program that would respond to the different needs of a heterogeneous society, which was rapidly growing. . . . I accepted the statement that an anthropologist must find a way while doing fieldwork to be accepted by the chief of the tribe. The state was at that time in its founding and formative stages. It was a time of expansion from the earlier foundations, from myth and religion. An anthropologist who wished to be relevant had to adapt to the psycho-historical context of the country. (Palgi 1993, 5)

In the article by Halper and Nudelman, different Israeli anthropological versions of applied anthropology are described, but similarities among them seem to be represented more than differences. All accept the standard conception of the applied anthropologist as a cultural mediator. An exception in this respect is Jeff Halper, who believes an anthropologist should be socially engaged and should demonstrate social and political responsibility for the society he or she studies. Halper has for several years been the chairperson of the Committee against House Demolitions (of Palestinians). He also took part in one of the flotillas or humanitarian aid to Gaza.

In another article relating to the question of applied anthropology in Israel, written by Ze'ev Kalifon (1997), it is argued that many Israeli anthropologists perform applied work, even if it is not defined as such by them. Their work, so the claim goes, corresponds to all the definitions of applied anthropology and exists within a broad range of practices. The articles included in this issue are meant implicitly to enhance the prestige of this branch of anthropology.

In the past, a number of initiatives attempted to develop applied anthropology as a specialization at Ben Gurion University, the Hebrew University, and Tel Aviv University, but these attempts were short lived. At Yezreel Valley College, a track in applied anthropology has been successfully operating for a number of years. Yoni Mizrahi and Malka Shabtai, who head the program, compiled an anthology of interviews with Israel's leading applied anthropologist, co-authored with their students (Shabtai and Mizrahi 2004)

Anthropologists Committed to National Targets and Establishment Goals Anthropologists during the two first decades of Israel's statehood were occupied with assisting the project of nation building and the founding of institutions, in an unquestioning and routine manner. In this, they do not differ from other social scientists in Israel and from social scientists in Third World countries at times of nation building. (See, for example, Özbudun-Demirer's 2011 work on Turkey.) The prevailing outlook during the 1950s and 1960s about the role of the social scientist, including the anthropologist and sociologist, was expressed in the declared goals for establishing a faculty of social sciences (the Kaplan School) at the Hebrew University. In 1947, the Senate of the Hebrew University recommended the establishment of the social sciences, presenting the following rationale: "The Yishuv is waiting for the university to undertake the scientific and professional training of the future forces that will fulfill important roles in the economic and social organization of the Yishuv" (Gross 2001). The founding document of the Kaplan school from 1952 states: "The Hebrew University wanted to fulfill a crucial role in nation building . . . [the establishment of a faculty of social sciences], leading to the solution of the state's crucial problems. This chiefly refers to the sociological, economic and demographic problems that relate to the development of a new society in Israel as a result of the ingathering of the exiles."[5] Some two months later, the governing board of the university decided that "this profession [social anthropology] is of special importance, because now, especially, after the great immigration, there is a huge opportunity for research, and there are also practical issues, and as every year goes by, the situation will change."[6]

At around the same time,[7] and in the same spirit, Raphael Patai proposed that the prime minister's office set up a bureau for applied anthropology (or, in his phrase, "useful anthropology [*antropologia shimushit*]"). The reasons for such an enterprise were described as follows:

> The urgent problems of absorbing the immigrants, and especially the Oriental Jews, and the cultural differences between the Jews and the minorities in Israel. Anthropologists can help with the hardships of acclimatization . . . which are liable to become greater. These difficulties cannot be reduced, of course, to the groups of immigrants from Oriental countries. . . but . . . it is among them that the problem has already reached the acute stage. The same is true, even to a greater extent, in respect to non-Jewish minorities, where almost no shared cultural features are to be found with the Jewish majority . . . the ministry chiefs . . . when deciding guidelines and general administrative approaches, which are liable to cause certain transformations in the lives of a certain ethnic community or group . . . may receive the opinion of the ministry about the estimated impact of that decision . . . when some kind of regulation or general ordinance is implemented . . . . The ministry itself can propose that the various governmental departments implement certain methods or means. (Patai, n.d.).

Patai's ideas fit in with the university's decision, as did Dorothy Willner's arguments about the contribution of anthropology to the absorption of immigrants. Willner, a social anthropologist, served as the head of the social research department in the Jewish Agency (Willner 1956). In her view, the anthropologist mediates between cultures and should be allocated a central role in the processes of intercultural encounters. However, in contrast to the respect given the anthropologist's knowledge by NGOs, governmental institutions showed little interest in their skills; this is corroborated by the fact that only a few anthropologists were granted positions in governmental ministries over the years. This fact also contradicts Kunda's claim that the type of administrative units that Patai proposed actually were established and were in operation—more modestly and under different conditions—during the years following the establishment of the state (Kunda 1992).

How did anthropologists view their role in institutional systems designed to implement policy? An anthropologist ought to make his or her knowledge available to society for the solution of social problems. Henry Rosenfeld describes the spirit of those times:

> Zionism is based on national capital that arrived from world Jewry. There is Zionist enthusiasm. The state institutions also require higher education. The state has bodies and institutions and people who are schooled, and they want to ride that wave. All those who wish to contribute are in a negotiating position: they want to receive (a livelihood, prestige, work, and an occupation). The growth of the population, new universities, and potential lecturers who need to make a living generate a demand for anthropology as well as for other fields of knowledge. Most of the social scientists who came here (e.g., Dan Patinkin, Louis Guttman) were themselves activists in Zionist youth movements and were naturally dedicated to the Zionist and socialist ideas. Those who were not Zionists did not come. They fit into the frameworks in which they had power (academia in Jerusalem), and turned to the path of committed research. Besides, a person searches for work, and should not be condemned for finding it in institutional frameworks.

Phyllis Palgi, who was the first (and for many years the only) anthropologist in the Ministry of Health, was born in the 1920s in South Africa, where she began her studies. She later studied in the United States, and immigrated to Israel in the late 1940s:

> I came to Israel in 1947. I thought I must work in the research field. In other words, I viewed my [Zionist] pioneering *Halutziyut* [commitment/identity] in that way, and it came out of a background. . . . My [Zionist] pioneering *Halutziyut* is a result of my prior background. During my studies in South Africa, I was involved in Zionist activism, and also in promoting Black rights.

> In South Africa, I was obliged to decide where I would be putting my energy in this life. And—in relation to which collective: either for the emancipation of the Black or for the Jewish people who needed a state of its own. Everything was done with good intentions. The leadership and the professional were in a trap of ambivalence: good intentions to receive and give entry to all the people (immigrants). The *olim* also had to make new Jews of themselves. The story about power dynamics is not true.

Palgi was appointed as head anthropologist, and worked for the mental health department of the Ministry of Health:

> I was part of the establishment, and that bothered me, but I had a lot of influence through consulting and teaching. Health was a neutral topic, and there is a greater degree of consensus about it, compared to other systems. I had a position as an anthropologist. Apart from the economic austerity measures, this was a period of contradictions, paradoxes, and emotional vagueness that focused on the ideological principle of the new state: the ingathering of the exiles. . . . In this context, I saw it as my role, first of all, to increase understanding among professionals, the administration, and decision makers, about the damaged survivor populations. I attempted to create legitimacy for the various customs of different ethnic groups . . . At the operations level, there was a need to develop varied means for helping the staff carry out its daily tasks. My entrance into the bureaucratic system was easier due to my appointment to the national planning committee of the mental health service, and later to the advisory committee to the Minister of Health. (Palgi 1993, 5)

In her account of the rich experiences, Palgi foregrounded the role of the anthropologist as cultural broker: "An example of mourning customs that appeared odd to the staff was the Moroccan custom to bring to the graveside professional wailers, who clawed their cheeks until they bled. Singing and dancing around the grave was another unfamiliar custom of Kurd Jews. Prior knowledge of various customs helped the staff feel less helpless and alienated."

Alex Weingrod was one of a handful of anthropologists in Israel in the early 1960s. He had grown up in a Zionist socialist family, which was "unassimilated, non-immigrant, but committed and activist." As a member of the

Zionist youth movement in the United States and a soon-to-be pioneer, he chose to study agriculture, but found himself bored by the subject. In 1949, he spent a year in Israel at the Institute for Youth Leaders from Abroad, in which the participants studied Hebrew, lived on kibbutz, and attended lectures on sociology, among other topics: "there was utter identification with everything that was happening here . . . as a Jew and a Zionist, I accepted the premises of this society, and even though it would have been fitting for me to be critical, I was without doubt within the consensus."

In a lecture that he presented at the fifty-year jubilee of Brandeis University, where he served as a lecturer, Weingrod exposed the duality and tension between his devotion to the Zionist project and his critical eye:

> Now the issues that I am raising are not only related to an Israeli episode in the sociology of knowledge, but also to the ways in which social scientists may serve, or better, be committed to, the ideologies of the society that they live in. I am not arguing that the social scientists, who were closely allied with the Israeli Establishment, consciously spun a set of understandings that served their interests—but they were more caught-up with the Zionist drama than withdrawn enough to be critical of its purpose as well as the immigrants' plight. This is the point that I wish to turn to next: how, if at all, can one maintain a critical outlook within the society that you chose to join? If you identify with and care deeply for the society that you chose to live within, then how do you maintain a critical stance? (1998b, 14)

In Chicago, Weingrod was exposed to the vibrant social sciences, which were oriented to leadership development and education for engagement. Some of the lecturers were social activists and trade unionists—"and in all of this I discovered anthropology and was attracted to it." The anthropology department was very active, and its dominant figure was Robert Redfield, whose name had come up as one of the candidates to teach anthropology at the Hebrew university. According to Weingrod, "I received a stipend and thought I would do research on Israel," under the instruction of Sol Tax, a prominent lecturer and anthropologist in the U.S. academy (Stocking 2000). Of his time working for the Jewish Agency, Weingrod attested, "We were young and full of enthusiasm and ready for a challenge. It was an historical moment. We wanted to do a new kind of non-established anthropology, which would make a contribution. By being involved, we could offer a realistic voice from the field."

Later in his career, Weingrod faced new dilemmas. In the beginning of the 1980s, he researched the pilgrimages to the graves of Tzaddikim (Jewish saints) and the religious devotion involved in the belief in saints and their miraculous deeds, along with the critique of these phenomena that was appearing in the Israeli media. The traditional response of anthropologists to the criticism was that the saint worship was a legitimate worldview and means for expressing religious sentiments, even if it was unacceptable to secular circles or to the Rabbinic establishment: "You follow your customs, let them follow theirs." But when this worldview began to include practices exploiting the power of amulets and imprecations to mobilize political support, the citizen in Weingrod protested: "Here, as a citizen, and not as an anthropologist, I am more than disturbed, and in fact am deeply concerned. I am worried about the growth of strength and legitimacy of fundamentalist religious movement in Israeli public life, and what this bodes for the state in which I live." Moreover, when he was conducting research on the Israeli–Palestinian conflict in Jerusalem, there was a rising wave of violence, which, he argues, prevented him and his colleagues from publishing the results of their research in the book they had planned: "The cruel realities of everyday life overwhelmed the anthropological project. The violence was too extreme, the rifts too deep—it is difficult to maintain a scientific outlook."

Weingrod presents a critical outlook that integrates his status as a citizen with his status as an anthropologist. As opposed to the stance he adopted while working for the Jewish agency, he later presented a form of research at home that is not based on a priori acceptance of the society's taken-for-granted norms, and which positions itself outside the consensus of ideological political camps (in this case, of both Zionists and post-Zionists). In his view, "a critical position is easier today than it was in the past, because the doubts and alienation among ourselves have increased. However, an anthropologist must persevere in his work, even under fire." Weingrod's account distills the core essence of the conflict between Zionist commitment and commitment to anthropology. It resonates, however indirectly, with critical anthropology on the one hand, and Israeli "establishment" anthropologists on the other.

Moshe Shokeid presents a similar ambivalence. He started as a regional sociologist in the Jewish Agency Settlement Department, and later studied for a Ph.D. in anthropology at Manchester, after which he returned to Israel to take up a position at Tel Aviv University. Throughout his academic career, Shokeid conducted a great many research projects about different aspects of Israeli society:

> It is difficult to be an Israeli sociologist or anthropologist. Unlike other places, these professionals, almost from the start, mobilized to document and assist the efforts for national renewal, but they were punished for doing so, and paid a high price for this. . . . The primordial sin of Israeli sociology has to do with the mobilization of its first generation to the national project of the ingathering of the exiles and creating a melting pot society, and the translation of the prophetic Zionist vision into the current terminology of the centers of sociology. . . . Without really thinking about it, ours was a mobilized sociology. Teachers and students believed that there was real value in this implementation of theoretical thinking, and that they were assisting the process of creating a melting pot society. . . . The sociologists of the 1980s and 1990 [did not understand] how the eyes of the researchers of the 1950s and 1960s were plastered over, preventing them from seeing that they had been in service of the Zionist establishment of dispersing the population, and of what may now be defined as the project of erasing the culture of Israel's ethnic minorities.

Unlike the sociologists, they [the anthropologists] recognized, for example, the religiosity of the *olim* as a central facet of their lives, which was not merely a manifestation of a phase that would pass automatically as the immigrants adopted modernity. Their research methods obliged them to encounter the continuity of this dimension in the lives of the *olim*. . . . The sociologists, and certainly the anthropologists, felt that they were fulfilling a mission. But it was precisely the anthropologists, whose point of departure was one that was more positive toward the culture and experiences of the *olim*, who were not absorbed in public consciousness. (2001, 80–83)

Yael Katzir, an anthropologist who studied in the United States, with the encouragement of her father, Aharon Katzir (the famous scientist whose candidacy for Israel's presidency was aborted by his murder in a terror attack), presented a point of view similar to that of Shokeid:

> I knew I would be an anthropologist from the age of nine. In the early 1950s there was a flourishing of anthropological literature that also reached my parents' library. The intellectual milieu of people

> who read and travelled around the world was influenced by the anthropological literature: Boas, Malinowski, Mead, Benedict, Sapir, Evans-Pritchard. My father was very sensitive to and aware of such schools of thought, and was impressed by the fact that anthropology [was a discipline] in which women were dominant. He sought for a scientific solution for the problems of multiculturalism in Israeli society; the relativist and heterogenic outlook appealed to him.

With her parents' encouragement and equipped with the worldview she had inherited from them, Katzir studied anthropology and carried out her fieldwork in Israel in a moshav of Yemenite Jews. Her well-known study deals with the place of women in the moshav and the processes of acculturation to Israeli reality (Katzir 1993).

Eric Cohen remarks (Cohen 1968) that although he never perceived himself as Zionist, he agreed to carry out research on the absorption of immigrants because, in his view, absorption problems were situated within the range of accepted anthropological research goals. In his research conclusions, he made a point of indicating the social price of the absorption policy. In his view, the anthropologist's work may succeed at refining the political mechanism and redirecting its goals. For example, it might cause the absorbing establishment to recognize the original institutions of various groups of immigrants, and take care not to destroy such institutions by implementing a nondiscriminate policy of mass absorption. However, Cohen argued, the social researcher has no control over the use the political institution will make of the research to promote entrenched political interests, and they may cite social scientific research selectively in order to publicize their achievements. For this reason, Cohen decided to avoid any research that was directly supported by public Israeli institutions, and preferred to secure external grants that would allow him to operate independently of decision makers, thus resolving the conflict between his humanist values and his values as a researcher: "I will refuse to conduct research on Israeli Arabs that is designed to promote Jewish national interests at the expense of the Arab minority." But despite this decision, he agreed to conduct a study on the occupied territories, although it was government sponsored, in the hope that it would assist a rapprochement between Jews and Arabs in the future (Cohen 1968, 10).

The study of Arab and Bedouin society, which attracted many Israeli anthropologists from the beginning of anthropology's institutionalization, is an arena in which such conflicts posed by various types of commitment and engagement are manifested. The first Jewish researchers in these fields were Henry Rosenfeld, Abner Cohen, and Emanuel Marx, followed by Joseph Ginat, Gideon Kressel, and later by Yifrah Zilberman and Dan Rabinowitz, who founded a research tradition that carried much weight within Israeli anthropology. The reasons for their interest in Arab society were various—some because of anthropology's role in assisting the Jewish majority to establish its control over a minority (Rabinowitz 2002), and some because they viewed Arab society as exotic, traditional, or as carriers of "Otherness," making them interesting and seductive candidates for classical anthropological study (Furani and Rabinowitz 2011).

Joseph Ginat, one of the researchers discussed by Rabinowitz, challenged these statements by claiming that his interest in Arabs in a political context was utterly separate from his academic interest in this group:

> I carry out applied anthropology in an establishment framework, within political systems. I conduct research on subjects related to conflict resolution and personally mediate in conflicts among Arabs. I began my career by recruiting votes for Mapai [the political labor party] among Bedouin in the Negev. As for my work as a consultant on Arab affairs in the Prime Minister's Office, there is no connection between my research and my role as consultant because I do not research the areas in which I provide consulting, and vice versa. There is a separation between work and research.

Ginat maintains ongoing ties with his research field: he visited his former subjects, mediated conflicts in the community, and assisted with their problems with Israel's governing institutions. According to him, crossing of the line would have been to assist someone who presented a security threat (not a political one). Ginat was academically interested in conflict-resolution anthropology, and he dealt with this topic at a center that he created for peace research in collaboration with the universities of Oklahoma and Bethlehem and with research centers in Jordan, as well as the Institute for the Study of Conflict at the Netanya College in Israel.

The outlook presented by Emanuel Marx in respect to his role as an anthropologist evolved over the years. In an interview with Aref Abu-Rabia, he described why he became an anthropologist:

> During the war around the establishment of Israel in 1948 I had seen a great deal of fighting. I had come out with a heavy conscience, and a wish to make amends. I thought that the study of Sociology and Oriental Studies . . . would provide a good foundation for a better understanding of Arab Society. . . . I thought that the two areas of study I had chosen complemented each other. So when the time came to write an M.A. thesis, I decided that the field study of the Bedouin society would integrate my studies. (Abu-Rabia 2001, 8)

In our talk about this topic, he said, "I thought that if I studied the Arabs, learned to know them, we might arrive at a better understanding."

In the introduction to his book on the Negev Bedouin (Marx 1967), Marx confessed that his attraction to the Bedouin had been that of a romantic. (This phrase is absent in the Hebrew edition of the book.) He received support for fieldwork and continued studies in the form of grants from the Israeli government and British foundations and, throughout his career, was involved in several planning projects (of the Bedouin town of Rahat, the airfields in the Negev, and also settlements in the Sharon region) in which he played the role of the broker anthropologist. In response to Aref Abu-Rabia's question (Abu-Rabia 2001) regarding whether it was appropriate for an anthropologist who conducts fieldwork to take the side of his informants when they are in dispute with the governing authorities, and what his view of the advantages and shortcomings of advocacy anthropology were, Marx replied,

> For a long time I believed that I was obligated to help the people I work with. That was a bad mistake, or the word "help" is practically identical with "control." To help people is to adopt an arrogant attitude toward them: you think that you are more influential, that you know what is best for them. What you do is to usurp their power. If you really want to be useful to people you work with you fulfill missions they entrust you with, provided you agree with their viewpoint. If they instruct you to see a government official on their behalf, that is allright, but you should never go beyond your brief. (2001, 22)

In his study of the town of Ma'alot in the early 1970s, Marx described the power and control of bureaucracy in Israeli society. Since that time, this topic has been underscored in his works as well as those of his students who study power relations in a bureaucratic context (e.g., Ofra Greenberg and Esther Hertzog). His critical view of the state's operations and institutions nonetheless did not lead him automatically to a commitment to social campaigns and struggles. Marx's trajectory involved a departure from the very heart of the governmental establishment to research on a non-Jewish society. Later, when Jews, immigrants, and the underprivileged residents of a peripheral town became his research subjects, he developed a critique of the governmental authorities. These transformations had to do, one can surmise, with processes of scientific maturation, but the character of the research field was that which influenced the reorientation of the spotlight from the "natives" to the interaction between the bureaucracy and the natives, and the development of a perspective that included dimensions of advocacy.

Anthropologists as Social Reformers and Advocacy Anthropology As mentioned earlier, some of the anthropologists adopted the image of an anthropologist who devotes his or her research efforts to an engagement that leads to commitment to social causes. The theoretical foundation for this approach is rooted in the critical paradigm of the social sciences, which defines the perception of reality as historical realism. Reality is constructed due to social, political, cultural, ethnic, and gender factors and is perceived by those who live this reality as "true" or "real." Even when this reality is invented or imagined, it is real to the social actors. The epistemology of this paradigm situates the relationship of researcher and subject as interactive relations, and assumes that the values of the researcher inevitably influence the research. The researcher is committed to helping and to acting on behalf of social change and moral reform as part of his or her contribution to the construction of a new society, and he or she is required to expose forms of social repression, and thus allow critique and change to occur. The researcher aims to empower the individual and to combat injustice by political means; he or she seeks to expose hegemonic processes and uncover the premises and the ulterior motives behind knowledge, explanation, rationalizations, and decisions. By exposing these dimensions, the researcher fulfills a subversive role against the possessors of repressive power. (For a discussion of this paradigm, see Guba and Lincoln 1998).

I identified among my interviewees two apparently opposing points of view that complement each other in respect to the critical paradigm upon which advocacy anthropology is based. One stems from identification with the distress of the weak victims of the establishment; the other views the anthropologist as one who, by virtue of his or her role in service of the governing authorities, can make heard the voices of the oppressed. Personal life experiences might have influenced the adoption of this perspective. Tamar El-Or says,

> My high school studies turned me into a sociologist. The messages, the teachers, the emphasis on being committed to one's society and the social composition of my class all produced elements of an emotional experience—not real anger, but an unmediated encounter with the social elite. I came to high school with lots of friends from my neighborhood, and there I also met the children of captains in El Al, from Ramat HaSharon and Herzliya Pituah, and Savion [well-to-do suburbs of Tel Aviv]. The atmosphere that dominated the classroom was that of the neighborhood kids and not of the elites. The encounter enabled me to understand the class structure of Israeli society. The encounter with the privileged class engendered a sense of injustice.

In her military service as an NCO in the personnel directorate (charged with HR responsibilities), El-Or traveled around the country and visited the homes of soldiers in "disadvantaged communities." Her acquaintance with these populations bred a critical worldview, but this did not translate directly into her choice of research topics. El-Or studied women without making a commitment to defend one aspect or another of their lives, but she emphasizes the need for a reflective anthropology and awareness of the positioning of the researcher: "The fact is that every person has a position and a location, and she or he must state where she or he is from."

Esther Hertzog was the director of the education department in the city of Or-Akiva:

> I was searching for a job, and I heard that a position was opening up in Or-Akiva to coordinate an adult education project. I knew that Or-Akiva was an underprivileged place, and I thought of this as a mission. The head of the regional council proposed that I manage the education department. I identified with the place and with the residents, the staff, the parents, the schools, and kindergartens, parent associations, and I learned a tremendous amount. It was the University of Life.

This local activity led Hertzog to volunteer for social causes in the context of political movements (including some political parties). "I was spending time in absorption centers, meeting lots of people, collecting data, and then I decided to write a doctoral thesis about the caseworkers who worked with Ethiopian immigrants, and it was suggested that I form a connection with an anthropologist who was interested in this topic." This was the phase in which she converted to anthropology, a discipline that suited her interest in social affairs. In her dissertation, Hertzog placed a strong emphasis on gender aspects and continued to carry out research on topics related to women's status and women's rights. She then developed a research interest (and practical interest) in the issue of removal of children from the custody of their parents into state institutions, the question of the kidnapping of the Yemenite children from their families at the early stage of their aliya, trafficking in women, pornography, and other causes: "All of my studies are ethnographic, because I base my analysis on real cases, on people I accompanied through their struggles."

Jeff Halper, a radical and outspoken representative of advocacy anthropology, examined the connection between ethnicity and education as part of his doctoral fieldwork: "I participated in a volunteering program in the Nahla'ot neighborhood of Jerusalem, and began to work for the municipality as a community worker in education. At the time, there was talk of students who were 'needful of cultivation'—i.e., disadvantaged, but instead the education system was involved in setting up students for failure." Concomitantly, Halper was an active member of the Israeli radical political movement. Halper defines himself as an applied and engaged anthropologist (Shabtai and Mizrahi 2004, 42–44). He initiated a number of manifestos at the IAA meetings, in favor of Bedouin or Ethiopian rights, or against the war in Lebanon. (See the chapter "The Israeli Anthropological Association as a Site of Anthropological Practice.")

Shalva Weil argues that anthropological research is relevant only if it deals with topics that contribute to the advancing the causes of the oppressed:

> Research does not belong in the drawer. Research is meant to advance populations in distress. That is why, in the framework of research in the Institute for Innovation in Education I have chosen to work on social issues concerning Ethiopian Jews, I run training seminars for personnel who work with Ethiopian immigrants, I manage training programs in excellence in leadership among the immigrants as well as programs for promoting immigrants from the

> Caucasus in the field of education. Research that cannot advance some cause is unworthy, especially if the focus is on ethnic groups. Ethnic research is no longer very fashionable today. At one time, everyone was researching ethnicity and everyone had some kind of social conscience, as a leftist, or with a desire to help. We are in a different era today, everyone is more egotistical, more materialist.

Weil's studies, beginning with her doctoral research on a community of Bni-Israel (Jews from the Mumbai region in India) living in the city of Lod, continued later with other immigrant groups, such as Ethiopian and Caucasian Jews. It was motivated by and premised on worldviews similar to those of anthropologists in the 1960s and 1970s, who believed they were contributing to the Zionist project by their mere acquaintance with immigrant groups. However, unlike these predecessors, she points out how her knowledge assists the immigrants themselves rather than the establishment charged with absorbing them. Therefore, the image of her professional life course is dual: she both advocates on behalf of the ethnic group (without critiquing the establishment), while also sharing the establishment premises concerning the anthropologists' contribution to the absorption and acculturation of immigrants in the wider Israeli context.

Curiosity About Others and Formation of a Professional Identity

The third theme in the motivations for choosing anthropology as a vocation is the curiosity that anthropologists developed over the course of their lives toward various "Others." It should be noted that the interviewees defined their perception of others as neither reflexive nor critical, but rather as an attraction and enchantment with the foreignness and difference that arouse curiosity. I wish to examine this curiosity toward the figure of others as an important motive for anthropological research and as a drive for developing an anthropological career. I shall not review the issue of how others are perceived, and how the definition of others contributes to critical discourse, but will consider rather what role the interest in others plays in the decision to become an anthropologist, and how this interest affects the anthropologist's path throughout his or her career. At the same time, I do not ignore the impact that the positioning of others has on the researcher's findings and its practical applications.

A Separation from the "Other" Anthropology's initial point of view toward the "Other," which was normative at its time, became a significant issue in the post-colonial anthropological discourse of the late twentieth century. The critical reading that took place in the centers of Anglo-American anthropology revolved around the way in which the Other was defined by both an Orientalist and colonialist gaze. The forefront of the anthropological agenda was occupied by a discussion of bureaucratic regimes, relations between dominators and the dominated, and the definition of the Other as an object of research. (Topics such as subject–object relations, Othering, and the reflexive discussion of these issues continue to concern critical anthropologists in Israel into the twenty-first century [see, e.g., Ram 1995; Loss 2001; Forum of Social and Cultural Studies 2002].) The relations between researcher and Other in the study of the Oriental Jews were based on the assumption that the researcher is the mirror image of the research subject. (This school of thought follows the Saidian critique of Orientialism to a large extent.) The researcher situates the subject in a position in which he or she can be subject to categorization. A critical reading of the latter exposes hegemony, power relations, and processes of repression and subjugation. Rabinowitz, for example, discussed the ways in which anthropology has studied Palestinian society. In his study of four pioneering figures of the Israeli anthropology of the 1960s, Loss (2001, 5), offered a dichotomous analysis of binary oppositions, based on the Saidian Orientalist thesis (Said 1978). Loss claimed that the study of Mizrahi Jews in Israel anthropology was premised on the basic division between the Oriental Jews (*edot ha-mizrah*) (i.e., the subjects) and the Sabra or Ashkenazi Jews (the researcher). In the rhetoric of attribution of oppositions, the "no" of the one becomes the "yes" of the other—positive versus negative. The most basic dichotomy is that of traditional/modern, to which are added the oppositions of urban/rural, secular/religious, rational/non-rational, and infantile/mature. It is clear that the adoption of such a point of departure assumes that anthropologists of that era, including Israeli ones, who define their research topic as "the Other," would thus regard the subjects of their research and present them accordingly in their works. I take issue with this approach. Anthropologists study other cultures and other people; Israeli anthropologists lived, and are living, in the company of others—not only as a methodological strategy, but as a state of mind.

Enchantment and Aversion in Relation to the "Exotic Others" Attraction to the exotic in anthropology has persisted since the founding days of anthropology, and it exists today too. The situating of others as exotic—or, as in a paraphrase of Victor Turner's famous phrase, unfamiliar and strange—has always been accompanied by a sense of adventure and by a clear-cut distinction between home and the field. The attraction to the strange and unfamiliar begets the need to interpret it in universal terms and to expose the similarities between the exotic others and the kinsmen of the anthropologist.

Is Israeli anthropology any different from other anthropologies in this respect? During the stage of establishing the discipline, in the 1960s and 70s, it followed the mainstream path of classic British and American anthropology, which were attracted to the exoticism of the distant Other in the Third World. Even then, most anthropology was performed on the "exotic Other" at home: Arabs, Mizrahi Jews, moshavim and kibbutzim. The Anglo-American anthropological development toward doing anthropology at home appeared later, in the 1980s, and joined the Israeli trend. Here, Israeli anthropologists found an outstanding focus for their interest: Other Jews. In both cases, the search for the different Other is accompanied by a search for the universal.

Brauer and Patai openly spoke about their attraction to the exotic; together with a commitment to document a world that was destined to disappear, they viewed this as the *raison d'etre* of ethnological and anthropological research. Their "Others" were Oriental Jews,[8] and the presentation of Mizrahi Jews as such was never encountered with criticism but was taken for granted.[9] The component of attraction to exoticism could also be found among the scholars who studied Arab and Bedouin society in the 1950s and 1960s.

In their introduction to the mid-1980s book *Oriental Jews (Yehudei HaMizrah),* the editors presented the role of the Mizrahi Jews in Israeli culture and society, as well as in historical, sociological, and anthropological research and in folklore studies:

> The balance of anthropological research in the field of Mizrahi Jews in the present, reveals the way in which the researchers followed the classic anthropological tradition, as well as their own desires, in order to discover exotic Jewish communities, or communities that were settled far from the center. A relatively large amount of effort was invested in the study of the most remote and traditional groups. . . . however the increasing scarcity of community and traditional research fields is leading anthropologists everywhere, and in Israel too, to take a stand against the discipline's romantic tendency to search for and attempt to preserve a vanishing world. . . . The differences between most anthropological works today and the early anthropological studies that were carried out in Israel during the

> [British] Mandate period and the period of the mass immigrations are conspicuous. Current research topics are less picturesque and less satisfy the appetite for exoticism, and therefore the effort required from the researcher to respond to the disciplines traditional demands, to provide a rich and detailed description, is even greater. (Deshen and Shokeid 1984, 20–21)

Until the beginning of the 1980s, the researcher's "Others" were colorful, picturesque, and steeped with "folklore." But even though the 1980s research of Mizrahi Jews had some kind of exotic color, the research findings and the way in which the researched communities were presented in the published ethnographic were devoid of any such exoticism. From that point onward, the gravitational center of anthropological research shifted to the urban, secular, and decidedly non-exotic middle classes. Another shift occurred in the middle of the 1990s, when enchantment with exoticism was to be found in Israeli society's different Others: the ultra-Orthodox (Haredim), the homeless, born-again Jews (*hozrim bi-teshuva*), newly secular Jews (*hozrim bi-she'ela*), extremely poor women, spirituality seekers, and more. One might say that the attraction to exoticism found substitute objects: the Bedouin dress was replaced by the seeker's Indian Sari, the *streimel*, and the rags of the poor and the homeless. At the Hebrew University, graduate students from other disciplines (social work, education, Jewish studies, and regional studies) turned to anthropology to acquire tools to study what they regarded as exotic (e.g., Hakak 2003).

What are the roots of the attraction to the exotic? These roots sometimes sprout early in the anthropologist's childhood. This was the case for Uri Almagor: "My father's library provided the encounter with what I would today describe in anthropological terms as 'the Other.' After the army, I took a job on a boat that sailed to the shores of Africa, and that's how I got to know the continent. I met Ghanaians who sailed with me, I wandered around wide regions of the continents, and I later decided to study anthropology." According to Almagor, his reasons for choosing his field site for his doctorate were "To choose a place that had not been influenced by Christianity and Islam. When I came to the Dassanetch (an Ethiopian tribe I studied for my doctoral fieldwork), and saw them, I said to myself that they were like people who had emerged from the nineteenth century. During fieldwork, I photographed without using a light meter, and took some one thousand slides and two thousand black and white photos." From anthropological documentation, Almagor moved on to the visual documentation of his immediate environment, and he continues today to photograph in the Jerusalem area and to develop his own pictures. Unlike other Africanists of his generation, he did not cease to take an interest in Africa after he completed his fieldwork. Rather, he went back and carried out a study of the Herero people of Botswana during 1975–1980. (Incidentally, this society was the subject of Erich Brauer's doctoral dissertation.) Almagor illustrates the type of anthropology that is driven by an adventurous and curious impulse toward the exotic. Photography and its practice perpetuate the difference between him and the photographed other, his research subject.

Yoram Bilu began his career as a clinical psychologist and, over the years, became more and more interested in cultural aspects of psychological therapy, which ultimately led him to carry out fieldwork among folk healers. Of his work as a clinical psychologist in the Jerusalem Corridor regional council, he says, "I made contact with a social worker who worked in the moshavim in the area. She spoke about the fact that the residents go to healers. That was an exotic world. She put me in touch with someone, and I began to collect material. I understood that this could support a doctoral dissertation. I never thought, when I was sixteen years old, that this would be my career. I never dreamed of going into anthropology." From that time onward, Bilu has made folk healers and folk medicine, Tzaddikim (righteous men) and their cults, past culture heroes such as Yaakov Wazana, and ultra-Orthodox society the subjects of his research.[10]

One finds examples of attraction to the exotic among the anthropologists who trained during the 1980s as well, even if their research interests did not necessarily focus on societies perceived as such. They experienced Mizrahim as Others in encounters that took place mainly during their military service, when Israelis of disparate Israeli social worlds meet each other. Orit Brawer-Ben David says, "I was born an anthropologist, I always loved observing people." Brawer-Ben David was born in a relatively wealthy suburb of Tel Aviv, to a father and grandfather who were known geographers. She attended the Scouts youth movement and a prestigious high school, and she led a social life that was circumscribed within the boundaries of the proximate community. Curiosity toward others was sparked during her army service, but, she says, before "I moved to live in Mitzpe Ramon, after my marriage, I had lived in a bubble. It was only there that my attitude changed. I wanted to communicate with all sorts of people of different types." Despite this attraction to others, she chose to study the close and familiar: the hiking trips conducted by the

Society for the Protection of Nature, which occupy the core of Israel's social and ideological center (Brawer-Ben David 1998).

I discovered similarities in the social profiles of Orit Brawer-Ben David and Maya Melzer-Geva. Melzer-Geva grew up in Haifa, on Mt. Carmel, in an Ashkenazi, elitist environment. Her parents, travel agents who had explored the world, presented her with photos and stories that exposed her to the world at large. She began to collect musical instruments from around the world, and she developed an interest in folklore. Along with an openness to remote cultures in her home, "there was no place for proximate [Israeli] exoticism. It was perceived as very threatening. Only when I was in the army did I visit [underprivileged] neighborhoods in Tel Aviv, as part of my job. I didn't know such place existed in the country." When she began her academic studies in the Hebrew University, she hoped to combine courses in folklore, within the faculty of the humanities, with courses in social anthropology. In the rigid structure of the university in the 1970s, crossing disciplinary boundaries was like crossing the Rubicon, but she succeeded at crossing and gained approval for her program. While studying for her B.A. and M.A. degrees, she focused on Georgian Jewry, who were Other culture to her and to Yitzhak Eilam, who was her instructor and the main researcher of this group. Her doctoral dissertation was also devoted to Georgian Jews (Melzer-Geva 2004).

Some anthropologists were averse to exoticism. Ben-Ari explicitly states that although he conducted his fieldwork in Japan, he was attracted to the urban aspect of Japanese society, and explicitly opposed the search for the traditional rural Japan. Ofra Goldstein-Gidoni, who also conducted research in Japan, was not attracted to the exotic in this society. She studied the wedding industry in the city, motivated by an interest in capitalist society and in the cultural, Western, and local aspects of the wedding ceremony. Haim Hazan has stressed that he studies the non-exotic others, arguing that every cultural group that is studied becomes Others. Hazan's Others were the elderly, to whom he has devoted most of his research energies.

The Attraction to "Other" Jews Among Israeli-born anthropologists, not one declared that his or her attraction to anthropology derived from his or her Jewish identity or that his or her interest in "Other" Jews was an outcome of a search for "exotic Jews." This is surprising when viewed against the attraction that Ethiopian Jews held for anthropologists after the former immigrated to Israel in the 1990s. Among scholars of Ethiopian Jewry, several are native-born Israelis (e.g., Malka Shabtai, Esther Hertzog, and Hagar Salamon), and some were not native Israelis (e.g., Lisa Antebi, Don Seaman, Shalva Weil, and Jeff Halper). Regardless of whether they were *Sabras* or not, for some anthropologists, the choice of studying the Ethiopian Jews stemmed from an attraction to Other Jews, whereas for others the motivations were different. Lisa Antebi noted that "to study Ethiopians was to study as remote a group as possible, but it was still [the study of] Jews."

Shlomo Deshen was aware of the connection between his identity as a Holocaust survivor, his disappointment from European Jewry, and his attraction to Mizrahi Jews. Of his childhood as a Holocaust survivor, he attests:

> Those years were erased for me. I developed a mechanism of disconnecting. I came from a preeminent Jewish German family. I felt the loss of Ashkenazi Jewry. I came to the country at the age of thirteen, and saw for the first time a Sephardic synagogue of Jews from the Caucasian mountains, in the moshav Be'er Ya'akov. The synagogue was always locked; I used to peer through the window. The first kernel of my anthropology was my encounter with this Other Judaism that had not experienced what I went through. I was deterred by Hassidism, which I associated with failure. Mizrahi Judaism contained none of this; the Hassidic leadership could have saved [the community in the Holocaust] but failed. Another experience was the arrival of Jews from Tripoli, who studied in a Yeshiva where Yiddish was the language of instruction. In the army, I first had beheld the sight of Moroccan Jews. That was in the mid-1950s. I was a religion NCO, and they were undergoing basic training, and they performed their own prayers independently—they demonstrated a communal spirit that cannot be found today.

In his early studies, Deshen focused on the community of immigrants from southern Tunisia, but later became interested in Mizrahi Jews generally, and published many studies, some in an anthology edited together with Moshe Shokeid (Deshen and Shokeid 1984). Deshen, an observant Jew within the secular establishment, who claims to have been successful at separating these two identities, has recently begun to notice "how exotic the secular students are," and has taken an interest in the way in which they celebrate their holidays.

Harvey Goldberg has also discussed his interest in various Jewish cultures in an autobiographical article (Goldberg 1985). Goldberg was raised in New York, in a mostly Jewish neighborhood where the community was centered around the Conservative synagogue. He attended an Orthodox yeshiva high school and was a member of the Conservative youth movement. While attending college, he audited courses at the Jewish Theological Seminary (JTS). From a young age, Goldberg cultivated Zionist sentiments, and he remembers the 1947 declaration of the state by the UN as a high moment of Zionist emotion: "For me, anthropology was a way to present tradition in a dignified way, and not only through another's eyes." During a year spent in Israel in 1958–1959 as a participant at a leadership program for young diaspora Jews, field trips were held "to learn the Land." For him, the intellectual study experiences went in tandem with his Jewish experiences: the description of the land of Israel as a semi-arid region was associated with segments of the daily prayers; the sight of a Bedouin woman holding her son's hand in the market in Be'er Sheva connected to the image of the matriarch Sarah. He encountered "utterly Other" Jews when he met Samaritans. At the end of the course, he served as a counselor in a moshav of Libyan immigrants in the Lachish regions, and this became an opportunity to encounter Jews who were very different from himself: "This adventure clearly integrated social scientific issues with knowledge about Middle Eastern Jews." Upon his return to the United States, he switched his college major to the social sciences—in particular, to anthropology, the discipline that attracted him the most. Following his experiences on the moshav, he had arrived at the insight that he was attracted to encounters with people and that he was curious about their culture. During his studies, he began to sense that there was a connection between culture and ways of interpreting Judaism, which were personally significant to him. Goldberg knew that in time he would return to study the community of Libyan Jews that he had met during his brief sojourn in Israel. The conflict between his radical proximity to Judaism and the radical exoticism of a tribal society was mediated by the ability to study "exotic Jews." Many years after completing his first field study in Israel, at the Porat moshav, Goldberg used to go back and visit his research site. In June 2000, I accompanied him on a visit to the moshav, where he had been invited by one of his old informants. After the encounter, he said, "I am going back to places that for me are like childhood. In the places of my childhood, nothing remains the same, but in the regions of my fieldwork I have memories which are like childhood memories." After many years in which they had not seen each other, moshav members addressed him by the name "the student Hayim" (his Bar Mitzvah name), just as he had presented himself to them upon their first encounter. The presentation of the Jewish self to the research subjects made apparent their commonalities. Goldberg's attraction to science is indirectly linked to his Jewish and Zionist national identity, which were both perceived by him, as a youth, being provincial. By practicing science he would be able to escape provincialism, by connecting to universal scientific discourse. At the same time, as an anthropologist who studied Other Jews, his Jewish identity only became stronger. The historical and cultural linkage between Judaism and anthropology became another of Goldberg's academic concerns. He has studied the history of the Jewish Theological Seminary in New York, and he has written about the Jewish component of the identity of famous American anthropologists (Goldberg 1997, 2005).[11]

Another anthropologist who experienced her own Judaism via anthropology was Shalva Weil, who grew up in Britain and studied there until completing her Ph.D. Her choice to study Other Jews was for her an explicit Jewish statement:

> I had a developed Jewish identity and therefore I chose a Jewish subject. There was a connection between my choice of profession and my religious outlook. I had always been interested in the Falasha [Ethiopian Jews], and I wanted to write a paper about them. On my honeymoon, I travelled in East Africa and in Ethiopia. But [at the university] they rejected the idea of [working on the] Falashas. Since I was a student at an institute for multi-racial studies, I had to choose a dark-skinned group for my master's thesis, and, instead of the Falashas, I chose to work on another group of dark-skinned Jews—Indians. I wanted to have a Jewish advisor. I had intended to write about their dual identity—Indians/Jews. For my dissertation, it was clear I would continue to work on Indian Jews, and I also searched for a Jewish supervisor in anthropology. I found Bill Epstein, who unlike others (who were Jewish but did not emphasize this fact) had rediscovered his Jewish identity.

After carrying out fieldwork on Indian Jews in Israel, Weil continued to develop an interest in Ethiopian Jews and also in communities of Jews in Asia. She was a member of a team that adopted the goal of identifying groups of Jews who were "descendants of the ten lost tribes."

Fran Markowitz came to anthropology from a different sphere of Jewish identity. A native New Yorker, and granddaughter of a Lithuanian rabbi, she herself had grown up in a middle class neighborhood that was not especially Jewish in character. In her youth she moved to Brooklyn and studied at a multinational school, where she took Judaism classes: "In Brooklyn I saw Jewish immigrants from the Soviet Union settle in the neighborhood. I wanted to specialize in urban anthropology by examining the processes of the neighborhood's Russification. From a young age, I knew that this was what I wanted to write my thesis about. I came to Israel for a post-doctoral fellowship, because I could not find a full time position in the United States. Here I had the opportunity to continue a comparative study of Russians in the U.S. and in Israel." All of these anthropologists who searched for such Others in non-Western countries, or who were interested in the "exotic Other" Jews, were members of the Ashkenazi Western Israeli society. A new model has been developed in recent years by Israeli anthropologists of Mizrahi origin who study their own communities, challenging Israeli anthropology's view of the Mizrahi Jews as "Other." Representatives of this group are André Levy and Pnina Motzafi-Haller. Tzur points to a similar process undergone earlier by historians who studied Oriental Jews (Tzur 2003).

The Flexible "Other" and the Imagined "Other" By definition, it is the anthropologist's Other who enables the act of research. Although defining the research site as Other is a productive attitude that can generate insights, only a few of the interviewees address their own Other in explicit terms. Don Handelman and Haim Hazan provided unique responses to the topic of the Other, by defusing the essentialism of the Other, and pointing to the flexibility and fluidity of the concept. Don Handelman said, "Who is the Other? Everyone is the Other. All people are Others. I don't employ the image of the Other—it is too easy an image. We search for valuable things but find only partial things and commentary. Nothing holds up. Certain things repeat themselves, but not for reasons that have anything to do with their scientific value."

Handelman notes that he chose anthropology because "anthropology allows me to dream and imagine." At the beginning of his professional career, he was attracted to anthropology because of the ability to create an imaginary Other. Later, when he became involved in Israeli affairs as a citizen, it became real and concrete.

Hazan also emphasized anthropology's unique power to imagine and produce interpretations with the imaginative faculties, thus leaving the boundaries of the Other open and flexible:

> I wrote about the elderly because I did not want to enter into a political agenda in Israeli society. In the anthropology of old age, I enjoy a central role without Israeliness. Most Israeli anthropologists who published works of import did so around central issues tied to some sort of agenda. . . . I have a sensibility and yearning for doing something that will reveal the human universals shared by all societies. Old people are removed, set at distance, and erased, and thereby have much greater degrees of freedom. This is an opportunity for exploration, because they do as they please.

Perhaps Hazan chose a sort of distance because it would allow him similar degrees of freedom. This was the strategy of Anatoly Khazanov, a Jewish anthropologist from the Soviet Union who stayed in Israel for a few years and later left for the United States; Khazanov explained that, in the USSR, he had chosen to study the ancient Scythian people as a strategy for escaping the discussion of contemporary nomads, which would have linked him to local politics.

MOTIVATIONS, IMAGES, DRIVES, AND LIFE COURSES OF ANTHROPOLOGISTS IN ISRAEL

The testimonies of anthropologists about the drives that impelled them in their life courses do not always reconcile with the interpretation of these motives by the same scholars when discussed them in their writing. My interviewees have written ethnographies, articles, and other publications in which they reveal some of their motivations to pursue anthropology. But these present only partial answers to the question of what drives them.

Ideologies Driving the Work of Anthropologists

Studies about the development of anthropology in Israel can be divided into two main categories: (1) research that describes the development of anthropology in Israel, and (2) critical studies that relate to the ideologies that guided the work of anthropologists, particularly in the period following the establishment of the state. Although the descriptive surveys appear to trace the milestones of the discipline neutrally and unreflectively, the critical surveys analyze the links between values and ideological positions, the structure of power relations, and the roles granted to anthropologists (and to other social scientists) within social and political systems during the pre-state Yishuv period and in the early state period.

The critical view of early anthropology in Israel, which paid attention to the researcher's place in society, emerged in the early 1970s and gained momentum in the 1980s. The timing of this retrospective gaze can be explained in light of the theoretical crises and political trends of the time, which both enabled and encouraged it. The crisis of representation and authority that affected world anthropology in the 1980s led to the undermining of anthropological conventions and to a renewed critical gaze at the anthropological pursuit. Advocates of anthropology began to write about the ethnographic-anthropological writing of their predecessors, and they overturned their premises. Ethnographic writing reflects the explicit and unstated perspectives and theoretical positions of the researcher, providing a window for the critic through which the anthropologist can be scrutinized. Additional sources for critics' insights are prefaces to the ethnographies, in which the writer may reveal his or her motivations, thoughts, and feelings about the field. Ben-Ari has pointed out the important social information that can be extracted from reading prefaces and especially acknowledgements (see Ben-Ari 1987).

In the style that was common before the 1980s, the writer hid behind a removed objectivity, pretending to be a "fly on the wall." Anthropologists' personal journals—such as Malinowski's famous diaries, which he kept simultaneously with his field notes (Malinowski 1967)—are also materials that provide substantiation for critics' claims.

A milestone in the critical trend was the writings of Talal Asad (1975), who argued that Abner Cohen's study of a Palestinian village (Cohen 1965) followed a mistaken paradigm of British functionalism that was based on colonialist motives and interests. Asad pointed to the importance of situating the researcher vis-à-vis his or her relationship to the society being studied; his critique became a classic example of writing about the place of the anthropologist in shaping colonialism in general and British functionalism in particular. According to Rabinowitz (1998), Asad's essay became a rallying cry of revolt against traditional British anthropology. The connection between colonialism and its Western representatives was further exposed by Edward Said (1978). Said's main contribution to anthropology was the rethinking of the relationship between the Western anthropologist and the Orientialist Other, and about the linkage between colonialism and social science.

These new intellectual currents fanned the flames of the critique of Israeli anthropology. Among the first sparks to ignite the fire was the work of Toin Van Teeffelen (1977, 1980), a Dutch anthropologist whose scholarship was based on the content analysis of Israeli anthropologists' publications and brief interviews with them. During a brief three-month stay in 1976, he conversed with some anthropologists, inside and outside academia, and read their English-language publications. In his study, a master's thesis he described as "exercise in the sociology of knowledge," he aimed to analyze the connection between a field of knowledge and ideology by examining at the Israeli case (Bellis 1978).Van Teeffelen accused Israeli anthropology of having developed a protective attitude toward Oriental Jews, and for not having expressed any type of critical stance toward Zionism. Van Teeffelen pointed to the deep link between anthropology and Zionism in Israel: both are based on a deep structure of romanticism and classicism. Romanticism erupts, he argued, when dramatic transformations take place, while classicism appears when the integrative and permanent features of culture are emphasized. According to his analysis, Israeli anthropology has manifested, even if covertly, an interest in post-state Zionism, in the Jewish experience in Israel, and in the goals of Zionist policy. Israeli anthropologists shared with their subjects a common ideology of a "return to Zion," pioneering, and nation building. They found it difficult to estrange or distance themselves from their subjects, thereby producing a romantic and uncritical anthropology. The adoption of Gluckmanian British functionalism as a leading theoretical approach reinforced the romantic and classicist principles of anthropology; it presented the project of immigrant absorption as a dramatic tension between success and failure, between modernity and tradition, and so on. As enlightened anthropologists, they emphasized the cultural heritage and identity of Oriental Jews, they criticized stereotypes and prejudices against Oriental Jews, and they criticized a number of Zionist concepts and practices in respect to the integration of Middle Eastern Jews in Israeli society; but all this, Van Teeffelen argued, was done out of a patronizing, protective, and arrogant position. In contrast to their study of Jewish society, anthropologists' study of Arab society, Van Teeffelen claimed, presented a much less holistic approach. They focused on patterns of marriage, blood feuds, religiosity, and so on. The Jewish researchers viewed the Arabs as "exotic Others," and their approach was Orientalist in the way it set up comparisons and oppositions with Western stereotypes. Van Teeffelen published his study in a volume edited by Stanley Diamond (a former scholar of the kibbutz) (Van Teeffelen 1980).

Most of the Israeli anthropologists responded to the publication with reservations that were voiced only internally amongst colleagues, with the exception of Moshe Shokeid (1992), who chose to reply to Van Teeffelen in the professional arena—in an anthropology journal. Shokeid broadened the discussion to address the issue of engaged anthropology, and claimed that in Israel the Manchester school had served as a template not only for studies of Jews but also for studies that focused on Arabs. The attribution of the sins of the functionalists and the evil of the colonialists to the Manchester school, Shokeid stated, serves to promote a group of researchers (including Van Teeffelen) who are chiefly interested in methodological innovation. In practice, he pointed out, there was little difference between the Manchester school and other contemporaneous approaches in respect to the manner in which its methods perceived the political status quo within its research fields. Shokeid wondered how it was possible that the moralizing criticism voiced by a novice anthropologist was embraced by veteran anthropologists (alluding to Diamond). In his attempt to turn Van Teeffelen's argument on its head, Shokeid employed Van Teeffelen's own rhetoric to confront him. In face of Van Teeffelen's claims, Shokeid exposed the ideological premises of Van Teeffelen's own views, and demonstrated how they led him to his academic conclusions. Van Teeffelen's intellectual, generational, and professional position was not unusual in the Dutch academy in the 1970s, when Dutch students succeeded in instigating changes in the hierarchical structure of the academy in their own country, influenced by Marxist ideas, which are also reflected in Van Teeffelen's writing. To Shokeid, the symmetry is clear: the place from which Van Teeffelen chose to voice his ideas and critique of Israeli anthropologists dictates his mode of analysis and his conclusions, just as the positioning of anthropologists dictates their modes of analysis and emotional identification with their subjects.

Among the anthropologists with whom Van Teefelen had met during his met brief stay in Israel was Don Handelman. According to Shokeid, Don Handelman complained in a letter to Diamond that his interview with Van Teeffelen had not been recorded, that the article held no traces of their topics of conversation, and that Van Teeffelen could have arrived at similar conclusions just based on reading textual materials and without carrying out any fieldwork. Van Teeffelen knew what he wanted to say even before coming to Israel, and only did the fieldwork to give his argument a veil of dignity and credibility (Shokeid 1993, 472). Handelman's remark reinforces my position regarding the necessity of the use of interviews for forming a complete and credible picture of the anthropological field in Israel.

As mentioned earlier, only at the end of the 1980s and in the early 1990s did the reflexive and critical perspectives of Anglo-American anthropology begin to reverberate in the halls of the Israeli academy and of Israeli anthropology. As a consequence, a spate of studies appeared that took a retrospective and critical look at Israeli anthropology, in parallel to similar sociological studies. Among the critical work, the studies by Uri Ram stand out (Ram 1995). Ram took a critical view of Israeli sociology. (Because he made no distinction between sociological and anthropological works, his claims are relevant to both.) Ram arranged the studies that had been carried out about Israeli society (1995, 52–57) according to their historical development. In the first phase of Israeli sociology, the studies were characterized by a "functionalist agenda," and a "systems approach," epitomized by Eisenstadt's book about Israeli society (Eisenstadt 1973). In the second phase, a more refined and critical version of the functionalist approached appeared—which Ram calls "improved functionalism." In this stage, the attempt to "bridge the theoretical monotony with the cultural diversity" (Ram 1993, 12) included most of the anthropological studies that were carried out during the 1960s in the spirit of the Manchester school. These studies accepted the premises of the structural-functionalist school's approach to modernity, but refined the approach in order to adapt it to deal with phenomena in Israeli society, focusing on its diversity. Ram cites anthropologists who reported the difficulties they experienced when trying to adopt sociological paradigms that were derived from functionalism. (See Marx's experience in this chapter.) In many cases, the premises of the modernization approach did not reconcile with the findings from the field, but the anthropologists, like the sociologists, did not contest their roles in assisting nation building (or as Ram puts it: "Shokeid concludes with a complex remark, that is characterized by its combination of moderate critique and reserved support for the credo of nation building" [Ram 1995, 57]).

In his book, Ram reveals that, like his colleagues, he too approaches his work armed with a theoretical and ideological burden, and declares that this critical study on the history and sociology of knowledge was carried out in the Hegelian-Marxist tradition (1995, xi). "I don't write out of no-where . . . I am a veteran—as much as my age allows—of the left-wing Israeli peace movements of soldiers and officers who refused to serve in the occupied territories." It should be noted that in the introduction to his book about Israeli society in Hebrew, Ram eschewed transparency and did not reveal his ideological positioning, nor did he deem it necessary to clarify to the reader that he does not come "out of no-where." Ram similarly does not share the fact that he was a member of Israeli leftist movement or divulge the premises of the school to which he pledges allegiance. In addition, if Ram's analysis is valid in respect to the sociologists, the same processes in Israeli society and at the forefront of socio-anthropological discourse should have affected Israeli anthropologists as well. Ram's claim that sociology and anthropology are essentially indistinguishable (based on his inclusion of both disciplines in his study of the 1960s, and his use of the term "socio-anthropology") is undermined by the fact that unlike sociology, Israeli anthropology did not cultivate an outspoken and distinct critical approach until the late 1990s. Israeli anthropology did not create a school that either named itself or was labeled by others as "the new anthropologists." In other words, no group of anthropologists emerged (however critical and subversive they might have been as individual researchers), that presented itself as an alternative to establishment anthropology. Critical writing exists—a critical *school* does not exist.[12]

In the late 1990s Yossi Loss wrote a critical study of "Israeli anthropologists, the academy and the Mizrahim" as part of his M.A. requirement (Loss 2001). In this study, he analyzed the motivations of four anthropologists who studied Mizrahi Jews during the 1960s: Moshe Shokeid, Shlomo Deshen, Emanuel Marx, and Alex Weingrod. Loss identified five motivations that drove their work: structural-functionalist, institutional, scientific, Orientalist, and Zionist. Loss focuses his discussion on the production of a gap between the researcher and his or her subjects in the sociopolitical context of Israeli society.

> The gaps between anthropologists as members of a developed, modern, rational, and secular Western group, and the subjects as members of a developing, traditional, emotional, irrational and religious Mizrahi group . . . by characterizing the gaps . . . I am able to extract the representations of the subjects from the representations of the researchers as both have been understood by the researchers (Loss 2001, 10).

Loss assumes that the gaps that anthropologists produce between themselves and their subjects, which are reflected in the texts that they publish, are expressive of the anthropologists' perception of reality, but not necessarily of empirical reality. They are a product of the writers' motivations, which are, according to his view, neither an intention or an awareness, but rather a complex of ontological, epistemological, and moral premises that predate the research: "Orientalism, the scientific ethos, Jewish religion, or Zionism" (Loss 2001, 11). A critical reading of the texts will expose, so Loss hopes, new dimensions that were not accorded salience before. Unlike Van Teeffelen and Ram, Loss came to anthropology from outside the discipline. He was trained in biology as an undergraduate and continued in the field of the history and philosophy of science. This external vantage point could have been productive, had Loss not made a schematic and insensitive use of the analytics tools of the critical school and of the Foucauldian power/knowledge approach. Loss seeks to locate his subjects in the context of the theoretical approaches that were prevalent in their times, but situates himself at a "panoramic" vantage point (as he describes Marx's perspective [Loss 2001, 107]). The demand for reflexivity from the anthropologist subjects is suspended when it comes to his own position. Loss does not provide a broad view of Israeli anthropology, but only of segments of it that relate to the study of Mizrahim in the 1960s and 1970s. His critical reading addresses only a narrow selection of researchers, periods, and texts.

Rabinowitz has contributed another critical view by discussing the way in which anthropology has studied the Palestinians (Rabinowitz 1998, 2002; Furani and Rabinowitz 2011). His work surveys Israeli and non-Israeli anthropologists who studied Palestinian society, and points to the contribution of Israeli Jewish anthropologist to the shaping of the image of the Palestinians and to the institution control of this society during different periods:

> The classic anthropological topics that preoccupied most of the Israeli anthropologists who wrote about Palestinians between the 1950s and the 1980s emphasized the cultural unity of the Palestinians. . . . The ideological orientation that characterized most of the members of the first generation of Israeli anthropology may be called "taken for granted Zionism." Their work was free, so it seems, of any overt institutional pressure to write about the justifications for Zionism or to point up the evilness or the wretchedness of the Palestinians. At the same time . . . [their studies] successfully reproduce, and with a great deal of inner conviction, the central rationalization of Zionism as an ethical movement motivated by a vision, and they uncritically embrace its dual task: the redemption of the Jewish people and the modernist reform of the Arabs. (Rabinowitz 1998, 150)

According to Rabinowitz, not only do the scholars of Arab society exhibit a Zionist orientation, some even began their professional paths as "Arabists"—specialists in respect to security matters. Indeed, the university was a second career for Emanuel Marx, Joseph Ginat, and Abner Cohen, after they had been in the employ of an agency whose goal was to regulate and supervise the Palestinians and the Bedouin. Yifrah Zilberman also came to the academy after having served in the security establishment, where he also dealt with the Palestinian population. Their interest in Palestinian society derived, so Rabinowitz argues, not only from intellectual curiosity but from a choice to study a population which they had been involved in controlling and repressing in their prior careers; their work later became a basis for culturalist approaches.

Pnina Motzafi-Haller (1997) entered into the discussion of identity politics and reflexivity in anthropology. In her article dating from the late 1990s, she presented her personal version of the politics of representation within and without the society that was the object of her study. She examined the centrality of the anthropologist's identity through her dual experiences conducting research in Africa both as a native anthropologist and a foreign anthropologist. In both instances, she discusses the complexities of her position, and writing and representation in ethnographic work. Motzafi-Haller states that during one of her visits to Israel as a graduate student, she met an Israeli anthropologist who to her mind represented the hegemony: a male Ashkenazi academic who suggested she study the Ethiopians, who were, he stated, "a big problem." She was thus granted an entry pass into a "club whose members, only 30 years ago, had described my parents and the immigrant group to which they belonged as a 'big problem'" (Motzafi-Haller 1997, 90). Motzafi-Haller's criticism focuses on the patronizing attitudes of Israeli anthropologists, which are apparent in the micro studies that documented this or that exotic group (this "ethnic" group was always Jewish Mizrahi or non-Jewish). She points to the advantages of her position as a researcher: "My real challenge as a 'native-researcher' was to avoid an essentialist description of the people whom I, as a native, was supposed to represent. The search for these [fieldwork sites] comes from a position of inner commitment . . . thinkers who identify themselves with excluded communities confront real dilemmas and are liable to have . . . personal motives, or simply to be wrong" (Motzafi-Haller 1997, 94).

The volume *Mizrahim in Israel* (Forum for the Study of Society and Culture 2002a), which was the product of a collaboration of scholars from the Van Leer Institute, presents an overarching critical view toward the anthropological study of Mizrahim, claiming in essence, that anthropology is a discipline which places at the center the practices of authenticization of Mizhrahi-ness. Its declared goal is to study others of the "transparent Israeli existence." The authors collected in the volume identify the following eras in anthropological research: in the 1930s

Mizrahi Jews were presented in the works (labeled as "folkloristic") of Brauer (mistakenly spelled "Bauer" in the original publication), Patai, and Ben Zvi. The Mizrahi Jews are presented as exotics, and the Yemenite Jews as Biblical, without any reference to the power-laden socioeconomic context of their lives; in the 1950s, "exoticism is replaced by the focus on the Mizrahi as a 'problem'" (Forum for the Study of Society and Culture 2002a, 292). In the 1960s and 1970s, the Mizrahi became the site of rich anthropological investigation. In the current era, the Mizrahi Jew is the "proximate Other," as opposed to the Arab who is the "distant Other." The Mizrahi's marking as "proximate" defines the boundaries of the Jewish collective, and the discussion focuses on the question of the flexibility of the new social order for the processes of nation building and the ingathering of the exiles (similar to the idea of a melting pot). The anthropologists of this era identified with Zionist ideology, with the social order, and with the status quo. Their writing therefore "lacks any challenging of the state's moral system which played a central part in the construction of inequality between different Jewish groups in Israel" (Forum for the Study of Society and Culture 2002a, 293). "The historical irony is that the anthropologists, who contributed more than any other research group to the reproduction and perpetuation of this conceptual scheme, which defined the Mizrahi as the failing 'Other' of the Israeli society, in fact felt empathy and later even a sense of reflexivity with the subjects of their research" (Forum of Social and Cultural Studies 2002a, 294).

In contrast to the position presented in *Mizrahim in Israel,* the notion that the anthropologist is a tool in the hands of the regime, assisting it to implement its policies, was challenged already in the 1950s by anthropologist Dorothy Willner, who worked in the Jewish agency. Her article (Willner 1956), which deals with the domain of anthropology, formulates the anthropologist's perception of his or her role. Although this role includes assistance to the new nation-building effort and the achievement of its goals, the anthropologist is not merely an executive arm of the immigration absorption policies, but is rather a mediator between the absorbing society and the immigrants. Willner was the first to write explicitly about the role of the anthropologist in absorbing immigration and viewed anthropology as a central tool for hashing out crucial problems concerning the absorption of immigration in Israel and finding ways of solving them. The problem was not with the immigrant:

> The representatives of these bodies [the government, the public institutions, and the political organization] generally tend to share cultural perceptions and a uniform scale of values, which are based

> on the norms of the generation which gave the Yishuv its dominant orientation and which now aspires, through its central institutions and their successors in the present, to instill them in the immigrants. This tendency to proselytize, the desire to instill a certain set of values, bolstered by the pressure enabled by the high level of centralization and bureaucratization, may create the same kind of negative and even dangerous reality in Israel, in which cultural contact brings about the internal destabilization of the weaker society, in our case of the society of the new immigrants. (Willner 1956, 90)

Note the use of the term "immigrants," instead of "Newcomers (*Olim*)," which was unusual for this period.

Willner identified the power of the state and of the governmental bodies in relation to the weakness of the immigrants, and the absorbing institutions' "tendency to proselytize," as she put it. She did not undercut the state's foundational values. But the findings of her fieldwork, which was carried out in an immigrants' moshav (Willner 1969), pointed on the one hand to the power of bureaucracy, and on the other hand to the immigrants who lacked resources. In the context of the immigrants' moshavim, the power was chiefly in the hands of the Jewish Agency workers and professional counselors/trainers:

> Their/Its undermining power increases in light of the fact that the immigrants themselves are in a relatively passive position from the moment they decided to immigrate. Apart from a few isolated individuals of means, or those with clear plans or skills that are recognized in the new society, the new immigrants have hardly any power to decide any of the issues that are crucial for determining their future. This imposed passivity deepens the rift between the immigrants and the absorbers and, for its part, damages the possibility of creating identification with the Israeli norms, an identification that is indispensable for creating real acculturation, as opposed to external mimicry. (Willner 1969, 91)

Willner's rhetoric enlists anthropologists to national tasks and calls on them to be mediators. Willner was not incorporated into the local academic system and did not leave behind a research or intellectual legacy that might have influenced future Israeli anthropology. It should be noted that Willner's article does not appear in anthropological curricula of the early 1970s, nor was it recommended in courses that dealt directly with absorption of immigrants. I am not trying to suggest that the subtle critique leveled at the national institutions was the reason for this, but the fact that she is not mentioned in critical reviews of national anthropology is unfortunate and betrays inattentiveness to its representations from the 1950s onward.

At the same time, the spirit of her words matches the perception of her role and of the motivations and images shared by most anthropologists from the 1950s until the late 1970s: an anthropologist who is devoted to the Zionist project, but is critical and skeptical about the way in which it should be implemented, and about the cultural and social price it entails. The images of the impulse for anthropological practice that my own interviewees presented matched well with Willner's image of the anthropologist.

The anthropologist is a nomad, a marginal figure living in a multicultural society, an immigrant who is committed to social struggles or is even the representative of establishment interests; he or she is presented as one who is located in the interim space between the subjects of his or her research and the large social forces. In anthropological texts that were at the focus of the critiques of critical anthropologists, one can locate expressions of resistance and subversions on the part of the research subjects to attempts at domination, the application of power, and the establishment's hegemony. Communities of immigrants who were dislocated from their earlier living loci created alternative cultural forms out of the give and take with the dominant society and culture, with the traditions and the existential conditions in which they lived. In the accounts of the interviewed anthropologists, one also finds an emphasis on their identification with the subjects of their research and their resistance to representing institutional interests. In his article about the study of the culture of the Oriental Jews, Deshen discusses the approach of social scientists in general and of anthropologists in particular:

> Many are accustomed to see in the immediate origin of Mizrahi Jews and the Arabs only a decline of classic Islamic culture, the demise of the Ottoman Empire and negative effects of imperialism in the guise of Levantine culture. Therefore, the recent past of the Oriental Jews is perceived by many laymen within the general framework of decline and demise. Social scientists of an historical orientation and historians reject this simplistic generalization. (Deshen 1979, 76)

From here, Deshen moves on to a practical and applied justification for studying Oriental cultures:

> This inquiry has the potential to instill both students and adults with the awareness that there are varied models for participation in the life of the country and in its building. Alongside the models of Nahalal, Holon, and Ramat Hasharon [Elite veterans' settlements], there are the models of the immigrant moshavim, the development towns, and the Amidar [public] housing projects. . . . It is to the credit of anthropologists in Israel that they have produced a number of studies that reveal the economic and cultural creativity and dignity, in places where few expected to find them. (Deshen 1979, 78)

These remarks imply that the distinction between enlistment for national goals and for social goals is not so clear cut, and it serves the ideological stances of both sides. The motivation of personal identity may lead to engagement, which is the basis of enlistment and commitment in various life arenas. The life course of the anthropologist is not built only out of the stations that comprise his or her professional life.

Anthropologist Identities

The founding generation did not possess a monolithic identity. They were immigrants from South Africa and the United States, traditional and secular, women and men, communists and liberals—they were not homogeneous. This diversity becomes even more obvious when one compares the immigrants to the native-born Israelis. A generational division keyed to identity characteristics will not assist us in clarifying the issue in question. Instead, I propose examining in what way identity inscribes anthropology and, conversely, in what way anthropology inscribes identity. It is useful to ask what the Israeli anthropologist's Other is and how the manner of defining this Other has determined his or her professional life course. If identity is indeed a cluster of identities, and the identity of the research object is not monolithic either, it becomes meaningful to ask which element of identity is conducting a dialogue with its elements of identity.

Images of the anthropologist and their motivations reveal the tension between the different and even contradictory components of identity. Despite the categorical presentation of these images as if they were mutually exclusive, in point of fact, everyone shares the same components: the difference is in the emphasis. The individual anthropologist finds that he or she must deal with contradictory worlds that maintain a constant dialogue: the search for others; the Israeli experiences that are ideologically motivated, caring, and engaged; and the connection to the scientific, cosmopolitan, and universal element. The emotional and cognitive "Others within us," are oriented to different aspects of the ideological practices that guide professional activity. The attraction to the discipline, for many, was as a way to satisfy the curiosity about others. Other practitioners of anthropology identified the roots of their search in their experiences as immigrants or in their lives in a multicultural society. They continued to wander between cultures and territories and viewed anthropology as a means for living simultaneously in multiple of worlds. Moreover, the fact that the great majority of Israeli anthropologists were at some point or another engaged in research about Israeli society is an indication of the power of the Israeli experience, which produces among the researchers a commitment to the community in which they live.

In addition to their interest in local realities, many anthropologists seek the actual engagement they find in the bureaucratic and institution university life, which provides a sense of belonging to the world community of academics around the world who share their own language and rites. The world disciplinary community is not a virtual one—it is real. Many members of the Israeli Anthropological Association (IAA) religiously make a yearly pilgrimage to the annual AAA meetings. They present their best crop of research and ideas at the meetings, and search for academic support among colleagues (especially U.S. colleagues). The practice of sabbatical leave, which begins with the post-doctoral fellowship and continues throughout the years of one's academic career, is a renewed reinforcement of the Israeli anthropologist's identity as "citizen of the world."

The Israeli anthropologist who ventures far to search for others, driven by curiosity and enchantment of the remote (the Hima in East Africa) or the proximate (the member of the Mizrahi immigrant moshav or the wedding-gift-giving practices of the middle class) organizes the relationship between him- or herself and others. The intergenerational gap is apparent in the relationship to the identity of the Others within us and to the link between curiosity for others and commitment to other identities. Similar to the general Zionist population of the first decades of statehood, the founding generation of Israeli anthropology viewed collective, national, or Jewish identity as the preferred identity within his or her cluster of identities. Other identities—community or personal—followed in descending order of importance. In the present generation, the hierarchy of identities has changed: the individual's personal (and familial) identity is central, and so is the simultaneous search for an international identity. The process of disintegration of collectivism in Israeli society, in a variety of realms (Almog 2000), is evident also in the case of Israeli anthropologists.

ANTHROPOLOGISTS IN ISRAEL: CHARACTERISTICS AND NUMBERS

Israeli anthropology embodies a small community in a small country. Israeli anthropologists number some 130 men and women, of whom only thirty hold positions in universities, and ten in colleges. My estimate is based on the number of those who have identified as members (full or partial) of the IAA since the 1980s. To this group, I added many anthropologists who are not members of the association but are active as anthropologists. This rate has remained stable in the past decades despite the expansion of anthropology in universities and its growing popularity. The size of the community has implications for the relationships between its members, as members maintain regular formal and informal connections; most know each other, and the network of relationships affects the development of one's personal career. Israeli anthropologists cooperate and compete, support and oppose, and work for and against ideas, people, and projects. A few have deliberately isolated themselves from the community. This has implications for recruitment, promotion, and development within institutional arrangements and the macro relations within the academy. The size of the community also may affect the quality of its products. Joseph Ben David, a sociologist of science and one of the founders of the sociology and anthropology department at the Hebrew University of Jerusalem, has discussed the connection between the size of an academic community, the size of the society in which it is active, and the quality of its science. He claims that Israel is a small academic community in a small country (Ben David 1964), and its size has limited its scientific development. In some academic areas, however, such as mathematics, Jerusalem became a secondary center of considerable importance (Katz 2004). In others, it has been marginal, as in the case of genetics and anthropology (Kirsh 2009).

The community of anthropologists is a new community: in its forty years of existence one or perhaps two generations have elapsed. Some of the veterans have already retired, but all are still actively involved in research and publishing, and even if they do not take center stage in the IAA conferences, they have considerable influence on informal anthropological activity. In the rest of the world, anthropology is considered a young science in comparison with the other social sciences, but in contrast to the metropole which has undergone epistemological upheaval and severe crises of identity, anthropology in Israel exhibits stability and continuity.

Another characteristic of the community is the entry of women into the discipline and the numerical equality between men and women at the lower and middle professional ranks. One can say that Israeli anthropology has undergone a process of feminization. In the 1970s, the proportion of women in the anthropological community was no more than twenty-five percent, but in the 1990s, the proportions leveled out. The main reasons for this were the general expansion of entry of women into the academy, including the social sciences; the increased professionalization of women in the academy, which is manifest in fields such as law and medicine; increased research at home, which makes it easier for women to maintain the anthropological practices of fieldwork while continuing to carry out domestic and familial roles; and the entry of women into "soft" methodologies such as ethnography. This change in gender ratios is the picture in the lower and middle professional ranks, but in the higher echelons of the hierarchy there has not been a noticeable change, and men are still almost uniquely represented here. (In 2004, the number of anthropologists at the rank of professor was no more than five.) This fact and the absence of Mizrahim and Palestinians in Israel's anthropological elite are the subject of strife in the discourse of identity politics in the Israeli academy. The banner of this campaign was raised by Smadar Lavie, whose articles in the AAA newsletter (Lavie 2003) pointed to the small proportion of Mizrahim and women, and of Mizrahi women in particular, in the Israeli anthropological elite. Israeli social justice organizations (such as "Ahoti," "HaKeshet HaMizrahit," and "Mosawa") filed a complaint with the Israeli State Comptroller in 2004 regarding this state of affairs. A copy of the complaint was sent to the AAA newsletter, which asked to publish it alongside a response by the IAA.

In the ensuing phase of the campaign, the complainant organizations surveyed the identities of the presenters and the topics presented at the IAA meetings. The findings from this inquiry were published on *Haokets*, a website for social and political commentary that serves as a platform for Mizrahi activism. The following is from an article published on *Haokets* subsequent to the 2005 IAA meetings:

> We have analyzed the distribution of participants in the conference, according both to discipline and the ethnicity/nationality/gender of the speakers. An examination of the distribution tables show that most of the participants in the meetings who hold academic positions, with or without tenure, are Ashkenazi. Only one of the anthropologists participating in the meetings is a Mizrahi who holds a tenured academic position, which he earned only recently. The number of female Mizrahi women anthropologists with a tenured

> academic position is zero. The number of male or female Mizrahi anthropologists holding a tenure-track position is zero. The number of Palestinian Israelis, male or female, holding an academic position of any kind, is zero. At the very least, the meetings therefore offer no response to the original complaint submitted by the Coalition to the State Comptroller in March 2004. Reading the meetings prospectus would lead one to conclude that the IAA prefers to fills the program of its yearly meetings with names that have a Mizrahi color, instead of changing the discriminatory policies of academic appointments in anthropology, and to stop appropriating our communal rights over our own cultures. (Hajaj and Farah 2005)

In the online comments that responded to this article, there appeared a one-liner written by a Mizrahi man (according to my own inquiries, a Mizrahi social activist), which, above all, is instructive for what it tells us about the elusiveness of identity. I quote: "Perhaps Abuhav will save the day?" (in Hebrew, this is a pithy rhyme: *ulai Abuhav tatzil et ha-matzav*). This was written in apparent response to my surname, which sounds Mizrahi or Sephardi. As the chair-elect for the next term of office in the IAA, this responder (who was not personally acquainted with me), seems to have thought that I hold the keys to remedying the injustice of representation of Mizrahi women in the higher ranks of Israeli anthropology. He did not know that my identity, according to all criteria, is that of a veteran Ashkenazi who belongs to the hegemonic sector of Israeli society, and obviously took his cue from my husband's surname, which I adopted in marriage. (For more on my personal identity, see the "[My] Introduction to Anthropology" section.) It was according to this same criteria—the examination of people's surnames—that the activist surveyors conducted their inquiry into the degree of ethnic and gender representativeness at the IAA meetings. I do not wish here to enter into the trap of discussing the anthropology of identities (invented, constructed, etc.), but I point to the advantages of accepting the self-definitions of the carriers of an identity. This principle led me to give voice to the anthropologists, who narrated their stories of identity themselves.

FIVE

ISRAELI ANTHROPOLOGY

The Discipline at Home

I held face-to-face meetings with Israeli anthropologists, asking them to tell me their story. I sifted through correspondence, research and teaching programs, papers on the future of anthropology, and random memos on day-to-day affairs. I read what they wrote and what others wrote about them. I wove a tapestry of Israeli anthropology with threads from both public and individual arenas. The length and breadth of this weave forced me to select a few choice parts for closer inspection: anthropology in research and teaching, anthropology in the IAA, anthropology as a career, and anthropologists' professional identity. Although it was not always possible to hide the seams, I tried to avoid creating a patchwork. In discussing each topic individually, I employed terminology uniquely suited to the analysis, and in this final chapter, I shall combine the conceptual threads of the various sections.

The idea that science and sociocultural realities are connected was proposed in the early twentieth century by key sociologists. Emil Durkheim pointed to the triangle of society-culture-science and to the integral links between its elements. Durkheim's intellectual heirs, Karl Mannheim, Robert Merton, and David Bloor, dealt with the links between society and science and wrote about the role of social and cultural categories in producing the conceptions that fix our interpretation of the world in terms of science. This is a bi-directional model, one that attempts to analyze the ongoing and dynamic relations of society-science-culture to draw conclusions about the contribution and role of science and of scientists to the construction of their society, and vice versa—about the influences of societal and cultural processes on the shaping of science.

Within the framework of a science-society model, discussion should focus on the factors that shaped, constructed, determined, influenced, and contributed to the development (and marginality) of Israeli anthropology during its lifespan. In addition, it should center on the intra-scientific and extra-scientific factors that were significant for anthropology during the different periods. My study, which was carried out at the beginning of the 2000s, provides a contemporary point of view. At the same time, because it offers a historical perspective, I have taken great care not to fall into the trap of reading the past through the lens of the present. The narrative was constructed with the help of anthropologists, who are its main characters, in addition to information I gleaned from historical documents. The story is not only about anthropology and anthropologists, but also about Israeli society's encounter with its own diversity. It has much to tell us about the intellectual and ideological dispositions of the Yishuv (pre-state) era, which decided what would occupy the forefront of scientific endeavor and what was considered dispensable (i.e., anthropology). It also provides suggestive hints as to what was deemed to be a Jewish, national, Israeli, or professional identity, and about the concrete and theoretical contexts in which anthropological knowledge about Israel is produced and disseminated. The analysis of social and cultural processes is carried out according to the axes of professional advancement, professional conduct, and the institutional site. In this context, knowledge is perceived as a system of socially constructed skills, practices and habits, which are exploited in order to attain strategic goals. A central focus has been placed on the modes of production and reproduction of social distinctions and hierarchies in which anthropologists maneuver and are maneuvered. In other words, attention is paid to the way in which the professionalization of anthropologist reflects cultural, national, and international characteristics.

The multiple viewpoints offered are as follows: the practices of individual professional behavior, the practices of making a livelihood inside and outside the university, and organizing as a professional association—all of which contribute to the construction of a complex portrait (on the advantages of multifocal perspectives, see Goldberg 1997). In taking this approach, my study joins the ranks of studies devoted to the history and development of scientific disciplines. But its unique contribution lies in its modes of producing the knowledge, which most certainly have affected the findings and conclusions. Past works about the development of Israeli anthropology relied only on texts, publications, ethnographies, books, reports, and articles by Israeli anthropologists, which served as a basis of data to be interpreted by those extrinsic to the arena studied. The current study has the added value of drawing on interviews with anthropologists. My own interpretation is produced in the framework of a discourse of which I am part, and within a research agenda that I have determined. The position presented builds a bridge between voices: the voice exemplified by "The Sin We Did Not Commit in the Research of Oriental Jews" (Shokeid 2001) and the one reflected in "You Have an Authentic Voice: Anthropological Research and the Politics of Representation" (Motzafi-Haller 1997). It is also a bridge between the voice of representatives of the founding generation and some voices of intermediate generation. The latter demands that the founders recognize past mistakes made in the their study of the topics of immigration, absorption, settlement, population, health, and education of Jewish immigrants, particularly those from Middle Eastern countries. This debate, carried out in scholarly journals, represents two polar positions on a continuum in which the silent majority occupies the interim positions. (Similar dialogues were held in scholarly journals in the 1990s; see Topel [1996].) The bridging stance that I have adopted is consistent both with my personality and with my own career: on one hand, I was present during the birth of anthropology at the Hebrew University at the hands of the founding fathers and mothers of the earlier generation, and have followed its development for many years, mostly from the outside. On the other hand, the new leaders and new voices are members of my age cohort and of my students' generation.

The tension between these two positions, in itself an expression of generational transition, does not only reflect a clinical intellectual dispute; it contains the passion of engaged, concerned, and ideological scientific endeavor, which is a characteristic feature of Israeli anthropological research. The main reason for this engagement is that most research is carried out "at home," within the borders of the State of Israel (Abuhav et. al. 1998; Marx 1983; Shokeid 2012). There are a number of reasons for and a variety of implications to the preference for research at home.

ISRAELI ANTHROPOLOGISTS STUDY THEIR HOME

When I first began my research I regarded anthropology at home as only a methodological issue, because it entails significant research dilemmas: whether and how one can examine a research problem under conditions of maximum proximity, what insights are lost from excessive proximity and what insights are gained from it, what are the ethical restrictions entailed by doing research in one's own social surroundings, and so forth. However, as my research progressed, I began to appreciate the extent to which anthropology at home defines the characteristics of Israeli anthropology: the issue crosses the bounds of a methodological discussion and is significant in its own right. I will discuss its basic significance and the dilemmas it presents from two tangential aspects: studies conducted as research at home by anthropologists in Israel, and my research as study done at home or even in my own room. That is to say, I will examine the connection between anthropology and the home of my colleagues and, at the same time, the influence of research at home on myself as an Israeli anthropologist studying her colleagues.

The Concept of "Home"

On the face of it, differentiating between anthropology "at home" and "away from home" appears to be a simple procedure: it is based on the territorial test—what is done within the political borders of Israel is defined as anthropology at home. When Weingrod (1998), Shokeid (1971a, 1971b), and Weil (1987) described themselves as "anthropologists at home," they referred to that definition as being self-explanatory. In a later study, however, Shokeid extended the Israeli home beyond its territorial borders and studied the Israeliness of Israeli expatriates living in New York (Shokeid 1988). Following this, the collection of articles on Israeli anthropology has also included works on Casablanca and New York (Hertzog et al. 2010). "Native anthropology," an equivalent concept in the literature on anthropology, expresses a similar idea: it focuses on the identity of the researcher and not to the location of the research site. For example, Nakhleh, who studied the village of his birth in the Galilee, refers to himself as a "native anthropologist" (Nakhleh 1979).

Several anthropologists split the concept of home into other components of their identities: gender, nationality, ethnicity, and so on. Expanding the significance of home accorded with the shifts in the centers of anthropology with regard to the research field, the methodology, and the power relations within it. Consequently, despite the fact that Israeli anthropology was generally conducted within the classical territorial definition of home, a shift occurred in the attitude regarding its concept.

Issues and Dilemmas

The discussion of issues and theories of "anthropology at home" began in the main anthropological centers in the early 1980s, focusing on three research dilemmas: transforming the obvious into the subject of the research and challenging its familiar corollary, the issue of "objectivity," and the issue of the very likelihood of a critical attitude at home and its inherent quality. I have referred to "objectivity" using quotation marks because the simplistic binary contrast of objective versus subjective has disappeared from the anthropological agenda. The demand for objectivity had arisen from positivistic fundamental assumptions that are less relevant nowadays. Today, the issue of objectivity has been replaced by other quandaries that apply to a discussion on the power of objectivity and on its potential leverage for obtaining insights, provided they are reflexive ones. The emphasis has shifted to discussing the diverse aspects of seeing at a distance or proximity, which are directly linked to the home and the outside. Distance/proximity constitutes both a stance and an emotional cognitive orientation; it comprises a discourse on prejudices and pre-study opinions, on the interpretation of the researcher and the researched, and on the power relations activated in the research context.

The Tradition of Research at Home

Anthropology at home was discussed at length by Messerschmidt in the early 1980s (Messerschmidt 1981). He delved into methods and dilemmas in anthropological research at home in the United States, noting the ever-growing inclination of anthropologists in the United States to conduct research within North America rather than abroad in the Third World developing societies. Research at home was presented as an innovation, in total disregard of the fact that, from the early days of American anthropology that studied the Indian tribes of North America in the middle of the nineteenth century, this was anthropology at the territorial home. For Messerschmidt and his colleagues, anthropology at home meant studying *non-native* Americans, a perspective that highlights the problematic nature of the definitions of "at home" and "away from home." Lewis has revisited and undermined Messerschmidt's claim (Lewis 1998) by showing many examples of anthropology at home that were not a post-1960s innovation, but rather earlier cases of work at home in complex societies.

Several years later after Messerschmidt started to use the term "anthropology at home" for the American context, Jackson (1987) gave the topic a British viewpoint. For example, Max Gluckman and his colleagues in Manchester had become interested in British society. (See the collection *Custom and Conflict in British Society* [Frankenberg 1982], whose title is a variation on the title of Gluckman's book *Custom and Conflict in Africa.*) According to Jackson, anthropology at home—meaning Western anthropologists studying their own societies—inherited the sociology that failed in its treatment of the same issue. Jackson was also aware of the development of native anthropology—members of societies under previous colonial rule who began studying their own societies, a trend that threatened the fundamental assumptions of classical anthropology and of the very existence of the discipline. (For a detailed discussion on the dilemmas involved in this, see Motzafi-Haller [1997].) When British anthropology, via its representatives from Manchester, first appeared in Israel in the late 1960s, anthropology at home was a unique world innovation. They joined the small number of local anthropologists who were mostly trained in America. Thus from the early 1960s up to the present day, the tradition in Israel of research at home is more common than research away from home.

In the 1930s and 1940s, professional anthropological research—which began with Granquist, who came from Finland to do research in Palestine—focused on Palestinian communities. Despite the geographical distance, one can discern in Granquist's research a certain kind of research at home, because as a conscious Christian, she represented a stream of Christian researchers who sought to find the roots of their Christian ancestors in the lifestyle of the local Arabs. British functionalists conducted studies in the Middle East but did not concern themselves with the local Jewish and Arabs communities because they were not "primitive" enough to warrant research on their account. It could therefore be surmised that the reason foreign anthropologists avoided research in Israel was that they felt that it was "too much at home" here. Unlike them, Brauer and Patai, native European Jews, conducted anthropological research on Eastern Jews in Palestine for romantic, exotic, and nationalistic motivations (Abuhav 2003). They posed them as the subject of ethnographic interest, to which was added the objective of conservation of past traditions that they feared were, according to their conceptions, gradually vanishing. Side by side with the aura of Otherness, which they attributed to Eastern Jews, their research was in practice very near home in terms of territory and sentiments. The Jews from Kurdistan and Bukhara who were the subject of interest to Brauer and Patai lived a walking distance away from their home in the nearby Jerusalem neighborhoods. In his personal diary (written in German), Brauer describes how he left his home and arrived after a short walk at the heart of his research field in the Shehunat HaBukharim or Mishkanot Israel neighborhoods:

> I arranged a meeting with a Bukharan. He did not come to the meeting and so I went to a concert performance of the Migdal David police band. In the afternoon I read an article in the library on children's games. I went again to the Bukharan neighborhood in order to try to gather material on children's games in Jerusalem. I also tried my luck in a school but the principal, Ms. Avishar, told me I would find nothing there. I went to a kindergarten in the Old City. . . . A boy led me to unfamiliar places in the alleys of the city. In Hebron Street, not far from the Church of the Holy Sepulcher, I met Meir and we went to our friend for a meal. (Brauer 1928–1935, Notebook 81, 203)

Several days later he wrote:

> I went in the morning to Abu-Hai in the Bukharan neighborhood, a couple of streets past the gymnasium. A Bukharan woman told me he was not at home. I went to the reading room in the library and searched for two books on Jewish folktales. I returned to the Bukharan neighborhood and the old man chased me away from the house mumbling something all the time about visiting Tel Aviv; he was probably lying. (Brauer 1928–35, 225)

And again:

> I left my home (in Rehavia) in the morning and went to Sa'adia Sweri, a Yemenite. He was not at home, perhaps at work. I became familiarized with a new district in Jerusalem: Mishkenot Israel. I saw miserable tin shacks in an alley with Yemenites living in them. In the afternoon I again returned to the Bukharan quarter and was again unable to meet the Bukharan I wanted to see. The children, too, did not come, but before I left the place a boy from Istanbul and a pretty girl, who is the daughter of the beautiful woman I saw previously, arrived. The mother is Kurdish . . . [the following day] I returned to Sa'adia Sweri who was not at home, but I was glad I visited Mishkenot Israel. Everyone is outside hanging up the laundry; the women are emaciated and appear to be unwell. There are no sewers there and they throw rubbish out into the street. I visited the open space between the neighborhood and Bezalel, where children were flying kites. I asked them about games they were playing but they just pestered me. I think it is easier to work with the Yemenites than with the Bukharan. (Brauer 1928–1935, 237–38)

Near-home anthropology in pre-state Israel during that period was also the result of lack of funds: Brauer and Patai had a desire to study the immigrants' communities in Jerusalem as a substitute for studying them in their lands of origin. Patai had planned to make a trip to Mashhad in Iran. Ruppin had wanted to set out for China and Brauer had dreamed of reaching Kurdistan. Though the field for Brauer, Ruppin, and Patai turned out to be at home in Jerusalem, they nevertheless realized that the social and cultural distance between them and the subjects of their study was as wide as East from West.

The tradition of study at home continued into the 1950s and 1960s, but with a different nuance. Rosenfeld, Feitelson, and Palgi looked around and found their research sites close by. Rosenfeld came to Israel because of his interest in the kibbutz and joined Ein Harod. As a kibbutz member, he collected ethnographic material on the community in which he was living: "I wrote 300–400 pages on the kibbutz but did not publish. The motivation to study the kibbutz arose from my acquaintance with it and the special communal pattern, together with my interest in the fate of the Jews." He left the kibbutz because of his disappointment with the changes that were occurring there. Although he had collected material on the kibbutz, his home as it had been at the time, he did not publish it. Is it at all possible to publish studies done on such an intimately small community by one of its members? A decade later, Kressel, a kibbutz member, studied his native kibbutz, G-R (Kressel 1974), and published two books on the subject. He informed the reader, in an incidental comment, that he had been a kibbutz member while doing the research (and continued the research after leaving). The reflexivity of doing the research at home is indicated in several sentences in the second book: "The research on G-R was done at an intensity of observation while being involved, which I was enabled to do as a kibbutz member. The problem with this method is over-involvement but its advantage is a deepened understanding" (Kressel 1974, 7). He shared with me his misgivings concerning the research on the kibbutz. It had not been an easy challenge for him because in contrast to most of the anthropological studies: research on the kibbutz involved equals. After their exploration of the kibbutz, Rosenfeld and Kressel moved on to study the Bedouin and the Arabs. Yassur was confronted with the same dilemma, although he is not an anthropologist. He carried out an ethnographic study on the Kfar Vitkin moshav, where he resides. The initial published version of the book on the moshav revealed the first names of the people he studied. As a result of opposition on the part of central figures in the moshav whose names appeared in the book, this version was removed from the bookshelves and replaced by another one with coded names (Yassur 1990).

The group of anthropologists who joined the research teams in the Jewish Agency Settlement Department and the Bernstein Project developed a slightly different model of anthropology at home. In the late 1950s and early 1960s the Jewish Agency was carrying out studies that, despite their claim to be sociological by definition, had been conducted with ethnographic methodology. This was an incubator for fostering an infrastructure of anthropologists in Israel who worked at that time in new immigrant communities and the agricultural sector in Israeli settlements. It also constituted anthropology at home in the territorial sense, although the researchers—apart from one—were immigrants. The two heads of the sociological research section in the Jewish Agency Settlement Department, Willner and Weingrod, were natives of the United States; under their management, Shokeid (an Israeli native), Nevo (a native of the United Kingdom), and Deshen (a native of Germany) carried out their studies. Shokeid subsequently wrote an article on the dilemmas entailed in fieldwork at home under the heading "Fieldwork as Predicament rather than Spectacle" (Shokeid 1971b) in which he brought up for the first time reflections regarding views on anthropological identities. Referring to a secular Jewish Israeli native anthropologist studying traditional Eastern Jewish immigrants, he wrote,

> Whatever the price, the mere possibility given to me to conform to some elementary values of my host society put me, I believe, in a better position to understand certain social and cultural aspects of that community. I may exaggerate or idealize the situation, but at times I also felt that the Romemites were proud to have me with them, and precisely because I was different in some ways and was identified with the veteran Ashkenazi "upper strata" of Israeli Society. (Shokeid 1971b, 116)

Or, elsewhere:

> In my own case, I am quite convinced that my command of Hebrew, as well as my familiarity with Jewish culture, influenced and supported my analysis. If I had had to rely mainly on an informant to translate the discussion among the Romemites, I would have certainly have missed much of the cultural content and the additional latent interpretations made during those discussions. (Shokeid 1971b, 119)

Palgi preferred to devote herself to the research on immigrants who came to the homeland at a time that was characterized, according to her, by the abandonment of past fundamentals, of myth, and of religion. She claimed that anthropologists who wanted to be relevant were obliged to adapt themselves to the psycho-historical context of the country (Palgi 1993). Like Brauer and Patai before her, Palgi was interested in Middle Eastern Jews, whom she met when they first disembarked from the ship, in immigrant camps, and in rural and urban settlements.

Looking back, Weingrod agonized over his "research at home" on an immigrants' moshav in the Negev that he had conducted about thirty years previously. His instructor in Chicago, Sol Tax, a Jew who wanted to consider himself as a citizen of the world, regarded Weingrod's interest in Jews in Israel as an indication of parochialism. Weingrod conjectured that if Sol Tax had lived in a more reflexive period, he would have said, "Anthropologists don't study people like them—they study people different from them" (Weingrod 1998b). For Weingrod, the distinction between home and field is not so clear. He shares his inner struggles with the reader: "Did I in effect study my tribe at home?" His reply is ambivalent:

> Yes, because I knew Hebrew and because I shared the basic assumptions of society with the people I studied: I was Jewish, a Zionist, and "within the consensus." In view of all these aspects I felt at ease going in and out of the moshav. But nevertheless also no, I chiefly studied the Moroccans and not the veteran Israelis, i.e. the employees of the settlement authorities who were of European descent.
>
> The other whom I observed-participated-interviewed comprised the immigrants—my project was to understand them and not to search for the exoticism of my own "native community." (Weingrod 1998)

Weingrod testified that at the time he was doing his fieldwork in the moshav of Moroccan expatriates, he did not, as many of his generation did, have any reflexive insights. These insights developed only years later.

Harvey Goldberg belongs to this same cohort of anthropologists of the Jewish Agency generation, even though he never conducted research on its behalf. In order to obtain his doctoral degree, he did fieldwork in a moshav of immigrants from Libya. Since then has continued to be interested for many years in this community. Like his colleagues, he was unaware of the tension between insider and outsider, between home and away from home. He conversed with his research subjects in Hebrew, which was both his and their second language. The Hebrew language served as a bridge between them and between them and the new reality in Israel. Like Weingrod, his absorption processes paralleled theirs.

The ten anthropologists, all Jews mostly from North America, who conducted field studies in Israel as part of the Bernstein Project, studied Jewish communities. Most of them examined the possibility of settling in Israel, but only three of them—Shokeid, Deshen, and Handelman—realized it. Was this anthropology at home? In what sense were the researchers and the researched similar, and in what were they different? Under what circumstances was their social affinity defined as research at home, and where were the borders and intervening definitions that created the impression of anthropology away from home? The participants in the Bernstein Project were positioned on the continuum between the native insider (Shokeid) and the stranger outsider (Abarbanel) who left after completing his fieldwork. Others, such as Arnold Lewis and Aronoff, stayed on after completing their first fieldwork and were interested in settling down here. Though they differed in the degree of their personal involvement in Israel, they both identified with the Zionist project despite their criticism of the way it was being implemented. Their studies exposed processes of redefining identities and organizing strategies against the heavy hand of the absorption bureaucracy. They were unexceptional in the tradition of British anthropology from which they burgeoned, where crossing the territorial bounds of their country to conduct fieldwork was customary. They differed, however, from their colleagues who went out to do fieldwork in Africa or in South East Asia in that they had a religious, cultural, ethnic, and ideological affinity to the people they studied, and most of them spoke the language with some degree of fluency and understanding.

At about the same time and even a little earlier, Jews studied the local Palestinian/Arab/Bedouin community. Were they studying at home? According to the territorial definition, the answer is in the affirmative. But on the scale of the cultural distance the answer is less straightforward. Marx, who came to Israel as a youngster, specialized in the Bedouin society of the Negev, and later did fieldwork in Ma'alot on the bureaucratic relationships between the (Eastern) immigrants and the local authorities. During his fieldwork Marx lived among the Bedouin of the Negev. Later, when he had left for the center of the country, the research site still remained "a few cigarettes smoking away" from his home. However, as in the case of other Jewish researchers who studied Arab society, the research had been conducted in the territorial home and not in the cultural home—others were well outside the range of his daily experience. I was astonished by his claim that "It was easier for me to understand the Bedouin than the people of Ma'alot." I offered Marx my explanation for this. When studying the Bedouin, he had the advantage of being equipped with concepts of the school of British social anthropology for understanding a segmentary society. In his research on bureaucratic violence, however, in which he was one of its pioneers, he was still suffering from the lack of conceptual frameworks, and this increased the difficulty of comprehension. Marx rejected this suggestion.

After completing a long fieldwork project in Africa for his doctoral dissertation, Eilam returned home. He switched the focus of his research to studying Jews from Georgia in order to promote his career in the university, which sometimes preferred specialization in a local topic, and because Israeli society was in need of anthropological know-how for the encounter with new immigrants from Georgia. Like his contemporaries who worked in the Jewish Agency and outside it, he was attracted by the challenge of becoming acquainted with groups of Other Jews who had come closer to his home and had integrated into it. Weil, who had a prior interest in the Jews from India in England, later immigrated to Israel and focused on the Jews of India in Israel. For the generation of the 1970s, as for the generation of the 1940s, home was defined as nearby territory and as a religious and ideological common denominator. Strangeness was defined on a cultural-cum-ethnological basis and constituted the minimum distance required to do what is considered good anthropology. The perception that a continuation exists between Israel's founding generation and that of later generations doing anthropology at home does not negate the cautious retrospective call on the part of the present-day observer. Here too, as in other contexts of my work, I have placed on the shoulders of the leading players my point of view in addition to theirs, but have endeavored to ensure that the latter should not overpower the former.

Unlike the universities of Jerusalem, Tel Aviv, and Bar Ilan, Haifa University has developed a unique model of anthropology that favors conducting anthropology away from home and has stuck to its principles to this day. It has formed a policy of world anthropology, members of the staff have been appointed chiefly according to the criterion of regional specialization, and it encourages focusing on fieldwork in research projects far from the borders of Israel. Saltman claimed that the development of anthropology at home has diminished the theoretical perspective regarding the profession. Each region creates diverse issues, and when a regional variety exists, so does a theoretical one. Saltman conducted a very adventurous anthropology project in Africa and in the Caribbean. Nevertheless, he never entirely abandoned research at home, and also examined issues connected with kibbutz ideology and with law.

In the anthropology at home of the founders' generation, one can discern two main trends: the dominant one is the anthropology of Jewish immigrants studying communities of Other Jewish immigrants, and others are that of Jews studying Arab communities (Marx 1985). The researcher immigrants showed empathy for the researched immigrants but lacked the reflexive contemplation to perceive the resemblance between themselves and the subjects of their research or to be aware of aspects of the power inequality between them. Avruch, who studied the Jewish immigrants from the United States, noted that upon their arrival here, they had to become accustomed to a simpler technology than that in their country of birth. He completely overturns the assumption that the new immigrants have to upgrade their degree of modernization (Avruch 1981). Both sides of the immigrant-studying-immigrant research underwent the drama of immigration, the processes of change in identity, and the acceptance in the new society. Was the similarity of their experiences the researchers' impetus for understanding others? Was the need to emphasize the difference between the researcher of immigrants and the researched immigrants the result of the research methodology and tradition? Or was it the result of blindness? I assume that the differences between the researchers and the researched in their social, occupational, and personal statuses also contributed to this blindness. The researchers did indeed endure the sufferings of integration into the new society, but the transition was easier on several accounts: the professional prestige they enjoyed as academics, the fact that they belonged to an international community of intellectuals from which they drew their legitimacy, the agreeable living conditions in their permanent domiciles, their previous acquaintance with the country, their freedom of choice, as well as their relative independence from the absorption authorities and their status as Ashkenazi Jews. As opposed to them, the subjects of their studies were categorized by the center as being exotic, problematic, traditional, and peripheral (except for studies on the veteran kibbutzim and moshavim). The similarity began and ended with the joint Zionist ideology and with their being Jewish. Shokeid, Goldberg, Weingrod, and others stressed the importance of an in-depth knowledge of Hebrew, which served them well in communicating with the immigrants they studied.

Shokeid laid bare his considerations for choosing the "Romema" moshav as a site for his study: "I admit that I did not think of this means of presenting Israeli society when I did my research on the moshav whose members were immigrants from the Atlas Mountains. I saw before my eyes the immigrants from North Africa who fascinated me by their strangeness. The fact that they were Jews added a special dimension to the exoticism of these distant relatives" (Shokeid 2002, 75). From the perspective of hindsight, Goldberg also reflexively contemplated his research on the immigrants from Libya in the moshav (Goldberg 1993b) and pointed to the unavoidable "extra-academic" involvement in research at home on those whom he ironically termed "my tribe." He regarded himself as one of a line of Israeli anthropologists of European descent whose search for the universal in the science of man afforded them a path to Jewish tradition by means of research on the Eastern Jews.

The prominent anthropologists of the 1970s spearheaded the rapid development of anthropology in the universities and trained a new generation of anthropologists who showed interest in new topics in new sites, but on principle remained at home and followed in the steps of their teachers. Certain anthropologists conducted research abroad—Hazan and Carmeli in England, Ben-Ari, Goldstein-Gidoni and Ivry in Japan, Bird-David in India, Cohen in Thailand—but the core of Israeli anthropological research still remained at home. They were later joined by Levy, who did research in Morocco; Motzafi-Haller, who did fieldwork in Africa; Avieli, who did his work in Vietnam; and a few others. Some of them such as Zilberman and Rabinowitz (both of whom did fieldwork on Palestinians) went abroad for academic studies and returned to Israel for their fieldwork. Despite the prestige of adventurous anthropology, most of the research in Israeli anthropology has remained at home. It is of note that although the universities have limited funds, they have encouraged students over the past few years to do fieldwork abroad. Consequently, studies in Nepal, the United States, Ethiopia, Japan, and other places have been added to the repertoire of fieldwork studies by Israelis.

There were additional aspects to the work on immigrants in Israel that came about as a substitute to doing research in the immigrants' homeland. From time to time, the need arose to bypass geopolitical restrictions or policies that prevented Israeli anthropologists from doing fieldwork in certain places. This strategy was inspired by a wide-ranging project under the management of Margaret Mead after World War II, "The Study of Cultures at a Distance" (Mead and Metraux 1953), designed to gain knowledge of distant cultures by means of studies of their members living in the United States. (The project was aimed in particular at societies that had been in conflict with the United States and to which access had been limited.) Women in rural Taiwan were similarly studied in order to overcome the difficulty of studying the same issue in China (Wolf 1972). The study by Zborowski and Herzog that employed this strategy dealt with the Jewish shtetl in Europe (Zborowsky and Herzog 1952).

The subjects of these studies and the new sites have established new relationships between the home, the field, and the outside. The American researchers Clifford, Marcus, and Fischer (Clifford and Marcus 1986; Marcus and Fischer 1986) drew up and defined existing trends—referential platforms that provided a meta-theory of ideas whose seeds had already begun to germinate in the middle of the 1960s. The development of their ideas focused on the ethnographic view at home—in other words, in the industrial society of the West, the researcher's home—and laid the relationships between the researcher and the cultural-cum-social reality open to a critical review. Marcus and Fischer emphasized the importance of research at the center versus at the periphery: on the elite powers in authority and not on their subordinates, on the probation officers and not on the youngsters under their supervision, on the immigration bureaucracy and not on the newcomers, and so on. Kunda suggests a renewed reflexive view on this topic (Kunda 1992).

The new insights generated by the reflexive thoughts on the status of ethnography and the consequent crisis they caused were of significant influence in Israel and contributed to undermining traditional ethnography and to making efforts to redefine methods, research fields, and research sites while concurrently continuing to use the traditional research patterns.[1] However, the discussion on native anthropology has not been the central topic of discourse here because the binary model of natives versus colonialists is difficult to realize in the Israeli context. Avoiding it is also linked to the distinctions between the native and the non-native entailing the politics of identities. The marginalization of the discourse on "native anthropology" in Israel could be explained by the unique nature of its anthropology, whose founding fathers were immigrants. The critical mass of natives trained in anthropology began to appear only after the 1980s.

The discussion of the definitions of nativeness has contributed to the task of clarifying the identities of Israeli anthropologists and to its characterization as anthropology, which is chiefly done by self-defined natives and not especially according to the criterion of color. Having said that, one can point to isolated cases in Israeli anthropology in which the previously researched is now the researcher. For instance, Aref Abu-Rabia from a Bedouin tribe in the Negev studied the Bedouin in the Negev. His community members were the subjects of a study by Marx as well as by Bailey, Kressel, Hundt, Kish, and Gefen. Y. Schaefer, J. Schaefer, and Shapira were kibbutz members studying the kibbutzim that had previously been the research interests of American anthropologists such as Spiro and Diamond. Nakhleh, who was born and brought up in an Arab village in the Galilee, has a professional anthropologist interest in the study of the village of his birth, a previous fieldwork site of Rosenfeld. Motzafi-Haller, a Mizrahi woman who also went to the United States for her academic education, is progressing in her research on Mizrahi women in Israel (Motzafi-Haller 2001, 2012). Outstanding in this respect is the low number of anthropologists emerging from the immigrant moshavim of the 1950s and 1960s, from development towns, and from among the Palestinians; this is linked to mobility processes in Israeli society and the low number of university students from communities who had been the subjects of anthropological research due to their peripherality. Lavie referred to this from a different point of view in her review of Israeli anthropology in the *American Journal of Anthropology* (Lavie 2003).

Narayan, the daughter of a German American mother who married an Indian (whose parents belonged to two distinct Indian social units) describes the complexity of the nativeness of her identity. She discussed how "native" native anthropologist is, and to what extent the issue is linked to politics (Narayan 1993). Her a priori assumption, like that of other native anthropologists, is that they could promote an authentic perspective of their communities. She declares that her dark skin is, for others, the decisive factor regarding her native identity. The problematic racist ambiguity has caused Narayan to renew the definition of nativeness by basing it on the manner in which the anthropologist is related to the research field. The anthropologist's recurrent return to the same research field turns him or her into a kind of native. Such a claim destroys the basis for essential distinctions between native and non-native, but confirms the feelings of numerous anthropologists who have done research abroad far from home and who describe the experience of identifying with the researched and their own transformation into a kind of native.

Nevertheless, contrary to Narayan's advice, one can also make use of the essential definitions of others/self, native/non-native, and home/abroad, and claim the ability to clarify things by means of the interpretive insights of the research field. Motzafi-Haller (1997) employs an autoethnographic strategy in order to bring her identity as a woman and as a

Mizrahi into the forefront of the discussion; she endeavors to understand where these identities stand within the process of her anthropological professionalization and why she experienced her research in South Africa and in Israel in different ways. Based on these insights, she developed theoretical arguments with regard to Israeli society:

> In this article, my search for satisfactory analytical paths, the theorization and writing about peripheral groups in a society is focused on two interconnected questions. The first one deals with where I stand as a researcher vis-à-vis the research topic. Here I questioned the connection between the personal and the emotional experience of the researcher who is part of the community being studied, and the way the research topic and the research methods are designed. Do I have the right to demand and express my "unique native-born voice"? What is this "native-born" voice and what characterizes it? Did the hegemonic academic discourse of my writing enable me to express myself and leave me any space into which I could enter, or did it efficiently silence my voice? (Motzafi-Haller 1997, 93)

In order to be able to cope better with the pain, the anger, and the frustration that she felt against the status of Mizrahim in Israeli society and against the paternalistic approach of the academic dialogue—of the anthropologists and of others—she decided to go to the United States for her doctoral studies and to work on African ethnography:

> I thought I was in need of a better understanding of the theoretical and analytical concepts and that the best way to acquire such knowledge would be to distance myself from Israeli materials until I attained it. My decision was based on the desire to return in the future and reenter the hegemonic academic discourse in Israel from the relative position of power of a "recognized academic" and not as an "angry Mizrahi woman."

The distancing from home, so she hoped, would enable her to entertain a calmer view while adopting concepts from the disciplinary lexicon. Though she realized the second mission, the anger remained undiminished. Perhaps living in such an ideological home with ethnic dilemmas foaming incessantly negates the possibility of allaying anger, of alleviating pain. Motzafi-Haller is not the only one to have experienced such highly emotional involvement. Lavie too has cast angry charges, accusations, and frustrations into the academic-feminist-Eastern discourse in articles in the press, panels in academic conferences, lectures, and numerous pages in Internet forums. Lavie abstains from defining herself as an Israeli anthropologist: "I admit that I have grown up here, researched here, and have remained here a number of years for personal reasons connected to my son's welfare." She adopted and internalized the principles of the anthropological discourse of the American academy where she studied and developed her skills over the years, and, upon her return to Israel, she has been using them in order to engender awareness of and opposition to the intentional discrimination against women, Mizrahim, and Palestinians in Israeli society in general and in the Israeli academia in particular. Motzafi-Haller and Lavie, like those before them, made use of the resources they acquired away from home in order to analyze the home. The first generation of anthropologists, however, studied Mizrahim who were regarded as a peripheral section of Israeli society. Motzafi-Haller and Lavie emphasize their Mizrahi identity and, as such, they study the hegemonic Ashkenazi center and its attitude regarding the social categories that lack power, namely women and Mizrahim. In an article written together with Swedenberg (Lavie and Swedenberg 1995), Lavie challenges the binary Easterner-Westerner formulation and speaks of essentialism and categorization of "mixing," of border zones and the politics of identities, yet makes use of exactly these same essentialist categories in formulating her own agenda.

Weil presented another direction for treating the home-research relationship in a discussion on anthropology at home. In one of her articles, which she wrote in collaboration with her then-husband Michael, they made use of his personal diary and the dialogue between them. Both texts were reflexive innovations (Weil 1987). Weil emphasizes that the home is not just a physical site; the meeting of anthropology and home could occur on the psychological and personal levels. She claims that anthropology is more than just a research site, but a world-embracing intellectual discipline involving additional people who define the home: family members, friends, and neighbors. In an innovative step, she presented the dialogue between herself and her husband as ethnography whose purpose is to show how the conversations they held during their fieldwork contributed to an understanding of the new phenomenon. The home is the absent-present family member during the fieldwork, and exposing its whereabouts when making decisions turns it into a partner in the research.

The husband's connection to the research and his contribution to the fieldwork, which are very frankly revealed here, are also not completely absent from other anthropological works in Israel, even if they are not expressly mentioned in writing. Family members are covert partners behind the scenes. For instance Dalia, Marx's wife, preferred to bring up their children in Israel, so they did not remain in England—a fact that, so he maintained, influenced the path of his career.[2] Some of the Israeli anthropologists left with their wives to conduct fieldwork outside Israel (Eilam, Saltman, and Levy in Africa; Goldstein-Gidoni and Ben-Ari in Japan). Goldberg, who was living in America then, came to Israel for his fieldwork. Doing ethnography around the corner leaves a great deal of room for family members to be involved and to participate. Even then, the degree of sharing with the spouse obviously depends on many other factors apart from the distance from the field, such as the spouse's commitment to the other's career, or considerations with regard to the welfare of the children. Weingrod expressed himself along the same lines:

> Because you are at home and Israel is small the distance between the research site and your permanent living quarters is short. The anthropological adventure is intimately connected to the researcher's day-to-day life. You are a citizen in the society you are researching, and share the "local wisdom" of the place and its self-evidence. And when society remains in a permanent conflict, and when you feel that you are participating in the illusion that by your actions you have helped cause a change, then the "field," the civil interests and the illusions all converge. The daily events fascinate me as an anthropologist on the one hand, and on the other hand depress me as a citizen of the state. And this is not just a problem of a split personality; the exotic and the everyday sometimes clash with the beliefs and the basic values. (Weingrod 1998b)

Levy emphasized the extent to which research and everyday life of the home combined and intermingled:

> At a class on rituals and ceremonies, I did a research on the hilulah event of Moshe Pinto in Ashdod. I was emotionally entangled. Pinto and my father died in the same month and are buried in the same

> cemetery and everything got mixed up. I watched the process of exalting a holy man and kept walking around the cemetery all the time. The event there did not solely concern Pinto. It also concerned me.

From the middle of the 1990s and, to a greater extent, at the end of the twentieth century, the rise in tension in the Israeli–Palestinian conflict made it became increasingly difficult for many Israeli anthropologists to accept the Israeli government's policy and to identify with the nationally based discourse. For researchers at home, the ideological component is crucial. Identifying with national aims was of value in the past, but today this component of identification is undergoing erosion and seeps into the conduct of fieldwork with regard to home and to theoretical approaches. Furthermore, the anthropologist's split soul is afflicted not only by the stances regarding the conflict, but also his attitude toward the beliefs of the people he studies. Kunda expressed a similar dilemma:

> As a "local," as a "native," as an "insider" I was obviously close to the culture I went out to investigate; but I was also obligated to the fundamental dominant worldview and underwent stress—particularly strong in the case of Israeli society, much stronger than other ethnographers are aware of, and dramatically amplified in times of war—to feel and to express empathy. . . . In other words I was tempted to set a border line between research work and politics and naturally, like many other Israelis, between themselves and military service; I also tended to construe these aspects of Israeli life as an irrelevant context for normal criticism, as a background noise whose thematic analysis, if such a thing is at all possible, would be very difficult. This kind of difficulty exists by definition for everyone who criticizes his own society and is caught in the ideological traps he endeavors to expose and which comprise categories that are repressed by the combined forces of personal pain and social pressures. (Kunda 1992, 22–23)

Along with his declaration regarding the difficulty posed by research at home and inner criticism of the society to which the researcher is committed, Kunda also emphasized the researcher's additional obligation:

> All of them, on top of their local obligation, are also committed to a foreign professional community as well as to a theoretical system

> and a language borrowed from other places. . . . Within the Israeli context this kind of distancing affords the illusion of engendering alienation but in effect turns into taking a Western stand in the local cultural domain. (Kunda 1992)

Thus, claims Kunda, the Israeli ethnographic critics of culture become "at one and the same time victims of local ideological forces and cultural hegemony, not to mention also of external intellectual colonialism and internal collaborators" (1992).

In his article on Israeli soldiers serving during the Intifada, Ben-Ari described an additional complex situation that an Israeli anthropologist could encounter when conducting a study at home. He served as a battalion adjutant on a policing mission in Hebron:

> Although I was rarely in direct contact with Palestinians while in Hebron, I found myself in a state of turmoil for weeks after my return. . . . Above all, however, I was very defensive about any criticism of the army or of the actions of soldiers in the territories. As I then only vaguely sensed and now more explicitly realize I took these criticisms and questions personally: that is, as attacks touching on my identity as an army officer, and through that as an Israeli, and as assaults on my commitment to the army and by way of that to my own society. (Ben-Ari 2010, 348)

Israeli anthropologists are trapped between the vise of local ideology to which they are committed and the world centers of anthropology that are their professional community and with which they hold an academic dialogue. The political discourse has become an inseparable part of the academic one, both as a philosophy of involvement and as processes of crystallization of the stances of foreign academic organizations who condemn Israel's activities and attempt to boycott cooperation with its scientists.

The use of an external terminology causes alienation, but is part of the rules of the game required in order to be accepted in academic centers abroad. A variation of this exists in the attempt to analyze the relationships between Israeli anthropologists and the people they are researching in the context of the power relationships between the representatives of European colonialism and the governed societies, as, for instance, in the case of Rabinowitz's research on the first anthropologists who studied Palestinians (Rabinowitz

1998). It is also true of a work by the Forum of Social and Cultural Studies (2002a) about the way the Mizrahim in Israel have been studied. Adopting the Orientalist perspective is unsuccessful in pointing out the complexity of the relationships between the researcher and the researched in the Israeli home. Anthropologists cope with the negative image and Israel's unpopularity in academic circles with various means.

Adopting a genre of narrative writing is an additional strategy for coping with the duality of home and abroad. Autobiographic or auto-ethnographic stories breathe life into positivist statements regarding Israeli society and its crises, and add to it another layer of understanding. Shokeid wrote two autobiographies, the first of a personal nature (2002) and the second professional (2012). In both, he integrated his anthropological writing with his political stances and dilemmas. By writing in Hebrew, he addressed these texts to insiders, the Israeli readers. Interestingly enough, Virginia R. Dominguez, a non-Israeli anthropologist who conducted fieldwork in Israel, exposed her problematic relations with the Israeli political reality in an article titled "To Fall in Love with the Criminal" (Dominguez 2013). It is a chapter in a newly published book that deals with "The Poetics and Ethics of Fieldwork" in Israel, in which contributors present the complexities of being in and out, far away and at home (Markowitz 2013).

Auto-ethnographies and narrative writing also enable researchers to overcome one of the difficulties inherent in fieldwork: the impossibility of being simultaneously in several places. The diverse versions of the same story, the numerous narratives, and the variations on the same reality are helpful in overcoming this difficulty: this strategy is known as multi-sited ethnography. Furthermore, narratives intensify the engagement in reflexivity and turn the personal story into the essence; for example, Motzafi-Haller (1997) and El-Or (2002, 1994) tried to tackle focal points of stress in Israeli society by means of the personal prism. The use of the narrative, which also blazed a trail to the cultural studies discipline, helps blur the distance between inside and outside, between the native and the non-native. Another accepted way of studying the home site is by observing representations, media, texts, chance meetings, and works of art. This kind of observing that can be regarded as mediation ethnography—between the classical field and its representations—enables the use of anthropological insights in broader contexts (Hazan 1997).

The classical definition of Western anthropology, which investigates not itself but others in the Third World (the "West versus the rest"), has over time undergone changes. The anthropological methodology, with its unique concomitant basic assumptions, has been transported nearer home. The development of the auto-ethnographic trend, which is a version of the negative connotation loaded expression "native anthropology," is one of the signs of the dramatic turn in the direction of post-modern anthropology. Those who were previously the researched have become their own researchers.

Engaging in anthropology at home contributed to its development and made it widely acclaimed in world anthropology for several reasons. First, the home of the early anthropologists was the national home, which recruited them both emotionally and physically into participating in its consolidation. Hazan found that "when Israeli anthropologists write about other places they enlist all their Israeli cynicism and irony. When they write about Israel they enlist sharpness and directness . . . and concern." Second, the close familiarity with the researched and the ability to converse with them in their actual and symbolic languages creates an anthropology of insights that a stranger would have found difficult to derive. It follows, according to Hazan, that "Israelis are bothered by problems of identity, and for them anthropology is a solution." The play between national and international identities, between Jewishness and Israeliness, between Western and Eastern, is strongly expressed in anthropological work in Israel. Like their researchers, the researched also agonize over similar identity quandaries; the anthropologist can therefore identify with the community studied, as Haim Hazan told me:

> When I tried to publish material about an Israeli old age home, they told me it was of no interest to the public, whereas at the same time anthropology on the kibbutz and the moshav was flourishing. The world assumes that Israeli anthropologists are dealing with Israel and that the natives are studying themselves. Israel is embarking on a political agenda and leading journals are accepting a greater number of leftist political articles by Israelis.

Outside researchers studying Israeli society were also not indifferent to it, "objective" about it, or distanced and estranged from it. I am referring to non-Jewish researchers who came to do only limited field research, but who developed personal relationships that made them become both emotionally and personally involved to varying degrees. Several had Israeli spouses, and some of them maintained a certain amount of contact with Israel. Again, their personal lives and their professional careers inevitably intertwined—keeping them apart was simply impossible.

In a conversation with me, Goldberg revealed that the encounter with the field site changed the focus of his interest. When he began his study on the moshav of Libyan Jews, he refrained from dealing with issues involving sensitive or emotional aspects such as religion and Jewish–Arab relationships in Libya, and topics of a sociological character such as absorption or acculturation. From the beginning, he preferred to study neutral issues. As a result of his encounter with the field site, he understood that he had to deal with historical topics that touched on the immigrants' lives before they immigrated to Israel, as well as with matters concerning religion. And thus he became the historian among the anthropologists and the anthropologist among the historians—the expert on Jewish studies among the anthropologists and the anthropologist among the experts on Jewish studies.

Goldberg, by his own testimony, feared that because of his bashfulness he would not be able to contain the expected excessive emotional burden, and adopted a strategy of distancing himself in time and distancing himself from the discipline, thus sidetracking the problematic effect of proximity on anthropology at home: "When I review the directions of my research, I discern that I have always been sensitive to the ideological stances lurking in the background of my research, and usually as a first reaction I have backed away from issues in which I felt I would lose my professional equanimity." Together with the restraint and the care in choosing the subjects of his research, he defines the place where he did his first fieldwork in Israel as his home today: "I no longer see the home in America as a home. Porat [the moshav where he did his fieldwork for his doctoral dissertation] is the home where I return to in my consciousness and in my memory." The common language for Goldberg and Disi Hajaj, one of his chief informants, was Hebrew, even though it was not either one's mother tongue. Despite their different accents, they understood one another and cooperated in formulating the Jewish texts that they could read together. The similarity and sharing of language, the basis of knowledge, the Zionist awareness, and the closeness of the territorial place constituted the infrastructure of the dialogue between them. Such togetherness could not plausibly have taken place between Evans-Pritchard and his friends in the Azande or the Nuer.

Shokeid expressed similar sensations about his studies in Romema:

> I studied a group of people to whom I was in some ways a foreigner, and in some ways not. These were Jews who had emigrated from the Atlas Mountains in 1956, and had settled in an Israeli co-operative

> village (which I called Romema). Born in Israel, into a family which had come from Eastern Europe leaving behind no close relatives about a half century earlier, I was intrigued by the mass exodus of Jews from many countries to Israel which had taken place after 1948. The majority were from Middle Eastern and North African countries whose social, cultural, and ideological background was very different from that of most of the "European" veteran population in Israel of whom my family was part. One of my main motives in studying the Atlas Mountains Jews was a deep curiosity to know about people to whom I am apparently related by ancient history and recent citizenship. I wanted to know about the culture, manners, and social life of these newcomers. I wanted to know about the vision of their new and ancient homeland they had had before immigrating to Israel, and their perceptions of the reality they met on their arrival. I wanted to know how they came to terms with their new physical, economic, social, and cultural environment. In contrast to most anthropologists I was, therefore, not basically detached from my field. (Shokeid 1971b, 114)

In her book on a training college for religious girls at Bar Ilan University, El-Or writes:

> Going to the midrasha]college] was going into my national, biographical, community, class and gender home. Nevertheless, it was a crossing of boundaries from the aspects of age, religion, political stances, education and erudition. Such a step is a never-ending movement of coming and going in time and space: in the morning at the midrasha, afterwards at home; there with my opinions from here—here with what I heard and saw there. . . . This kind of movement creates and demolishes at one and the same time the "here" and the "there." On the one hand it reconstructs the groups among whom the researcher moves as "actual" groups on each occasion and helps in creating a boundary between them. On the other hand it becomes clear during the movement that the boundary is elusive and that the groups are not essential, as could have been assumed before the movement toward them and outward from them. (El-Or 1998, 77)

The distinctions in the literature between non-native anthropology—Euro-American, outsider, Western—and native anthropology do not provide me with a sufficiently appropriate system of concepts. Israeli anthropology, in its making, was one of immigrants studying immigrants. When Weingrod, Goldberg, Kuper, and Weil came here, they were newer immigrants than were the immigrants they studied. Palgi arrived here together with or very close to the arrival of those she researched. Who then is the native born and who is the native here? The concepts likely to clarify the distinction between distance and closeness, between the home and the outside, are linked to numerous identities. I am adopting El-Or's stance, which is based on definitions of gender, education, and professional likenesses and not on exclusively territorial distinctions that are also supposed to be cultural distinctions between the researchers and the researched.

AN ANTHROPOLOGIST STUDYING ANTHROPOLOGY AT HOME: THE REFLEXIVE DIMENSION

As stated earlier, through the concept of anthropology at home, I have sought to examine the underlying assumptions of Israeli anthropologists. I too am performing anthropology at home, an undertaking that should reduce the margins of the epistemological distance needed to produce insights about the research arena. In my research, I submit to a sort of "home arrest" that chains me to the local soil, while yet allowing me to manage my everyday ethnographic affairs, as a condition of knowledge production. "Understanding the subjects" or "speaking their language" were for me taken-for-granted categories, for I was raised in the same disciplinary habitat. The differences between me and my subjects are embodied first and foremost in the differences between my own position and theirs in the academic hierarchy.

As a veteran Israeli anthropologist in Israel, I am not an immigrant who is obliged to learn how to teach the knowledge gained in his or her native tongue and to turn it into foreign-language anthropology. I have served rather as a Hebrew teacher, an anthropologist, and a translator of Israeli society for Harvey Goldberg and Shalva Weil, immigrant anthropologists who came to teach anthropology here. My socioeconomic affiliation with the veteran Ashkenazi center of the country brings me into kinship with anthropologists such as Tamar El-Or and Hagar Salamon. Like many of my generation who did not move far beyond the underlying premises of their Zionist parents, it was not difficult for me to identify with Israeli anthropologists of my parents' generation or with those of the younger one who were partners to the anthropology of the national homeland. Like them, I am trapped in the webs of "local wisdom." Since I began my studies at the

Hebrew University of Jerusalem, its brand of home anthropology has been treated with derision by sociologists from the same department, and it has lacked funds with which to develop. As a small and marginal group, it developed a unique *esprit de corps*, which included a commitment to and involvement with anthropology, a bent toward adventurousness, and criticism of positivist methods. These beginnings have left their mark until today. As zealous collectors are wont to do, I made sure to purchase every book or publication in anthropology in Hebrew, whether translated or original, and thus I began to build, from my own personal beginnings, a rich library of anthropological literature in Hebrew. Sensitivity to boundaries, a commitment to the discipline, and emotional involvement—the characteristic features of Israeli home anthropology—are also features of my personal identity. What then permits me as an "insider" to examine things from within? What grants me an advantage as a researcher in the inner confines of my own home? I offer a broad but detailed view on the one hand, and a deliberate turn to general anthropological insights on others. The very formulation of a research question allows me to position myself in an "extra-domestic" Archimedean point and to view the home from a broad range of vantage points. Israeli anthropologists' interest in the development of Israeli anthropology is neither systematic nor consistent—most are intimate only with their own personal quarters—but among them are others who wander and explore the other rooms and halls in the house, depending on personality, seniority, and motivation.

Taking upward flight, with the aid of these two wings—the broad view from within, and the conceptual disciplinary leverage—allows an even more abstract and conceptualize glimpse of things, aiming to transcend the taken-for-granted and to liberate the ideas allowing one to looking inward from the outside. In this, I follow Narayan (1993), who claims that distance is a cognitive position that produces a measure of cold, generalized, and deliberate objectivity, thus inevitably also producing stereotypes. Such a stance, therefore, ought to be replaced by experiential and emotional knowing, which also provides a broader scope for the informants' own interpretations.

Anthropology at home in Israel has weighty theoretical, practical, and disciplinary implications. First, the life courses of researchers have revolved around local research. Second, the IAA has acquired its character from its particular Israeli features. Third, the development of research and teaching in the academy has been influenced by the Zionist project and by the perception of the role of anthropologists in Israeli society.

IDENTITIES, MOTIVES, AND DRIVES: ANTHROPOLOGISTS MAKING CAREERS

Some of the chief issues that grabbed my interest in this study were the motives, life courses, and identities of Israeli anthropologists. My findings revealed three main images anthropologists used to describe their life courses: the anthropologist as "immigrant," in the sense of a nomadic, marginal sojourning in a multicultural society; the anthropologist as "committed," in the sense of engagement, identification with other people, and social reform centered on particular social causes; and the anthropologist as one who is "curious" about other cultures—Jews and non-Jews, and an attraction to exoticism and adventure. The anthropologist confronts contradictory worlds that maintain a constant dialogue between themselves. He or she desires to learn about others in the context of an Israeli experience that is at once ideological, concerned, and engaged. On the other hand he or she aspires to connect to the sphere of the cosmopolitan, the scientific, and the universal. "The others within us" contend with a host of emotional and cognitive "others," interacting in ways that are sometimes complementary, and sometimes oppositional, and that affect the practices and ideologies that guide our professional activity.

Some of the interviewees found that the roots for their search for other cultures were located in their own experiences as immigrants or in their lives in a multicultural society. Some anthropologists ventured far to search for the other ways of life, motivated by curiosity and enchantment with the exoticism of the distant-far; others were intrigued by the near-far. The distinction between these two categories is based on a different organization of the relation between the subject and the researcher. The most important element in the founding generation's cluster of identities is the collective-national or Jewish identity. This is followed, in descending order, by communal identity and personal identity. The (Jewish) anthropological pioneers were participants in the Zionist project, which was a motivating factor, alongside their scientific and professional commitment. The scientific pursuit dovetails with the national and with the local without producing an internal contradiction. The commitment to participation in national projects fell in line with those elements of Zionist identity that they acquired when they themselves were immigrants, and this was how they defined their motives for coming to Israel. A professional identity was the basis of one's identity as a breadwinner and as one who takes pride in one's work.

After the first phase of nation building, with the apparent institutionalization and routinization of many social, cultural, economic, and political processes, anthropology too became institutionalized within academic frameworks and achieved legitimacy. The successors of the founding generation hailed from the British and American scientific communities, membership in which afforded them a universal, cosmopolitan identity and, in some cases, provided them with the leverage for exiting local parochial communities to affiliate with extra-Jewish culture. Even if the Zionist identity of the anthropologists remained intact, anthropology's goals and research concerns changed. Thus, for example, a discussion of the nature of Israeli ethnicity replaced the dilemmas about ways of assisting the absorption of immigrants. The exposure of most anthropologists to the scientific community at anthropological centers, due to attending international conferences and spending sabbatical leaves overseas, reinforced the cosmopolitan (specifically—the Anglo-American) aspects of the identity of Israeli anthropologists. This is facilitated also by the availability of technological means to communicate globally and transcontinentally, as well as by the growing acknowledgement of the importance of maintaining ties with the broader academic world.

The following phase led to the reinforcement of group identity (the community of intellectuals, membership in voluntary associations, etc.) as well as of local identity, at the expense of national-Zionist identity. In the current generation, the inner hierarchy of identities has shifted in comparison with the founding generation: the individual's personal (and familial) identity occupies the center, as does the desire to adopt the cosmopolitan and transcultural identity of a "person of the world," while national identity has sunk to the bottom rung. The professional, international, academic identity has risen to the fore. Many anthropologists view themselves as part of a community of intellectuals who are committed to ideas that have emerged out of Western scientific centers, ideas that have, to a great degree, guided their own research goals and theoretical approaches. Affiliation with these communities has taken the place of aspects of national identity, whose force of attraction has been on the decline or which perhaps is taken for granted. These transformations in the community of anthropologists are consistent with changes in the character of Israeli identity—the deconstruction of monolithic identities into different "I"s that are in dialogue with one another (see the extensive discussion by Bar-On [2008] and Almog [2000]). The decline of the hegemony of the Labor party, together with the rise of the power of groups who were formerly on the margins, has led to two results: a growing commitment on the part of anthropologists to continue this political-social process, and, via their research and teaching, to strengthen the weak and marginal groups in society. They are committed to opposing the increasing power of the right-wing political leadership and of religious groups. Most Israeli intellectuals are traditionally "left wingers," who have found it difficult to accept the policies pursued by the governments since the electoral "turnover" (*Mahapakh*) of the late 1970s. On matters of war and peace, many anthropologists have preferred to identify with the peace movements and to bypass their national identifications by connecting with cosmopolitan identities or post-national ones. Many perceived their vocation and identity as anthropologist as an enlistment to social causes and to the exposure of power relations—in other words, by espousing a subversive, critical anthropology. Some members of this group reduce the volume on their critical voices, whereas others mute it, painting their identities in paler hues. As an escape from national identity whose legitimacy within intellectual discourse has diminished, the professional cosmopolitan identity has crystallized, implying identification with socially minded views and with universal reformers such as "green" movements or international peace movements. In parallel, there is a trend toward reclusiveness within a local social and class-based community that has constructed a cosmopolitan lifestyle, not only in the professional dimension, but also in the social/class dimension that characterizes it as urban, secular, and joined at the hip to processes taking place in the Anglo-American centers. The character of this identity, which portrays the Israeli scientists in the Israeli intellectual elite, has been called a "glocal" identity in the sociological literature (Ram 2008).

In wake of the intensification of the conflict with the Palestinians, the international opposition to the government's policies, and attempts to boycott the Israeli academic establishment in some professional centers, the tension between local identities and professional ones has increased. It is manifest in the anthropological conferences of recent years, in which stormy debates rage over the place and role of anthropologists, on the politics of categorical identities, on the place of women or Mizrahim within academic anthropology, and on professional ethics.

THE ROLE OF NATIONALISM IN THE CREATION OF ANTHROPOLOGICAL KNOWLEDGE IN ISRAEL: A COMPARATIVE VIEW WITH OTHER DISCIPLINES

Related to the relationship between Israeli anthropology and national identity is the question of the role that a discipline such as anthropology plays in the formation of a new society, in a state whose institutions are in process of formation, just as the science burgeoning there is in search of its own particular identity. The search for science at home was the outcome of national identifications, but also contributed to creating them. We are witness to the process of the "Israelization of anthropology" alongside the "anthropologization of Israel," in which anthropology enters into various realms of Israeli society.

The issue of nationalism and Zionism is a central motif in each of the arenas of anthropological practice. Moreover, in the past ten years, it has become fashionable for intellectuals and scientists in Israel to take an interest in this topic, just as the past and the history of science may be viewed as a fertile ground for new and fascinating research. For those who were involved in the fields of physics, biology, and chemistry, their activity took place in the framework of the national project and contributed immensely to the security and military industries, as well as to agriculture and general industry. In these sciences, the "contribution" to the state was both intentional and self-aware, its aims were explicit and out in the open, and it was perceived as a positive contribution. However, a generation later, the critical outlook had been accepted here as well. The outstanding studies representing this trend are those by Kirsh and Falk, on the field of genetics at the Hebrew University (Kirsh 2003, 2007, 2009; Falk 2006). At the same time, critical interest in the disciplines of the social sciences and the humanities has also grown, and they themselves have become more reflexive and self-aware. Among them, there has been a salient tendency to expose the nationalist motivations of those who have shaped science in archeological, sociological, folklorist, and geographical research projects. Because the comparative discussion of these fields and anthropology in Israel may contribute to the understanding of the latter, I shall set aside the discussion of Israeli anthropology momentarily to acquaint ourselves briefly with its neighboring disciplines and obtain the desired comparative perspective.

Under the academic structure prevalent in Israel, sociology is the closest discipline to anthropology. In fact, writing about Israeli sociology very often subsumes anthropology without distinguishing between them (e.g., in the work of Ram [1995] and Danziger [1994]). In a discussion of Israeli sociology, Ben Yehuda (1997) argues that for many years the analysis of "Israeli society" was focused on political processes within Jewish society and was supported by the theoretical scaffolding of the functionalist approach. During the state's first thirty years, sociological research was perceived as supporting Zionist processes of nation building and was connected to the construction of new Jewish and Israeli identities. It included topics such as absorption of immigrants, settlement in new (development) towns, or kibbutzim. This, as Ben Yehuda argues, was done at the expense of paying attention to conflicts—including the Jewish–Palestinian conflict—or to domination, hegemony, and exploitation. Gradually, opposition to this theoretical trend developed, and voices that challenged it began to be heard.

The "new sociologists" in Israel illuminated the question of the role of sociologists in processes of nation building. Their chief arguments were as follows: since the early days of sociology in Israel, the discipline toed the line with the institutional ideology and social policy, and thus contributed to the established power relations between the dominant elite and the weaker sectors of society: minorities (Arabs), immigrants (*olim hadashim*), residents of peripheral towns, and so on. These ideological struggles also had implications for the granting of academic positions.

According to Ronen Shamir and Dan Avnon (1999), Martin Buber was removed from his position as head of the first department of sociology, after he had served only for two years in this office, because he had offered a critical sociology that was marginalized by the functionalist model promoted by Eisenstadt. The theoretical model represented by Eisenstadt, which was dominant in Israeli sociology during its constitutive years, began to be opposed in the 1970s, with the publication of the journal Notebooks on Research and Criticism (*Mahbarot Lemekhar Ulebikoret*) by sociologists and anthropologists of Haifa University, as well as the work by Smooha (1985). Their perspective on Israeli sociology (and anthropology) was summarized and developed by Ram in the early 1990s (Ram 1995) when he put forward a systematic critical reading of Israeli sociology, and pointed out the way in which it was enlisted to the hegemonic agenda of the Zionist national project. He and Baruch Kimmerling (2001) were partners to the assault on the old school, accusing it of ideological bias, which simplistically may be called Zionist, national, and supportive of the hegemony of the government and of the elites. These agencies were interested in promoting the "modernization" of the new immigrants and enabling the "development" of social projects; in service of these goals, they recruited scientists, including educators, psychologists, economists (anthropologists), and sociologists. In their works, the critics pointed to the nexus of power and knowledge production: the position of a researcher as a member of the elite makes him or her tend to produce knowledge that is of use to hegemonic forces, and therefore to entrench their power. The cloaking of the establishment in a mantle of science helps it continue to promote its own goals, which reinforce its own power while weakening those already in a position of weakness.

One of the most noticeable responses to these critical stances was by Moshe Lissak (1996), a senior sociologist at the Hebrew University. In his publications and also from various discussion platforms, Lissak rejected the arguments that the early sociologists who were the target of criticism had adopted the ethos of the dominant elites. He argued instead that the attempt to disengage from the social and cultural milieu of the research was precisely the important challenge that he and his colleagues had successfully met. The rift, Lissak argued, was not one separating the critical sociologists from establishment sociologists, but rather one that divided those representing functionalist and positivist approaches from those representing post-modern approaches that challenge the premises of the objectivity and scientificness of the social science. Lissak referred the critics of sociology to some of the founding figures of Zionist historiography, such as Dinur and Baer, as well as to archeologists such Yadin, to seek there what they had attributed to the sociologists.

Following Lissak's advice, I turned my gaze to Israeli archeology to look at its role in the establishment of a central ethos and in support of nation building. Israeli archeology, which studies the "facts on the ground" (as in the title of Abu al-Haj's book, which points to the connections between the archeology of Jerusalem and sovereignty claims [Abu El-Haj 2001]), was a powerful instrument for the establishment of Zionist and national claims over the Land of Israel. The ethnographer and archeologist Nahum Slousz (1871–1996) and one of the Jewish archeologist pioneers to excavate in Israel stated that the goal of archeology was to expose the roots of Jewish existence in the Land of Israel.[3] Shavit (1997) shows how archeology provided a new picture of the past and constructed a new historical narrative as part of a broad cultural framework in a historical, linguistic, ethnographic, literary, and geographical context, which includes collective memory, historical myths, and more. This narrative provided Jews with the missing link between the Biblical period and the present. Israeli archeological research has found its main incentive in religious Christian, Muslim, and Jewish motivations to explore the land, as part of a national enterprise of nation building and a search for roots (Bar-Yosef and Mazar 1982). The role of archeology in Israel was to enhance the connection between the nation and the land, especially by turning museums and archeological sites into educational centers and points of interest for the public at large (Silberman and Small 1997). A few researchers have pointed to the importance of archeology in Jerusalem in the context of the comprehensive discussion about its position as a religious and symbolic center for the various nations (Bar-Yosef and Mazar 1982; Abu El-Haj 2001). Although Jewish archeologists have prioritized engagement with "Jewish archeology," Palestinian archeology has been neglected (Broshi 1987). An anthropological dimension of archeology has been highlighted by Alex Weingrod (2002), in his article "The Dry Bones," on the ritual and cultural importance of the human remains of important figures from the past.

Michael Feige has drawn an interesting comparison between archeology and anthropology in Israel by demonstrating the part played by them in shaping the image of the development towns as representative of the periphery. Feige's intention was to challenge the notion of the great contribution made by social science and humanities scholars to the constitution of Israeli nationhood (Feige 1998). Archeology had an integrating role, not only in connecting the nation to the Land of Israel, but also in linking together its disparate regions and spaces.

The field of folklore, which interfaces with anthropology in many respects, is also considered a knowledge field that helped to promote national goals, national identities, and the development of national sentiments. The national movements of the middle nineteenth century were nourished by the collection of stories, legends, poetry, and other representations of popular culture, which sharpened the sense of the national collective's particularity as well as of the commonalities among its members. This approach was fueled by romanticism, which was then a dominant cultural trend, together with nationalism: both supported folklore while also enjoying their support of the use of key concepts such as "invented tradition" or "imagined communities." These concepts, which gained currency in the discourses of the humanities and social sciences in the mid-1980s, highlighted the processual element in the production of the collective imagination of communities, as they attempt to justify their actions in the present and interpret both their past and the processes of formation of nationhood. The study of the folklore of Jewish groups in pre-state Israel and Israel was perceived as a practice that emphasized the unique particularities of Jewish ethnic groups on the one hand, but also underscored their common Jewish basis, on the other. But folklore, like anthropology, experienced its own adjustment problems within the Israeli academy. Dan Ben-Amos (1990) wondered why for many years the discipline of folklore did not achieve academic independence in Israeli universities, although there were folklorists employed in various departments, especially in Jewish studies. This can be explained by several factors: historical, ideological, social, and methodological. The most crucial of these is the tension between the particular and unique elements that are the basis of Jewish studies and of Zionism, and the comparative element that informs the discipline of folklore, which searches for universal patterns and universal features of folk thought. Moreover, the traditional focus of folklore researchers in Israel was "the marginal Other," a slot occupied for many years by Oriental Jews. The project of collection of folktales focused on Jews of the Orient, although it did not ignore the Jews of Eastern Europe. In their study of folklore at the Hebrew University, Hasan-Rokem and Yassif (1990) presented the development of the discipline at the Hebrew University as a tension between particularity and universality, between nationalism and globalism, between past and present, Israeliness and "exile," the high and the low, and between the Jewish and the comparative. The extent to which this issue was problematic can be gathered from the fact that Yiddish studies were rejected for many years at the Hebrew University, because the university wished to ignored what it perceived as expressions of "exile" and of "exilic" existence.

Like sociology, archeology, and folklore, the discipline of geography in Israel also contributed to the shaping of national identity. The interpretive models according to which Israeli geographers worked (and still work) in Israel are based on a fundamental concern with the construction of Israeli identity. Members of the first generation emphasized the important of studying the Land of Israel as a homeland; the second generation developed research around questions of development, dispersal of population, and the implementation of policies intended to gain technological domination of territory. At the same time, a growing research direction was the study of the historical geography of the Zionist and pre-state era (Schnell 2000). Critical voices began to be heard in the 1980s, regarding the policies of discrimination against Mizrahim and populations in peripheral settlements—including in Arab settlements (Schnell 1994; Pringle and Yiftachel 1999). In order to bolster their ideological positions, geographers of the first generation selected from Western scientific discourses those scientific models that would suit their purposes as Zionists. Schnell points to the strong involvement of Israeli geographers in promoting national identity and planning national space through the adoption of romantic, positivistic, and other models out of the basket of paradigms offered by Western social sciences and humanities. A comparative look at the different disciplines reveals that nationalism was at work as a solid ideological force, even if not always at a conscious level. The border between the desire to advance an academic field and the desire to advance a national project was usually obscured.

ANTHROPOLOGY BUILDS A NATION: A COMPARATIVE VIEW OF ANTHROPOLOGY'S CONTRIBUTION TO NATION BUILDING IN TURKEY

In order to expand and elaborate the discussion of the relationship between anthropology and nation building, I shall present an additional case study—the Turkish republic—where anthropology was similarly enlisted to the project of nation building.

Shared Factors

The comparison between Turkey and Israel is based on a number of shared factors.

Sharing a Common Region Ferdinand Braudel's concept of the "Mediterranean region" regarding its sociocultural similarities, discerned in the *longue durée* among societies residing in its shared space, bolsters the legitimacy of the comparison of these two Mediterranean countries (without ignoring the conspicuous differences in terms of the size of the territories and populations). Israel and Turkey share neighbors, a climate, and flora and fauna (in the southern region of Anatolia), and both are significant players in the geopolitics of the region.

Significant Revolutions The Kemalist and Zionist revolutions brought about radical changes in lifestyles, values, political structure, and social ideology. Crisis and revolution demand social and political reorganization, enlisting and harnessing intellectual might and the academic elite to help realize change. After the Turkish War of Independence ended with the Treaty of Lausanne in 1923, the Caliphate regime of the Ottoman Empire came to its final endpoint, and a new alternative was constituted in the form of a democratic, national, Western, and secular state. After the revolution, steps were taken to establish a republic with an elected parliament and a modern central government. With the abolishment of the Caliphate, the status of the Islamic administrative institutions was considerably reduced, Islamic social and cultural symbols were limited, state and church were separated, the Turkish language was strengthened by the replacement of the alphabet, and an academy of the Turkish language was created. National dimensions were also expressed in aspirations to "return to the sources" of Turkish culture and national folklore; it was within this ideological framework that the ancient Anatolian cultures were preserved and cultivated—in particular the preservations of Anatolia's material and the cultivation of a historical consciousness of its past. Alongside these, significant symbolic steps toward "Westernization" were taken, including the adoption of a European dress code, the adoption of the Latin alphabet, the introduction of surnames, the establishment of a weekly day of rest on Sunday, and more.

The Zionist revolution demanded from the Jewish people a radical change of lifestyle and societal values, as well as the geographical relocation from life in exile to a new existence in a new-old land. This ideological movement led to the immigration of hundreds of thousands of Jews from all over the world to a geographical region in which they encountered the local Palestinian population. Rejecting the values and lifestyles associated with the countries of origin, and creating an alternative founded chiefly on ideals of secularization, modernity, and democracy required the construction and enhancement of the cultural, ethno-racial, religious, and linguistic elements that were shared by Jews, as well as differentiation from the local Palestinian population in terms of those very same elements. These processes entailed the rejection of whatever was perceived as "traditional" life ways and the adoption of "modern" ones, as well as a focus on features of the so-called "advanced" West, as opposed to the "backward" East. The establishment of the State of Israel emphasized these trends even more powerfully, with the empowerment of the national enterprise and the construction of the state as a Jewish and democratic state.

The Kemalists were faced with the challenges of secularization, the bolstering of a national identity that was to be shared by the different ethnic groups residing throughout the republic, and the development and strengthening of a capitalist economy and Westernization. The Zionist revolution was faced with similar challenges: the construction of a shared identity for Jewish groups of different origins, and the task of institution building in a new state and society.

Modern versus Traditional The routinization of revolution in both societies and the embedding of their respective ideologies did not forge ahead without instigating a crisis. The intellectual and academic elites were expected to assist the processes of development, industrialization, urbanization, ethnicity, and more. In both societies, the problem of the tensions between the so-called modern and traditional were presented to these cadres of intellectuals, to seek their advice on how to cope with such tensions and enact policies that would be conducive to state goals, while also addressing the question of the location of identity between East and West.

Anthropology's Contribution to Nation Building

In Turkey, the relationship between anthropological knowledge and nation building did not begin in 1918 at the end of the War of Independence, or in 1923 with the establishment of the republic. Even before these two events, social notions had infiltrated and affected the emergence of ideas about Turkish nationality by means of emissaries such as the sociologist Gokalp. Similarly, well before the beginning of professional anthropological research in 1930s/1940s Palestine, Zionist leaders were well aware of ideas that were pertinent to anthropological concerns, including the fundamental inquiry into the bases of Zionist identity. Nevertheless, the time periods I have selected to compare are the beginning of professional anthropology in Palestine/Eretz Israel (in the Israeli case) and the institutionalized anthropological activity close to the time of the establishment of the Turkish republic.

At the beginning of the period in question, in both the Turkish and Israeli cases, knowledge produced by the field of physical/medical anthropology, perceived as scientific and accurate (in comparison to social and cultural knowledge), was enlisted to bolster ideological premises that would furnish a basis for policy. These premises concerned the construction of a shared past for different ethnic groups and the forging of a single national identity. The image of anthropology during the period of the pre-state Israel had a significant impact on these forms of engagement. In the eyes of the academic elite and the Zionist leadership, anthropology was a field concerned with human beings' physical measurements (physical anthropology). The physiological and genetic traits of Jews were of interest to those establishing the founding premises of Zionism, and they were intent on comparing different communities of Jews in order to establish a shared physical heritage. Ethnology (or, in our current terms, social and cultural anthropology) and folklore were accorded the roles of documenting and preserving the culture of Oriental Jews before they, along with their unique traits, disappeared through the encounter with "modernity." In both Turkey and Israel, the discipline of anthropology has splintered into its various branches in the past few decades, and specializations are developed in separate academic faculties, while the relationship between the social and the cultural has been split asunder. Even today, in Israel, from time to time one hears sporadic claims about "the existence of a priestly gene," or the "shared genetic heritage of Israelis and Palestinians," or the "genetic similarities between Mizrahi and Ashkenazi Jews," appearing as title of articles surveying the findings of genetic research on Jewish communities around the world. But there is no organized scientific tradition or any substantial activity dealing with questions of ethnic and Jewish identity, as a basis for state policies.

Policymakers, the public at large, and even some of the anthropologists themselves generally hold the view that anthropologists are specialists in possession of concrete knowledge about the society and culture of strange and "exotic" groups. They are thought of as experts who are familiar with the culture of these groups, or at least as have the ability to study and gain familiarity with them. For policymakers, detailed knowledge of a studied group is an asset or a resource that can be used to both shape and implement policy. In the Israeli case, anthropologists were perceived as experts on the "Other," capable of deciphering the cultural codes of "exotic Jews" or helping the state deal with conflicts with Bedouin, Arab, and Palestinian populations. In Turkey, the regime was troubled by the implications of modernization and Westernization processes on traditional culture, and because anthropological knowledge was thought to be capable of precisely depicting encounters between the traditional and the modern, and between East and West, the notion that anthropologists would be able to assist with such processes gained currency. But this view embodies an essentialist assumption about the unique characteristics of the communities in question; differences between their various components are obscured; complexity and inner tensions and contradiction are ignored—in fact, everything that makes anthropology the art of the complex is disregarded. On the other hand, among anthropologists who are frustrated by the fact that their signature skill set may actually prevent them from making unequivocal statements, there is (both worldwide and in Israel) a growing tendency to engage in social activism that embraces a clear political agenda. The anthropologists' research skills are applied to eliciting the voices of the underprivileged or the oppressed, to exposing mechanisms of power and domination, especially state power, at the cost of abandoning the aspiration of presenting a complex worldview.

Turkish nationalism coalesced around the notion of Turkishness, as an identity binding together the nation that had sprung up atop the ruins of the Ottoman Empire. Its conceivers had formulated the identity's contours—as a modern, Western state, within Turkish territory, which would become the homeland of the people and its culture, over and against local religious and ethnic loyalties. In other words, this was a claim for the creation of a melting pot out of diverse cultural, economic, and political differences. The birth of Turkish ethnography was meant to constitute a foundation for the enhancement and preservation of elements of culture that were defined as Turkish, in order to bolster Turkish identity. To this end, the "Turkish society" was created: its goal was to collect and transmit materials related to the history, languages, and ethnography of Turkish civilizations. After World War I, the Kemalist elite formulated the goal and challenge of creating "a nation beating with one heart, and sharing one fate," out of the ethnic and religious diversity of the empire's population. The dual tradition of physical/cultural anthropology of the late nineteenth century provided an answer to this aspiration, with its fusing of blood and land—the biological with the cultural.

One outcome of the enlistment to the Turkish national project was the establishment of research and information centers within the universities. The first anthropological research institute was founded in 1925 at Ankara University. The institute carried out mostly research in physical anthropology, alongside a few sociologically oriented statistical surveys and a few folklore studies. Physicians trained in Europe learned how to measure cranial circumferences, skeletons, and other physical attributes such as height and weight. Mustafa Kemal personally charged the institute's staff with examining the physical traits of the heads of 64,000 Turkish men and women. The Ministry of Education allowed researchers to measure students, and a government directive was issued to measure prisoners and soldiers. The institute came out with an anthropological journal, *The Turkish Review of Anthropology*, which appeared from the mid-1920s until the late 1930s, and was the official publication of a research institution under the auspices of a state university, where no scientific research could be undertaken without government approval.

The republic's elite attempted to use the institute's publication to prove the existence of a Turkish race, by deploying the positivist scientific methods of physical anthropology. At the same time, despite the apparent contradictions, comparative studies were carried out on the "various races living in Istanbul," in which physical characteristics of Turks, Jews, Armenians, and Greeks were examined—people who, in fact, were distinguished from one another on the basis of religious affiliation. Although the comparative studies on the "Turkish race" did not produce interesting findings, the importance accorded to the these studies and the resources allocated, make sense, according to Özbudun-Demirer (2011), when judged against the background of a number of factors: the superior value accorded to research founded on biology and Western science, the effort to prove that the Turks were indigenous to Anatolia by associating them with the Caucasoid/Alpine race, and the attempt to confirm the claim that the founders of the ancient civilizations—Egyptian, Sumerian, and Hittite—were all Turkic in origin. Thus, the Turks were not to be seen as a "barbaric" people, but rather as the descendants of the founders of civilization. Hence the search for a basis of legitimacy for the unification of Anatoly, the Caucasian regions, and the Balkans—they were all descendants of common ancestors. The findings of the racial studies, were, therefore, a means for understanding and reconstructing history, and for constructing a shared past.

In the wake of World War II, research in physical anthropology diminished, as race theory was condemned and racist elements were rejected from participation in the activities of the Turkish historical society. Ethnographic or folklore studies were carried out both by amateurs and at the instigation of the regime. The regime's opportunity to educate both the people and the intelligentsia was through "Turkish circles," whose purpose was to engage with Turkish popular culture. Their activities included the collection and preservation of historical remains, language, and culture, and the ethnographic and ethnological study of diverse ethnic and cultural units. In addition, the ruling party created a network of the people's houses that shared the same purpose as that of the Turkish circles: to research, represent, and preserve products of local and popular culture, and to transmit and instill knowledge about Western culture and new technologies. The amateur ethnographers documented the "vanishing" rural life. It must be remembered, Özbudun-Demirer argues, that the amateur ethnographers never forgot that they were "agents of the Republic" much more than they were "objective researchers" (Özbudun-Demirer 2011, 125). It appears, then, that the nation-building project had two versions: the racial version, oriented chiefly to the construction of an imagined history, and the cultural version, oriented to the constitution of a unity within the plurality of people sharing the same living territory.

Ethnographic studies were also carried out on a relatively small scale. These were in fact defined as folklore studies, conducted not by professional anthropologists, but chiefly by historians. Between the 1940s and 1960s, studies of village life abounded, in the style of the rural community studies developed at Chicago University. For the most part, they were carried out by sociologists who had studied or specialized in North America, such as Boran and Berkes. Some of those engaged in this area of research were senior members of the ruling party or founders of scientific institutions and of scientific societies. For example, Boran gave up her academic career at the university to pursue political activity and became the leader of the Turkish Labor Party. The research projects were conducted with the aid of survey and fieldwork methodologies; the studies asked questions about the effects of urbanization and industrialization on the structures of communities and on other aspects of their lives. The Turkish regime was very concerned with the implications of modernization and Westernization processes for traditional society. It therefore supported research in impoverished suburbs of Ankara, a city that had undergone far-reaching transformations. Simultaneously, the rural sector remained a consistent object of research, which was mostly questionnaire-based and quantitative in nature. Encouraged by the various governments, Turkish universities became the underwriters of impressive research products, particularly in the fields of history, archeology, literature, and language. But even in the social sciences, the academic investment was noticeable: directed chiefly toward political aims and not pure research (Magnarella and Türkdoĝan 1976; Erdentuğ and Magnarella 2001; Tandoğan 2008; Özbudun-Demirer 2011).

The contribution of Turkish anthropology to republican nation building was manifest, therefore, in a number of phases. At the time of the dissolution of the Ottoman Empire, a discourse of evolutionary development, inspired by Western models, served the intelligentsia as a metaphor for the modernization of the Empire. During the period of the Second Constitution, the path was cleared for absorbing ideas from Western sociology, which was focused at that time on concepts such as development and modernization. Ottomanism retreated and was supplanted by ideas of creating a modern nation state. Ethnography was enlisted to this cause to construct and establish the "spirit" of the unified nations. With the establishment of the republic, physical anthropology dominated the academy, and race studies were conducted in the medical faculties. Between the 1920s and the 1930s, it was expected that the social sciences, anthropology included, would harness themselves to the realization of two goals—assisting the formation of a citizenry in line with the vision of the republic, and the Turkification of different ethnic groups. In the field, projects of collection and preservation were perceived as folklore and popular and national culture. Özbudun-Demirer claims that despite the plentiful resources allocated to anthropological research—for training, museums, laboratories, and field studies—anthropologists "[i]nstead of studying real human beings (physically and culturally) they seemed to have embarked upon *creating* citizens: 'Brachycephalic-Alpine-Turkish . . . *and* secular' a fact which renders it more appropriate to qualify the anthropological discourse of the formative years as rhetorical rather than scientific." (Özbudun-Demirer 2011, 128).

ISRAELIZATION OF ANTHROPOLOGY AND ANTHROPOLOGIZATION OF ISRAEL

The "anthropologization of Israel" refers to the process of anthropology's entering into the discourse about culture and society in Israel, the field's rising popularity, as well as the increase of knowledge about anthropology within and without the academy. The "Israelization of anthropology" means research at home on behalf of national goals or local weakened sectors within the society of Israel. The two expressions are not only a conceptual pair displaying an aesthetic symmetry: they occur simultaneously and reciprocally affect each other, allowing Israeli anthropology to be painted in its own unique colors.

In the early 1970s, we were forced to explain to our interlocutors what anthropology was; those who had already heard the term asked whether we studied skulls and bones. Since then, by means of a slow and gradual process, the field of social and cultural anthropology settled into Israeli society, mostly via the media; however, its presence today is negligible in comparison with other social science disciplines such as economics or psychology. The cinemas used to feature films whose protagonist was an anthropologist venturing on some research adventure into the jungle. A few anthropologists have been invited to respond in media forums on television or radio slots devoted to "exotic" practices or to "ethnic" groups. Phyllis Palgi was hosted on an episode of the television show *This Is Your Life*, in which she revealed the anthropological profession to a large public. Later, the new-journalism style used various interpretations of "anthropology" to denote any insight about human behavior, or in regard to a non-participant observer of human situations.[4] In recent years, Resling Publishing House has begun a (welcome) trend of publishing canonical anthropological works into Hebrew; despite the modest sales, these books have contributed to raising awareness about anthropology. Other publishers have added a number of translated works to the Hebrew bookshelf of anthropological writing. The main anthropologists translated have been Victor Turner, Claude Lévi-Strauss, Margaret Mead, Marvin Harris, and Clifford Geertz. The translation of anthropological literature from foreign languages into Hebrew began at the turn of the century and has continued until the present; the selections in each period reflect a variety of considerations: dominant ideologies, the popularity of the authors, and the publisher's agenda (Abuhav and Shilo 2011).

In the course of 2011, anthropology students and faculty formed a group they called "Anthropology Awakening," whose aim was to try to make anthropology more familiar to the general public and in public discourse. The first initiative in this activity was the launch of a website to serve as a platform for presenting anthropologists and their research to the general public, while attempting to disseminate awareness of the website and its content through the media, cultural, and educational institutions and so forth. At present, the site is home to more than eighty anthropologists. The second initiative of the group was to create a Facebook page on anthropology in Israel and elsewhere, called "Behevrat Ha'adam—In the Company of Men," and disseminate conference information, reports on anthropology, articles published by Israeli anthropologists or about Israel, original articles, and so forth. The page has two main aims: to form a community of anthropologists and lovers of anthropology, and to expose anthropology and the work it does to a wider audience. The page currently has more than 600 friends, from senior professors, through undergraduate students, to people unconnected to either anthropology or academe. The group's intention in the future is to offer a series of anthropological lectures to the general public, to build "a home for anthropology" that will serve as an open arena for anthropology.

In the past two decades, there has been a significant increase in the demand for anthropological studies, a rise in the number of anthropological studies, and, in general, a strengthening of the status of anthropology within the departments of sociology and anthropology in the academy. Nonetheless, in the past five years, there seems to be a decrease in interest in pursuing anthropology studies.

The fact that Israeli anthropology is conducted "at home" brings it closer to the public at large. If in the past the subject of Israeli anthropological research was the "Other" (the member of an "ethnic group," or a resident of a development town), today research focuses on "us"—the Israeli middle class. The potential reader is also the subject in studies about the average person: his or her military service (Lomsky-Feder and Ben-Ari 1999), what he or she eats (Tene, forthcoming), his or her residential neighborhood (Birenbaum-Carmeli 2001), the gifts he or she brings to a wedding (Abuhav 2010c), or the use of "key words" in children's communication (Katriel 1993). The degree of exposure and access to anthropology has risen by nearly every measure, yet its status does not equal that of the other social science disciplines.

The Israelization of anthropology is a process that embodies internal contradictions. On one hand, research at home has always been a characteristic of Israeli anthropologists. On the other hand, there have been critical voices heard of late, from some of the immigrants and some of the native anthropologists, calling for a refurbishing of this home. The adoption of approaches and schools of thought from Anglo-American centers, and their local naturalization without undergoing significant adaptations, leads to the obscuring of the unique Israeli characteristics of local anthropology. Yarden Enav-Weintraub has critiqued the view of the "Israeliness" of social anthropology in Israel (Enav-Weintraub 2007). The forces at work in both directions—the anthropologization of Israel and the Israelization of anthropology—have been both the cause and effect of the growing power of the discipline in the Israeli context. Concurrently, a distancing from nationalism is under way, as well as processes that bring world anthropology closer to Israel.

APPLIED ANTHROPOLOGY WITHIN AND WITHOUT THE ACADEMY

The first serious anthropological work to follow the pioneering work of Brauer and Patai began as applied research. Anthropologists performed jobs from the Jewish Agency and conducted studies with an applied orientation on the subjects of education and socialization. Later, when anthropology began to enter its institutional academic phase, the extra-academic studies almost disappeared, and the proportion of the non-applied studies within the academic sphere increased. As opposed to the United States (the source of inspiration for contemporary Israeli anthropology), there are no Israeli museums that employ anthropologists. The power and role of museum anthropology in America, in tandem with university anthropology, was equal to that of academic anthropology in the shaping of the discipline. In contrast, Israeli museums do not include anthropologists in their personnel, although the number of ethnic museums has grown in recent years, such as the museum for the heritage of Babylonian (Iraqi) Jewry, or the Center for the Heritage of Libyan Jews.

A number of anthropologists (Jeff Halper, Malka Shabtai, Yoni Mizrahi, etc.) attempted to establish a specialization in applied anthropology as part of the B.A. and M.A. programs at the Hebrew University, Ben Gurion University, Tel Aviv University, and Yezreel Valley College, but this attempt was short lived. In the world at large, and in Israel in particular, the prestige of applied anthropology is inferior to that of academic anthropology. Nevertheless, Kalifon (1997) an anthropologist who has practiced applied anthropology, argues that Israeli anthropology is, in essence, applied anthropology, even if never defined as such. Research at home can help shape policies, whether or not they have been commissioned by extra-academic bodies and organizations. By virtue of being "anthropology at home"—of the home and about the home—it raises questions regarding the here and now, which have an "applied" cast to them. It is true that in Israel the research frontier is often affected by whatever is defined as a social problem, but nevertheless, Israeli anthropology should not be seen as applied in nature, because it is not designed for utilitarian purposes. The availability of plentiful resources (especially those provided by American Jewish foundations) for the study of Ethiopian Jews who arrived in Israel in the 1990s attracted many anthropologists to become involved in research projects on the encounter between them and the Israeli society . However, most of the anthropologists' recommendations or the insights that could have been extracted from their work were never implemented. (The most notable of these studies were those by Salamon [1997–98, 1999]; Weil [1997]; Hertzog [2010]; Ben Ezer [2006]; and Shabtai 1999, 2001].)

BETWEEN THE GLOBAL AND THE LOCAL, CENTER AND PERIPHERY, METROPOLE AND PROVINCES

The tension between the metropole and the local and between the center and periphery is one of the central motifs of Israeli anthropology, and, in my own work, this is manifest in the context of the personal and professional identity of Israeli anthropologists and in the theoretical development of anthropology in the realms of research and teaching, for which the relations between the world centers and the Israeli periphery have been central. Most Israeli anthropologists were trained in anthropological centers abroad and view themselves as part of an international community of professionals with which they have aspired to connect and identify. The universities encouraged young researchers to go abroad to study either during or after their doctoral studies; they expected these young anthropologists to recharge, expand their horizons, and innovate. The connection to the scientific community provided them with an escape from local affiliations that seemed marginal and parochial. Anthropology, as an intellectual pursuit, drew them out of the local insular bubble in which they lived and connected them to a multicultural and universal project. At the same time, life in Israel guided their feelings of identification with and of enlistment on behalf of local goals, whether Zionist, national, or social. The tension between these two identities, the local and the international, fertilized the research. In wake of general processes of the dissolution of collective identities in Israeli society—among the veteran and the new, the subversive as well as the establishment anthropologists—there has been a distancing from local (national and Zionist) identities. Every time the conflict with the Palestinians flared up, in wars or uprisings (intifadas), the local community was forced to confront the challenge presented by the international anthropological community, which put its national identity to another test: the opposition to Israel's policies in the international academy led to an attempt to boycott Israeli scientists. Israeli anthropologists, like other scientists, faced the dilemma of identifying with the international community and participating in a self-boycott, or opposing and fighting the boycott despite their opposition to Israeli policies in respect to the Palestinians and the occupation.

Another variation on the opposition between the international and the local is the tension between center and periphery. The use of these terms in sociological literature, which had been widespread since the 1960s, has diminished due to critical-theoretical reasons. But despite criticism of these concepts, which focuses on their tautological distinctions (that which is in the center is defined as the center) that serve to enhance processes of marginalization of the marginal and reinforcement of stigma, I do find that in the disciplinary context, these terms contribute to the understanding of the processes of crystallization and continuity of Israeli anthropology. The local version of anthropology had migrated here from centers of knowledge, due to both pull and push factors—first from central Europe and later from Britain and America. Until the 1970s, the field did not find its own place and remained marginal wherever it attempted to take root. Over time, it adapted to its new homeland, and although this home skimped at providing resources for its sustenance, anthropology insisted on surviving. The transformations it underwent during its adaptation to the local context did not distance it from the Anglo-American center, which continued to provide the preferred and respected model of scientific theory and practice—a position it still holds today. In the arena of the IAA, this was clearly felt, for the IAA operates according to the organizational model of the AAA. Resources for research, decisions regarding the promotion of anthropologists in the organization, and models for promotion are all influenced by the center and dependent on it. The constant movement from the local center to world centers of knowledge enables updating and the rapid mobility of ideas and people, but this mutuality is not symmetrical. The center influences the periphery, and the local system is dependent on the world one.

The connection to world centers has led to Israeli academic institutions' adoption of those centers' organizational models. Such models have been the source of the Israeli academy's approach to training processes, promotion, specialization and differentiations, professional stratification and evaluation by colleagues, peer review, publication strategies, and more. The continual contact between overseas institutions and Israeli ones—via reciprocal visits, sabbatical leaves and post-doctoral fellowships, participation in conferences, and reading of publications—nourish the institutional similarities and perpetuate it. One can surmise that the close contact between the center and periphery is among the factors that prevent the parochialism and provincialism so feared by the early anthropologists and by the Israeli academy in general. However, because Israeli anthropology researches at home, the ties between Israeli anthropology and other peripheral anthropologies are weak. The few Israeli anthropologists who have studied non-Israeli societies maintain consistent ties with their colleagues through the mediation of the center (the AAA or the European Association for Social Anthropology).

ISRAELI ANTHROPOLOGY AND COLONIALISM

The relationship between anthropology and colonialism became almost a truism with the emergence and growth of post-colonial approaches. The issue of the validity of the statement that "anthropology is the handmaiden of colonialism" came up frequently in the conversations I had with my anthropologist interviewees, as well as in academic public contexts. A significant proportion of critical anthropology takes the connection between anthropology and colonialism as its point of departure; therefore, the relationship between the two in regard to Israeli anthropology deserves comment. Although this issue is very complex, I shall address a limited number of aspects in the present context, and point to a number of directions for further thought.

Said's book *Orientalism* (Said 1978) has contributed, inter alia, to a critical view of the social sciences and humanities and their role in shaping colonialist and Orientalist images. Those who are critical of Orientalist approaches have directed their spears at different targets: for our purposes, the discussion of ethnographic writing and the role of Orientalism in the production of the ethnographic text is the relevant one. It is here that the power relations between the colonizer and native, the Occidental and the Oriental, the modern and the traditional, the metropole and the periphery are embodied. Analyses in this vein conclude that Western colonial ethnography is tainted by epistemic violence that produces narratives that serve the colonialist's domination of his subjects. This appraisal has bred doubts about ethnography's claim of representing objective reality. Said, who viewed the social sciences as a source of hope for undermining the Orientalist gaze, was warmly embraced by anthropologists the world over, and was even invited as a guest of honor to the annual meetings of the IAA in 1999.

The critical discourse was also applied to the first Israeli anthropologists, who studied their own societies while attempting to adapt this discourse to Israeli reality and to the relationships between researchers and subjects in the context of this reality. Even the most critical analysts realize that colonial motives are not manifest explicitly and consciously; rather, the allegation is of echoes of colonialism within the ethnography and reverberations within discourse, apparent only in the conceptualization and observations of the studied reality. Colonialist premises are therefore likely to inform any one of the research arenas I surveyed: the motives and life course of anthropologists, the modes of production of ethnographic knowledge, and its products in research and teaching at the universities and in the IAA.

As a condition for discussing colonialism in Israeli anthropology, one must first clarify who the colonialist is and who the native is. Who is the dominator and who is the dominated? The identification of the colonial object is not a simple matter. Although the anthropology of the pre-state period took place within a formal and explicit political colonial context—the British Mandate for Palestine—British colonial anthropology did not take an interest in its subjects in Palestine, which did not become a destination for anthropological studies in the vein of British structural functionalism.

Another possible test is the analysis of the involvement of overseas philanthropic foundations and private capital in anthropological activity as a colonial practice. Israeli anthropology received donations from wealthy Jews in Europe and North America, who funded its activities even before the discipline was institutionalized as a knowledge field within the universities. In the 1930s at the Hebrew University, Brauer and Patai received research funds from the university's Friends associations in England, Canada, and the United States and also from the Foundation for Assisting Refugees from Germany. The donors were partially successful in their attempts to influence appointment policies, research directions and modes, as well as the setting of the research and academic agendas. The Hebrew University's Friends associations in England and the United States formulated the goal of supporting the study of Oriental Jewry, arguing that these cultures needed to be documented before they vanish, and invoking the ideological justification of enhancing the unity of the Jewish people by revealing the commonalities shared by the tribes and ethnic divisions of which the people of Israel are comprised.

A few decades later, this trend was reversed: the wealth of one Jewish magnate from overseas transformed the entire character of Israeli anthropology. The faces of Israeli anthropology changed in the late 1960s when the British Lord Bernstein decided to create a generous fund for anthropological research to help advance the fledgling state. In this respect, the money of wealthy overseas donors influenced and shaped the nature of that emergent anthropology. Although the donor did not intervene in determining the research topics, and even gave Gluckman and Marx carte blanche in deciding the research topics (most of which were focused on current problems and the national agenda), the motives behind this act of philanthropy were explicitly and unmistakably Zionist.

In my interviews with Israeli anthropologists, I sought to clarify whether the self-accounting of their life courses and personal drives gave any credence to the colonialist argument. To the critic's retrospective gaze, the choice of Zionism and nationalism may appear as a patently colonial starting point, but models that were appropriate for their time (until the mid-1920s) and place (the European anthropologists' view of the colonies) should not be automatically projected as is onto a different context. My work has shown the contrary—how anthropology was rejected because it was not sufficiently colonialist: the objects of research were not "primitive" enough to become subjects of a classic ethnographic study. Even when anthropologists undertook projects that were motivated by national sentiments and ideologies, their findings did not support the interests of the governing systems. The materials upon which the critics have based their claims are texts written by anthropologists, and the researchers' own identities. These claims are focused on the quasi-colonial relationships between Jewish/male/Ashkenazi anthropologists and their subjects—the "Oriental Jews" and the "Arabs." Orientalist images were indiscriminately projected onto the anthropological treatment of these categories, without adapting them to the research realities and factors such as authority and resources. (On the complexity of the Orientalist-native relationship, see, for example, Goldberg's [2004] discussion on the Mizrahi and the Orientalist.)

A strong statement about how problematic it is to project theories from one social reality onto another can be found in the work of Alatas about the relevance of Western social sciences to developing societies (Alatas 2001). In this framework, he questions the possibility of applying grand theories, such as those of Marx and Weber or postmodern approaches and the critique of Orientalism. Alatas advocates the importance of constructing a relevant theory that draws its concepts from existing theories but adapts them to the local historical contexts and to cultural practices—a maneuver that could place the relations of researchers and subjects in the relevant period in a different light. Although in Israel the research subjects were Oriental Jews and the researchers were Ashkenazi, the latter's identity did not deterministically and unambiguously shape their relations to the world. They evinced a basic attitude of empathy, concern, identification with, and solicitude toward the research subjects. At that time, the discussion of research–subject relations had not yet arisen; it would emerge in the 1980s and lead to questions of exploitation and power relations in the research relationship.

Another attempt to examine the colonialist nature of Israeli anthropology could draw on of Ben-Ari's observations (Ben-Ari 1998) about the anthropology of Asia. Ben-Ari points to a number of possible relationships between anthropology and colonialism: (1) anthropology as a discipline that produces science that is applicable to colonial policy, (2) links between anthropological theory and the needs of the colonial government, and (3) the role of anthropology in creating colonial discourse. Let us examine how Israeli anthropology can be characterized by each of these models.

The first model—creation of applicable science—is a crucial element of Israeli anthropology, beginning with the 1960s and that era's preoccupation with the settlement policy for the new immigrants, and ending with the continued support of the establishment that settled the waves of immigrants in the 1970s and 1990s. The policies of the settlement agencies, such as the Jewish Agency, formulated goals that were different from conventional colonialist goals. The structure of power relations enabled the Jewish Agency to impose control and power over the immigrants. Its policies, however, still cannot be called colonial in the manner of those of the European empires. Even if we accept the claim that the Anglo-American functionalist theories that took the brunt of the critique of scientific colonialism were ascendant in Israeli sociology in the 1960s, and, as Ram and others have argued, that they dictated the policy of "absorption of immigrants" during the years of state building, the picture in anthropology was a different one. Unlike the sociology of that era, the functionalism of Gluckman's Manchester school, which formed the theoretical foundation for a number of the Israeli anthropologists who contributed to settlement processes, did address dimensions of power and conflict in its analyses. The local anthropology challenged the automatic linking between functionalism and colonialism.

In regard to the second model, the image of anthropologists in the eyes of the new state's agencies was indeed that of cultural mediators suited to serve the state's purposes. But this was not the mission that the anthropologists took upon themselves.

In respect to the third model of the relationship—the role of anthropology in creating colonial discourse—Israeli anthropology employed the concepts of this discourse sparingly, beginning with the premises of the anthropologists' research and how they viewed their subjects, through the resistance to take part in the implementation of social policy, and ending with their written products.

I conclude, therefore, that the use of the term "colonial anthropology" is oversimplified and is not adequate for describing the complexity of the context of Israeli anthropology, nor can it serve as a lens with which to examine it. What is required is an open, multifaceted, and more subtle perspective. Nor is "colonialism" a uni-dimensional phenomenon. Thomas (1994) points to the fact that colonialism infiltrated every area of life—it pervaded the everyday, and not only via the actions of administrators, policymakers, and scientists. A complex viewpoint would deconstruct this concept and require us to indicate the way in which anthropological understanding is constructed within a colonialist context (the British Mandate, the funding by the Jewish Diaspora, settlement, nation-building projects, etc.).

The history of Israeli anthropology arising from the arena of university research and instruction is a far cry from anything that could be described as a prosperous, influential, or powerful field. On the contrary, the story of anthropology at the universities is one of a marginal discipline, which appears as a sporadic thought and then dissipates. When it finally becomes palatable and is incorporated into the academy, it is carried at first by individual, lone anthropologists. Anthropology's breakthrough occurred at a time when awareness of the problems dealt with by ethnographic research began to grow. A triad of knowledge, power, and a discipline that supports exploitation and domination cannot be said to exist in Israeli anthropology, because at least one of the elements is missing. An opportunity for such a mechanism to have worked might have developed in the 1960s, but there were not enough anthropologists active on the scene to achieve such an end. When a supporting system was in place, there was no knowledge and therefore no power; when there was power and knowledge, there was no supporting system.

The discussion contesting the adequacy of the colonial paradigm for describing the Israeli case also teaches us about the care required in a retrospective reading of history. Retrospective reading is a contemporary interpretation of a historical scientific discourse, which is embedded in a particular context. The eagerness to locate power and exploitation in the motives of scientists clouds the anthropological instinct to attempt to understand social phenomena in their social and historical context. One cannot underestimate the usefulness of critical gaze and reflexivity, yet findings must rest on stable and substantive grounds and be reflective of the relevant era.

ANTHROPOLOGY "ON BEHALF OF" AND ANTHROPOLOGY "FOR THE BENEFIT OF"

Engaging with issues of identity, which has been one of the focuses of my work, involves observing a knowledge field from a personal and human perspective. What underlies the anthropological project? Who are its carriers? What is their driving force? What I have learned is that the anthropologists whom I studied work "on behalf of" and not "for the benefit of." They practice a concerned, engaged anthropology that enlists itself on behalf of—and not "for the benefit of"—national, social, or other causes.

Like everyone else, anthropologists are subject to uncontrollable and random processes, which often determine the direction in which their career develops, but they possess more power and agency than is attributed to them by critics. With some exceptions, most have taken advantage of the privilege of choosing which projects to pursue and which to reject, of selecting from among funding sources for their studies, and of refusing projects and assignments whose goals were in conflict with their ethical principles, policy values, or ideological beliefs as practitioners. Each has his or her own personal agenda that he or she wished to advance, as well as a particular and unique drive composed of the singular mix that makes each individual what he or she is. At the same time, an organized framework of constraints and conditions places limitations on researchers. Both these forces are simultaneously at work, and the tension between the two elements produces the differences, enables innovative anthropology, and evokes the greatest interest.

The agenda of Israeli anthropologists is liberal; is sensitive to minority rights, individual rights, and human rights; and involves enlistment to public campaigns with an ethical focus. These characteristics are largely due to the anthropological training in the educational and professional matrices of U.S. and British anthropology. A minor sector of Israeli anthropology can be described as politically militant. These concerns are reflected in the choice of research fields and teaching subjects, in scientific and academic activity, in the connections forged with social movements in Israel and overseas, and in the IAA's practice of publishing public statements and social-political declarations.

The apparent homogeneity of this overall picture does not tell the whole story. Even if the veteran anthropologists share much with the younger generation, there are still points of controversy separating them. What direction will these controversies take? Will a "new anthropology" arise in Israel?

Israeli anthropology develops step by step, bringing more and more individuals to its company. And it offers unique and fresh perspectives to current society and the future Israeli society.

APPENDIX

List of IAA Guests by Year

1975	Alex Weingrod
1976	Cyril S. Belshaw
1977	David Schneider
1979	Eric Wolf
1980	Victor Turner
1981	Barbara Myerhoff
1982	Gerald D. Berreman
1985	Dale F. Eickelman
1986	Mark Nathan Cohen
1987	Bruce Kapferer
1988	Barbara Kirshenblatt-Gimblett
1989	Michael Silverstein
1990	Vincent Crapanzano
1991	Byron J. Good
1993	Sherry B. Ortner
1994	Nancy Scheper-Hughes
1995	Ulf Hannerz
1996	Arthur Kleinman
1997	Arjun Appadurrai
1998	Kirin Narayan
1999	Edward Said

2000	Daniel Miller
2002	Jean Comaroff
2003	Valentine Daniel
2004	Lawrence Cohen
2005	Michael Herzfeld
2006	Akhil Gupta
2007	Emiko Ohnuki-Tierney
2008	Russell Bernard
2009	Michael Lambek
2010	Matti Bunzl
2011	Janet Carsten
2012	Fred R. Myers
2013	Bruce Kapferer

NOTES

CHAPTER 1

1. Marta Topel, a student of Cardoso de Oliviera, focuses her doctoral dissertation (1998) on the Jewish identity of many Israeli anthropologists and on the way in which Israeli anthropology addresses problems of ethnicity and nationalism, and characterizes the community of Israeli anthropologists as one of scientists on the periphery addressing this community's connection to the centers of anthropology.

CHAPTER 2

1. Erich Brauer, memo concerning the creation of an ethnological collection, 1938, Hebrew University archive, Brauer file.
2. University Senate, June 25, 1939, Hebrew University archive, Brauer file.
3. For an extensive discussion of Patai, see Hirschler (1983); Schwarzbaum (1983); Loewe and Hoffman (2002); and Schrire (2010). For an autobiographic perspective, see Patai (1992).
4. R. Patai, memo concerning the need to study the social anthropology of the Jews, November 4, 1943, Hebrew University archive, Patai file; R. Patai, memo concerning the ethnological study of Jewish ethnic groups in the Orient, October 24, 1944, Hebrew University archive, Patai file.
5. Vaada Matmedet, meeting 7, January, 7, 1949, Hebrew University archive.
6. Letter from S. D. Goitein to Patai April 36, 1949, Hebrew University archive, Patai file.
7. *Ukhluseinu ba-aretz* (Ben Zvi 1929).
8. Brauer to Schocken, October 4, 1940, Hebrew University archive, Brauer file.
9. Letter from Roberto Bachi (substitute chair for the social sciences committee) to the rector, November 27, 1950, Hebrew University archive, file 2256.
10. April 24, 1950, Hebrew University archive, file 2276,
11. The university to Guy de Rothschild, director of the Friends of the University in Paris, September 2, 1960, Hebrew University archive, file 26610.
12. Studies published by the center: Rosenfeld (1958, 1964a, 1964b, 1968).
13. Additional sources on the Bernstein project: Marx (1975), Goldberg (1976), Van Teeffelen (1977), Shokeid (1976, 1988/9), Shokeid and Deshen (1980), Ben-Ari (1997), and Handelman and Evens (2006).
14. The Mexican anthropologist Battalla (1990) also used the metaphor of marriage and couple pairing to describe the relations between anthropology and the state in Mexico.
15. Letter from Eric Cohen, Dean of the Social Sciences to the Rector, June 27, 1982, Hebrew University archive, Patai file.

16. For more on the contribution of the Bernstein Project and the Manchester school to Israeli anthropology, see the section "The Bernstein Project: Max Gluckman."
17. Israel Anthropological Association newsletter, 1975. p. 2.

CHAPTER 3

1. For a detailed account of the IAA annual meetings, see Abuhav (2005b).
2. Shokeid discusses this indirectly in a chapter of his book titled "Who Is Afraid of Ethnography?" (Shokeid 2002, 191–203).
3. See the list of IAA guests by year in the appendix.
4. A number of invited guests have refused to come because of political inclinations and criticism of Israeli occupation, of its policy toward the Palestinians, or due to a plain fear to visit in a war zone. In the midst of the Second Intifada, Arjun Appadurrai lectured at the annual meeting, traveled to Egypt for a brief visit, and was supposed to return to Israel for a round of lectures at the universities. However, he cancelled his return and travelled directly back to the United States, because of his family's insistence that he put his personal security first.

CHAPTER 4

1. Alex Weingrod to Harvey Goldberg, 1999.
2. Deshen gave this speech at a memorial event for Yitzhak Eilam at the Hebrew University in the spring of 1978. Citations are from this speech.
3. See, for example, the works by Yacobson (1987), Simhai (2000), and Maoz (2002).
4. The interviewees used the concept of multiculturalism' as a central concept. They did not distinguish between multiculturalism and a multicultural society. I use the concepts interchangeably.
5. The founding of the Kaplan School, July 16, 1953, Hebrew University archive, Kaplan School file.
6. Poznanski to Hoffman, July 7, 1952, Hebrew University archive, the Faculty of Social Sciences file.
7. The document bears no date. Because Patai was active in Israel until 1949, I assume he composed this document at the beginning of the 1950s, when he was abroad but still exercising influence on affairs in Israel.
8. See my discussion in chapter 2 of the development of anthropology in the universities in the 1930s.
9. See Forum of Social and Cultural Studies (2002a, 290–91), Tzur (2003), and Shavit (2003).
10. See, for example, Bilu's Ph.D. dissertation (Bilu 1978).
11. For further discussion of the Jewish component in anthropologists' identities, see Feldman (2004) and Frank (1997).
12. On the problematic blend of Israeli anthropology with sociology, see Goldberg and Bram (2007).

CHAPTER 5

1. For a summary discussion on these processes in worldwide and American anthropology, see Darnell (2001) and Barnard (2000).

2. See Aref Abu Rabia's interview of Marx in its English version (Abu-Rabia 2001).
3. Slouschz was an ethnographer, linguist, literary scholar, and archeologist who contributed much to each of these fields in the Jewish and Eretz-Israeli context. For more, see Goldberg (2004).
4. In this pseudo-anthropological style of journalism, the reporter sits in the café, for example, and observes a conversation at the next table. In his own eyes, he is an anthropologist for the moment. On the link between anthropology and the representation of the development towns in the media, see Yassif (1998).

BIBLIOGRAPHY

Abarbanel, Jay S. 1972. *The Co-operative Farmer, and the Welfare State.* Manchester: Manchester University Press.

Abu El-Haj, Nadia. 2001. *Facts on the Ground: Archaeological Practice and Territorial Self-Fashioning in Israeli Society.* Chicago: University of Chicago Press.

Abuhav, Orit. 2003. "Pnei Adam: Al Trumtam shel Erich Brauer Veraphael Patai Leheker Ha'antropologia shel Hayehudim [The Human Countenance: The Contribution of the Ethnologists Erich Brauer and Raphael Patai to the Anthropology of the Jews]." *Mehkarei Yerushlaim Befolklore Yehudi* 22: 159–77.

———. 2004. "Anthropology in Israel: Professionals in Stormy Days." *History of Anthropology Newsletter* 31 (2): 9–16.

———. 2005a. "Antropologia Behithavut: Hauniversita Ha'ivrit Umada Ha'adam [Anthropology in Process: Hebrew University and the Human Science]." In *Toldot Ha'universita Ha'ivrit Beyrushalayim,* edited by Hagit Lavski, 573–93. Jerusalem: Magnes.

———. 2005b. "Antropologia Ve'antropologim Be'israel: Mabat Mibifnim [Anthropology and Anthropologists in Israel: Looking from the Inside]." PhD thesis, Hebrew University, Jerusalem.

———. 2005c. "Raphael Patai." In *Encyclopedia of Modern Jewish Cultures,* edited by Glenda Abramson, Vol. 2, 657-58. Oxford: Routledge.

———. 2008. Erich Brauer: "Ha'etnolog Ha'rishon shel Medinat Israel" [Erich Brauer: "The First Ethnologist of Israel"]. Tel Aviv: Mofet.

———. 2010a. "Israeli Social Anthropology—Origins, Characteristics and Contributions." In *Perspectives on Israeli Anthropology,* edited by Esther Hertzog, Orit Abuhav, Harvey Goldberg, and Emanuel Marx, 1–16. Detroit: Wayne State University Press.

———. 2010b. *Karov Etzel Aherim: Hitpatkhut Ha'antropologia [In the Company of Others].* Be'israel: Resling.

———. 2010c. "Wedding Gifts: The Wrapping and Content." In *Perspectives on Israeli Anthropology,* edited by Esther Hertzog, Orit Abuhav, Harvey Goldberg, and Emanuel Marx, 235–58. Detroit: Wayne State University Press.

Abuhav, Orit, Esther Hertzog, Harvey Goldberg, and Emanuel Marx, eds. 1998. *Israel—Antropologia Mekomit [Israel—Local Anthropology].* Tel Aviv: Tcherikover.

Abuhav, Orit, and Gila Shilo. 2011. "Language Choice, Nationalism and Ideology: The Anthropological Texts Translated to Hebrew as a Case Study." *Annual of Language & Politics and Politics of Identity* 5: 73–90.

Abu-Rabia, Aref. 2001. "The Long Walk III—Pastoral Nomads and Anthropology: An Interview with Emanuel Marx." *Pastoral People* 5 (1): 7–27.

———. 2009. "Childbirth in a Traditional Bedouin Society." In *Perspectives on Israeli Anthropology,* edited by Esther Hertzog, Orit Abuhav, Harvey Goldberg, and Emanuel Marx, 453–65. Detroit: Wayne State University Press.

Agar, Michael H. 1996. *The Professional Stranger: An Informal Introduction to Ethnography.* New York: Academic Press.

Alatas, Sayed F. 2001. "The Study of the Social Sciences in Developing Societies: Towards an Adequate Conceptualization of Relevance." *Current Sociology* 49 (2): 1–19.

Al-Haj, Majid, Michael Saltman, and Zvi Sobel, eds. 2005a. *Social Critique and Commitment: Essays in Honor of Henry Rosenfeld.* Lanham: University Press of America.

———. 2005b. "Henry Rosenfeld: Some Signposts and Bibliography." In *Social Critique and Commitment: Essays in Honor of Henry Rosenfeld,* edited by Majid Al-Haj, Michael Saltman, and Zvi Sobel, 345–55. Lanham: University Press of America.

Almagor, Uri. 1978. *Pastoral Partners: Affinity and Bond Partnership among the Dassanetch of South-West Ethiopia.* Manchester: Manchester University Press.

Almog, Oz. 2000. *The Sabra: The Creation of the New Jew.* Berkeley: University of California Press.

Aronoff, Myron. 1974. *Frontiertown.* Manchester: Manchester University Press.

Asad, Talal. 1975. "Anthropological Texts and Ideological Problems: An Analysis of Cohen on Arab Villages in Israel." *Economy and Society* 4: 251–81.

Avieli, Nir. 2011. *Rice Talks: A Culinary Ethnography of Hoi An, Vietnam.* Bloomington: Indiana University Press.

Avruch, Kevin A. 1981. *American Immigrants in Israel: Social Identities and Change.* Chicago: Chicago University Press.

Baldwin, Elaine. 1972. *Differentiation and Co-operation in an Israeli Veteran Moshav.* Manchester: Manchester University Press.

Barkan, Elazar. 1992. *The Retreat of Scientific Racism: Changing Concepts of Race in Britain and the United States between the World Wars.* Cambridge: Cambridge University Press.

Barnard, Alan. 2000. *History and Theory in Anthropology.* Cambridge: Cambridge University Press.

Bar-On, Dan. 2008. *The Other within Us: Constructing Jewish-Israeli Identity.* Cambridge: Cambridge University Press.

Bar-Yosef, Ofer, and Amihai Mazar. 1982. "Israeli Archaeology." *World Archaeology* 13 (3): 310–23.

Barzilai, Sarit. 2004. *Lifrotz Mea She'arim* [To Storm a Hundred Gates]. Tel Aviv: Yediot Ahronot.

Basker, Eileen, Barbara Beran, and Moris Kleinhauz. 1982. "A Social Science Perspective on the Negotiations of a Psychiatric Diagnosis." *Social Psychiatry* 17: 53–58.

Battala, Guillermo Bonfi. 1990. "Problems Conjugales? Una Hipótesis Sobre las Relaciones del Estado y la Antropologia Social en México." In *A Antropologia na América Latina,* edited by George Cerqueria Leite Zarur. Mexico: Instituto Panamericano de Geografia e História.

Behar, Ruth. 1996. *The Vulnerable Observer: Anthropology that Breaks Your Heart.* Boston: Beacon Press.

Bellis, James M. 1978. Review of *Anthropologists on Israel: A Case Study in the Sociology of Knowledge,* by T. Van Teeffelen. *American Anthropologist* 80: 706–8.

Ben Amos, Dan. 1990. "Jewish Studies and Jewish Folklore." In *Proceedings of the 10th World Congress of Jewish Folklore,* Vol. II, Section D, 1–21.

Ben-Ari, Eyal. 1987. "On Acknowledgements in Ethnographies." *Journal of Anthropological Research* 43 (1): 63–84.

———. 1997. "Anthropology in Israel." *American Anthropological Association Newsletter,* January, 37–38.

———. 1998. "Colonialism, Anthropology and the Politics of Professionalization." In *Anthropology and Colonialism in East and Southwest Asia: A Japanese and Dutch Experience,* edited by Jan Van Bremen and Akitoshi Shimizu. Honolulu: University of Hawaii Press.

———. 2010. "Mask and Soldering: The Israeli Army and the Palestinian Uprising." In *Perspectives on Israeli Anthropology*, edited by Esther Hertzog, Orit Abuhav, Harvey Goldberg, and Emanuel Marx, 335–50. Detroit: Wayne State University Press.

Ben-Ari, Eyal, and Yoram Bilu, eds. 1997. *Grasping Land: Space and Place in Contemporary Israeli Discourse and Experience*. Albany: State University of New York Press.

Ben-Ari, Eyal, and Edna Lomski-Feder, eds. 2000. *The Military and Militarism in Israeli Society*. Albany: State University of New York Press.

Ben David, Joseph. 1963. *Rural Planning and Village Community in Israel*. Paris: NESCO.

———. 1964. "Mada Be'ertz Ktana" [Science in a Small State] *Ha'universita* 10 (2): 14–17.

Ben-Ezer, Gadi. 2006. *The Migration Journey: The Ethiopian Jewish Exodus*. New Brunswick: Transaction.

Ben Yehuda, Nachman. 1997. "The Dominance of the External: Israeli Sociology." *Contemporary Sociology* 26 (3): 271–75.

Ben Ze'ev, Efrat. 2000. *Narratives of Exile: Palestinian Refugees Reflections on Three Villages: Irat Haifa, Ein Hawd and Ijzim*. Oxford: Oxford University Press.

Ben Zvi, Itzhak. 1929. *Ukhluseinu ba-aretz [Our Populatiod in the Land]*. Warsaw: Hava'ad Hapoel shel Brit Hanoar ve "Merkaz Ha'alutz" Ha'olami.

Bernstein, Dvora. 1978. "Hasotzyologia koletet et ha'aliya [The Sociology Absorbs the Aliya]." *Mahbarot Lemehkr Ulebikoret* 1 :5–19.

Bilu, Yoram. 1978. "Psikhiatria Mesoratot Be'israel [Traditional Psychiatry in Israel]." PhD thesis, Hebrew University, Jerusalem.

———. 1980. "The Moroccan Demon in Israel: The Case of 'Evil Spirit Diseases'." *Ethos* 8 (1): 24–38.

———. 1990. "Jewish Moroccan 'Saint Impresarios' in Israel: A Stage-Developmental Perspective." *Psychoanalytic Study of Society* 15: 247–69.

———. 2000. *Without Bounds: The Life and Death of Rabbi Ya'aqov Wasana*. Detroit: Wayne State University Press.

Bilu, Yoram, and Eyal Ben-Ari. 1997. "Kadosh Betzemtai Mashma'ut" [Sacred in Interpretations' Junction]. In *Mitos Vezikaron*, edited by David Ohana and Robert Wistrich, 290–303. Jerusalem: Van Leer.

Bilu, Yoram, and Yehuda C. Goodman. 2010. "'What Does the Soul Say?': Metaphysical Uses of Facilitated Communication in the Jewish Ultra-Orthodox Community." In *Perspectives on Israeli Anthropology*, edited by Esther Hertzog, Orit Abuhav, Harvey Goldberg, and Emanuel Marx, 529–55. Detroit: Wayne State University Press.

Bird, Nurit. 1982. "'Inside' and 'Outside' in Kinship Usage: The Hunter-Gatherer Naiken of South India." *Cambridge Anthropology* 7 (1–2): 47–57.

Bird-David, Nurit. 1994. "Sociality and Immediacy: Or, Past and Present Conversations on Bands." *Man*, n.s., 29 (3): 583–603.

Bird-David, Nurit, and Asaf Darr. 2009. "Commodity, Gift and the Mass-Gift: On Gift-Commodity Hybrids in Advanced Mass Consumption Cultures." *Economy and Society* 38: 304–25.

Birenbaum-Carmeli, Daphna. 2001. "Between Individualism and Collectivism: The Case of a Middle Class Neighborhood in Israel." *International Journal of Sociology and Social Policy* 21 (11–12): 1–25.

Birenbaum-Carmeli, Daphna, and Yoram S. Carmeli, eds. 2010. *Kin, Gene, Community*. New York: Berghahn.

Boas, Franz. 1911. *The Mind of Primitive Man*. New York: Macmillan.

———. 2004. *Anthropology and the Modern Life*. New Brunswick: Transaction.

Boissevain, Jeremy. 1974. "Toward the Sociology of Social Anthropology." *Theory and Society* 1: 211–30.

Borofsky, Robert. 2002. "The Four Subfields: Anthropologists as Mythmakers." *American Anthropologist* 104 (2): 463–80.

Bošković, Aleksander, ed. 2008. *Other People's Anthropology: Ethnographic Practice on the Margins*. New York: Berghahn.

Bourdieu, Pierre. 1984. *Distinctions: A Social Critique of the Judgment of Taste*. Cambridge: Harvard University Press.

Bowman, Glenn. 2012. "Nationalizing and Denationalizing the Sacred: Shrines and Shifting Identities in the Israeli-Occupied Territories." In *Sacred Space in Israel and Palestine: Religion and Politics*, edited by Yitzhak Reiter, Leonard Hammer, and Marshall Breger, 195-227. New York: Routledge.

Brauer, Erich. 1925. *Züge aus der Religion der Herero: ein Beitrag zur Hamitenfrage, Institut de Volkerkunde, Erste Reihne: Ethnographie und Ethnologie*. Leipzig: R. Voitländers Verlag.

———. 1928-1935. *Personal Diary*. Jerusalem: National Library.

———. 1934. *Ethnologie der jemenitischen Juden*. Kulturgeschichtliche Bibliothek, 1st series (Ethnologische Bibliothek), Vol. 7. Heidelberg: Carl Winter.

———. 1938. *Denksxhrift: über die Errichtung einer Juedischen Ethmologischen Saalung*. Proposal, found in archive.

———. 1947. *Yehudei Kurdistan* [The Jews of Kurdistan]. Jerusalem: Hamchon Haweretzyisraeli Lefolklor Ve'etnologiya. [Heb.]

———. 1993. *The Jews of Kurdistan*. Edited by Raphael Patai. Jewish Folklore and Anthropology Series. Detroit.

Brawer-Ben David, Orit. 1998. "Hevra Veteva Betiyulei Ha'hevra Lehaganat Hateva [Society and Nature in Hahevra Lehaganat Hateva Treks]." In *Israel—Antropologia Mekomit*, edited by Orit Abuhav et al., 451–82. Tel Aviv: Tcherikocer.

Brettell, Caroline B., ed. 1993. *When They Read What We Write*. Westport: Bergin and Garvey.

Broshi, Magen. 1987. "Religion, Ideology, and the Politics and Their Impact on Palestinian Archaeology." *Israel Museum Journal* 6: 17–32.

Bruner, Edward M. 1986. "Introduction to the Anthropology of Experience." In *The Anthropology of Experience*, edited by Edward M. Bruner and Victor Turner, 3–30. Urbana: University of Illinois Press.

Bucher, Rue, and Anselm Strauss. 1951/1966. "Professions in Process." In *Professionalization*, edited by H. M. Vollmer and D. L. Milles, 185–96. Englewood Cliffs: Prentice Hall.

Bunzl, Matti. 2003. "*Völkerpsychologie* and German-Jewish Emancipation." In *Worldly Provincialism: German Anthropology in the Age of Empire*, edited by H. Glenn Penny and Matti Bunzl, 47–85. Ann Arbor: University of Michigan Press.

Cardoso de Oliviera, Roberto. 2000. "Peripheral Anthropologies 'versus' Central Anthropologies." *Journal of Latin American Anthropology* 4 (2); 5 (1): 10–30.

Carmeli, Yoram S. 1987. "Played by Their Own Play: Fission and Fusion in British Circuses." *Sociological Review* 35 (4): 744–74.

Carmeli, Yoram S., and Kalman Appelbaum. 2004. *Consumption and Market Society in Israel*. Oxford: Berg Publishers.

Carmi, Shulamit, and Henry Rosenfeld. 1979. "Nichus Emtza'im Tziburiyim vema'amad Beynoni Totzar Hamedina [Appropriating of Public Means and Middle Class Made by the State]," *Makhbarot Lemekhkar Ubikoret* 2: 43-83.

———. 2010. "Israel's Political Economy and the Widening Class Gap between Its Two National Groups." In *Perspectives on Israeli Anthropology*, edited by Esther Hertzog,

Orit Abuhav, Harvey Goldberg, and Emanuel Marx, 377–412. Detroit: Wayne State University Press.

Chambers, Lain. 1994. *Migrancy, Culture, Identity.* London: Routledge.

Clifford, James, and George E. Marcus, eds. 1986. *Writing Culture: The Poetic and Politics of Ethnography.* Berkeley: University of California Press.

Cohen, Abner. 1965. *Arab Border Village in Israel: A Study of Community and Change in Social Organization.* Manchester: Manchester University Press.

Cohen, Eric. 1968. "Comments on: 'The Social Responsibility of the Social Scientist,' by Gutorm Gjessing; 'New Proposals for Anthropologists,' by Kathleen Gough; 'Is Anthropology Alive?' by Gerald Berreman." *Current Anthropology* 9 (5): 410.

———. 1971. "Arab Boys and Tourist Girls in a Mixed Jewish-Arab Community." *International Journal of Comparative Sociology* 12: 217–33.

———. 1988. "Qualitative Sociology in Israel-A Brief Survey." *Qualitative Sociology* 11 (1–2): 88–98.

———. 2000. *The Commercialization of Craft of Thailand Hill Tribes and Lowland Villages.* Richmond Surrey: Curzon.

———. 2007. "Youth Tourists in Acre: From a Disturbance to Initiation into Life-Long Preoccupation." In *The Study of Tourism: Anthropological and Sociological Beginnings,* edited by Dannison Nash, 50–59. Amsterdam: Elsevier.

Colligan, Sumi. 1980. "Religion, Nationalism and Ethnicity in Israel: The Case Study of the Karaite Jews." PhD dissertation, Princeton University.

Collins, Randall. 1990. "Changing Conceptions in the Sociology of the Professions." In *The Formation of Professions,* edited by Rolf Torsteindahl and Michael Burrage, 11–29. London: Sage.

Cottrell, Leonard S., and Eleanor B. Sheldon. 1964."Problems of Collaboration between Social Scientists and Practicing Professionals." *Annals of the American Academy of Political and Social Sciences* 346: 121–31.

Dalshheim, Joyce. 2011. *Unsettling Gaza: Secular Liberalism, Radical Religion, and the Israeli Settlement Project.* Oxford: Oxford University Press.

Danziger, Gilad. 1994. "The Study of British and Israeli Race and Ethnic Relations, 1950–1970: A Comparative Analysis." PhD thesis, London School of Economics and Political Studies, University of London.

Darnell, Regna. 1971. "The Professionalization of American Anthropology: A Case Study in the Sociology of Knowledge." *Social Sciences Information* 10 (2): 83–103.

———. 1974. "The Nature of Anthropology." In *Readings in the History of Anthropology,* edited by Regna Darnell, 11–18. New York: Harper and Row.

———. 1998. *And Along Came Boas. Amsterdam:* John Benjamins.

———. 2001. *Invisible Genealogies: A History of Americanist Anthropology.* Lincoln: University of Nebraska Press.

Department of Sociology and Anthropology. 1971. Tochnit Limudai Antropologia [Anthropology Program]. Jerusalem: Hebrew University.

Deshen, Shlomo. 1970. *Immigrant Voters in Israel.* Manchester: Manchester University Press.

———. 1979. "Ha'antropologim Veheker Hatarbuyot shel Edot Hamizrah [The Anthropologists and the Study of the Cultures of the Eastern Ethnic Groups]." *Peamim* 1: 76–84.

———. 1992. *Blind People: The Private Life of Sightless Israelis.* Albany: State University of New York Press.

Deshen, Shlomo, Charles S. Liebman, and Moshe Shokeid, eds. 1995. *Israeli Judaism: The Sociology of Religion in Israel.* New Brunswick: Transaction.

Deshen, Shlomo, and Moshe Shokeid, eds. 1974. *The Predicament of Home Coming.* Ithaca: Cornell University Press.

———. 1984. *Yehudei Hamizrah* [The Jews of the Middle East]. Tel Aviv: Schoken.

Deutsch, Nathaniel, and S. An-Sky. 2011. *The Jewish Dark Continent: Life and Death in the Russian Pale of Settlement.* Cambridge: Harvard University Press.

Diamond, Stanley. 1957. "Kibbutz and Stetl: The History of an Idea." *Social Problems* 5: 71–90.

———. ed. 1980. *Anthropology: Ancestors and Heirs.* The Hague: Mouton.

Dominguez, Virginia. 1989. *People as Subject, People as Object: Selfhood and Peoplehood in Contemporary Israel.* Madison: University of Wisconsin Press.

———. 2013. "Falling in Love with a Criminal? On Immersion and Self-Restraint." In *Ethnographic Encounters in Israel: Poetics and Ethics of Fieldwork,* edited by Fran Markowitz, 201–20. Bloomington: Indiana University Press.

Durkheim, Emil. 1915. *The Elementary Forms of Religious Life.* London: Allan and Anwin.

———. 1958. *Professional Ethics and Civic Morals.* New York: Glencoe.

Edgar, Andrew, and Peter Sedgwick, eds. 2000. *Cultural Theory: The Key Concepts.* London: Routledge.

Eilam, Itzhak. 1972. *The Social and Sexual Roles of Hima Women: A Study of Nomadic Cattle Breeders in Nyabushozi County.* Manchester: Manchester University Press.

———. 1980. Hagruzinim Be'israel: Heibetim Anropologiyim [The Georgian in Israel: Anthropological Aspects]. Jerusalem: Hebrew University.

Eisenstadt, Shmuel Noah. 1949. "Ha'antropologia Ha'hevratit—Likvi'at Mekoma Bein Madai Ha'hevra [The Social Anthropology—Its Status among the Social Sciences]." *Eyun* 1 (4): 286–306.

———. 1954. *The Absorption of Immigrants.* London: Routledge and Kegan Paul.

———. 1964. "Ha'mehkar Ha'antropologi shel Hevrot Murkavot." *Keshet* 6 (2): 137–52.

———. 1973. *Ha'hevra Ha'yisraelit—Reka, Hitpatkhut and Be'ayot* [Israeli Society—Background, Developments and Problems]. Jerusalem: Magnes.

Eisikovits, Rivka A. 1983. "No Exit: Residential Treatment and the 'Sick-Role' Trap." *Child Care Quarterly* 12 (1): 36–44.

———. 2008. *Immigrant Youth Who Excel: Globalization's Uncelebrated Heroes.* Charlotte: Information Age.

Efron, John M. 1994. *Defenders of the Race: Jewish Doctors and Race Science in Fin-de-Siècle Europe.* New Haven: Yale University Press.

El-Or, Tamar. 1994. *Educated and Ignorant: Ultraorthodox Jewish Women and Their World.* Boulder: L. Rienner.

———. 1998. *Bapessach Haba: Nashim Ve'oryanut Batzionut Ha'datit* [Next Pessach: Literacy and Identity of Young Religious Zionist Women]. Tel Aviv: Am Oved.

———. 2001. "Tna'im shel Ahava: Avodat Ha'imahut Sviv Hamahane [Conditions of Love: Motherhood Work around the Camp]." *Teoria Ubikoret* 19 (79): 114.

———. 2002. *Next Year I Will Know More: Literacy and Identity among Young Orthodox Women in Israel.* Detroit: Wayne State University Press.

———. 2006. *Mekomot shemurim* [Reserved Seats: Gender, Religion and Ethnicity in Contemporary Israel]. Tel Aviv: Am Oved.

———. 2012. "The Soul of the 'Biblical Sandal': On Anthropology and Style." *American Anthropologist* 114 (3): 433–45.

Enav-Weintraub, Yarden. 2007. "From 'Israeli Anthropology' to 'Anthropology of Israeliness'." In *Reflection of Man,* edited by Radmila Lorencova and Jennifer Spiers, 35–53. Praha: ERMAT.

Epstein, Shifra. 1983. "The Celebration of a Contemporary Purim in the Bobover Hasidic Community." PhD dissertation, University of Michigan.

Erdentuğ, Aygen. 1998. "The Pioneering Anthropologists of Turkey: Personal Profiles in Socio-Political Context." *Turkish Study Association Bulletin* 22 (2): 13–44.

Erdentuğ, Aygen, and Paul Magnarella. 2001. "Turkish Social Anthropology since the 1979s." *Oriental Anthropologist* 1 (1).

Evens, Terence. M. S. 1995. *Two Kinds of Rationality: Kibbutz Democracy and Generational Conflict.* Minneapolis: University of Minnesota Press.

Faist, Thomas. 1997. "The Crucial Meso-Level." In *International Migration, Mobility and Development: Multidisciplinary Perspectives,* edited by Tomas Hammar et al., 187–217. New York: Berg.

Falk, Raphael. 2006. *Tziyonut Vehabiologia shel Hayehudim* [Zionism and the Biology of the Jews]. Tel Aviv: Resling.

Feige, Michael. 1998. "Archeologia, Antroplogia Ve'itzuvo shel Hamakom Ha'israeli [Archaeology, Anthropology and the Shape of Israeli Space]." *Zion* 63 (4): 441–59.

Feldman, Jackie. 2008. *Between the Death Pits and the Flag: Youth Voyages to Holocaust Poland and the Performance of Israeli National Identity.* New York: Berghahn.

Feldman, Jeffrey David. 2004. "The Jewish Roots and Routes of Anthropology," *Anthropological Quarterly* 77 (1): 107–26.

Firth, Raymond. 1936. *We, the Tikopia: A Sociological Study of Kinship in Primitive Polynesia.* London: George Allen and Unwin.

Fischer, Shlomo. 2012. "Fundamentalist or Romantic Nationalist? Israeli Modern Orthodoxy." In *Dynamic Belonging: Contemporary Jewish Collective Identities,* edited by Harvey E. Goldberg, Steven M. Cohen, and Ezra Kopelowitz, 91–111. New York: Berghahn.

Forte, Tania. 2001. "Shopping in Jenin: Women, Homes and Political Persons in Galilee." *City and Society* 13 (2): 211–43.

Fortes, Meyer. 1968. "Antropologia Chevratit [Social Anthropology]." *Ha'entziklopedia Ha'ivrit* D: 695-705.

Forum of Social and Cultural Studies. 2002a. "Epistemologia Shel Mizrahiyut Be'israel [Epistemology of Mizrahim in Israel]." In *Mizrahim Be'israel,* edited by Hannan Hever, Yehuda Shenhav, and Pnina Motzafi-Haller, 15–27. Jerusalem: Van Leer Institute.

———. 2002b. "Mangenonei Kinun Veyitzur Hayeda Hakanoni al Mizrahim Be'israel [Mechanisms for Founding and Producing of the Canonic Knowledge on Mizrahim in Israel]." In *Mizrahim Be'israel,* edited by Hannan Hever, Yehuda Shenhav, and Pnina Motzafi-Haller, 208–355. Jerusalem: Van Leer.

Foucault, Michel. 1980. *Power/Knowledge: Selected Interviews and Other Writings, 1972–1977.* Edited by Colin Gordon. New York: Pantheon.

Frank, Gelya. 1997. "Jews, Multiculturalism and Boasian Anthropology." *American Anthropologist* 99 (4): 731–45.

Frankenberg, Ronald, ed. 1982. *Custom and Conflict in British Society.* Manchester: Manchester University Press.

Frazer, James. 1922. *The Golden Bough: A Study in Magic and Religion.* London: Macmillan.

Furani, Khaled, and Dan Rabinowitz. 2011. "The Ethnographic Arriving of Palestine." *Annual Review of Anthropology* 40: 475–91.

Geertz, Clifford. 1973/1990. *Parshanut shel Tarbuyot* [Interpretation of Cultures]. Jerusalem: Keter.

———. 2002. "An Inconstant Profession: The Anthropological Life in Interesting Time." *Annual Review of Anthropology* 31: 1–19.

Gerholm, Tomas. 1995. "Sweden: Central Ethnology, Peripheral Anthropology." In *Fieldwork and Footnotes*, edited by Han Vermeulen and Arturo Alvarez Roldan, 159–70. London: Routledge.

Gerholm, Tomas, and Ulf Hannerz. 1982. "The Shaping of National Anthropologies." *Ethnos* 47 (1–2): 3–35.

Gibton, Dan. 2001. "Teoria Me'ugenet Basade [Grounded Theory]." In *Masorot Uzramim Bamekhkar Ha'eihuti*, edited by Naama Sabar Ben-Yehoshua, 195–228. Tel Aviv: Dvir.

Gilad, Lisa. 1982. *Yemeny Jewish Women: The Changing Family in Israeli New Town*. Cambridge: Cambridge University Press.

———. 1989. *Ginger and Salt: Yemeni Jewish Women in Israeli Town*. Boulder: Westview Press.

Ginat, Joseph. 1982. *Women in Muslim Rural Society: Status and Role in Family and Community*. New Brunswick: Transaction.

———. 2009. *Beduin "Bisha'h" Justice: Ordeal by Fire*. Brighton: Sussex Academic Press.

Glaser, B. G., and A. L. Strauss. 1967. *The Discovery of Grounded Theory: Strategy for Qualitative Research*. New York: Aldine.

Gluckman, Max. 1970. "Foreword." In Shlomo Deshen, *Immigrant Voters in Israel*. Manchester: Manchester University Press.

———. 1971. "Foreword." In Moshe Shokeid (Minkovitz), *The Dual Heritage: Plitical and Familial Interaction of Immigrants from the Atlas Mountains in an Israeli Village*. Manchester: Manchester University Press.

Goitein, Shlomo Dov. 1955. "Portrait of a Yemenite Weavers Village." *Journal of Jewish Studies* 17: 3–27.

Goldberg, Harvey E. 1972. *Cave Dwellers and Citrus Growers: A Jewish Community in Libya and in Israel*. Cambridge: Cambridge University Press.

———. 1976. "Anthropology in Israel." *Current Anthropology* 17(1): 119–21.

———. 1984. *Greentown's Youth*. Assen: Van Gorcum.

———. 1985. "Anthropology and the Study of Judaism: An Autobiographical Perspective," *Pard'es* 2: 99–115.

———. ed. 1987. *Judaism Viewed from Within and from Without: Anthropological Studies*. Albany: State University of New York Press.

———. 1990. *Jewish Life in Muslim Libya: Rivals and Relatives. Chicago: Chicago University Press.*

———. 1992. Review of Storms from Paradise: The Politics of Jewish Memory, by J. Boyarin. *Maghreb Review* 17 (3–4): 180–91.

———. 1993a. *The Book of Mordechai: A Study of the Jews of Libya*. London: Darf.

———. 1993b. "History and Experience: An Anthropologist among the Jews of Libya." *Going Home*, YIVO Annual, 21: 241–71.

———. 1995. "The Voice of Jacob: Jewish Perspectives on Anthropology and the Study of the Bible." *Jewish Social Studies*, n.s., 22: 36–71.

———. 1997. "Becoming History: Perspectives on the Seminary Faculty at Mid-Century." In *Tradition Renewed: A History of the Jewish Theological Seminary of America*, Vol. 1, edited by Jack Wertheimer, 353–437. New York: Jewish Theological Seminary.

———, ed. 2001. *The Life of Judaism*. Berkeley: University of California Press.

———. 2002. "Modern Jewish Society and Sociology." In *The Oxford Handbook of Jewish Studies*, edited by Martin Goodman et.al., 975–1001. New York: Oxford University Press.

———. 2003. *Jewish Passages: Cycles of Jewish Life*. Berkeley: University of California Press.

———. 2004. "The Oriental and the Orientalist: The Meeting of Mordecai Ha-Cohen and Nahum Slouschz." *Jewish Culture and History* 7: 1–30.

———. 2005. "The Science of Judaism and the Science of Man: Some Jewish Threads in the History of Anthropology." In *Text and Context: Essays in Modern Jewish History and Historiography in Honor of Ismar Schorsch*, edited by Eli Lederhendler and Jack Wertheimer, 283–317. New York: Jewish Theological Seminary.

———. 2010. "Cultural Change in an Israeli Immigrant Village: The Twist Dance in Moshav Porat." In *Perspectives on Israeli Anthropology*, edited by Esther Hertzog, Orit Abuhav, Harvey Goldberg, and Emanuel Marx, 31-40. Detroit: Wayne State University Press.

Goldberg, Harvey, Eileen Basker, and Orit Ziv [Abuhav]. 1980. *Antropologia: Adam, Hevra, Tarbut* [Anthrolology: Man, Society, Culture]. Tel Aviv: Tcherikover.

Goldberg, Harvey E., and Chen Bram. 2007. "Sephardic/Mizrahi/Arab-Jews: Reflections on Critical Sociology and the Study of Middle Eastern Jewries within the Context of Israeli Society." *Studies in Contemporary Jewry* 22: 227-56.

Goldberg, Harvey E., Steven M. Cohen, and Ezra Kopelowitz, eds. 2012. *Dynamic Belonging: Contemporary Jewish Collective Identities*. New York: Berghahn.

Goldberg, Harvey, Samuel Heilman, and Barbara Kirschenblatt-Gimblett, eds. 2002. *The Israel Experience: Studies in Jewish Identity and Youth Culture*. Jerusalem: Andrea and Charles Bronfman Philanthropies.

Goldberg, Harvey, and Hagar Salomon. 2002. "From Laboratory to Field: Notes on Studying Diversity in Israeli Society." *International Social Science Review* 3 (1): 123–37.

Golden, Debbie. 2006. "Structured Looseness: Everyday Social Order in an Israeli Kindergarten." *Ethos* 34 (3): 367–90.

Goldstein, Jan. 1984. "Foucault among the Sociologists: The 'Discipline' and the History of Professions." *History and Theory* 23: 170–92.

Goldstein, Marcus S. 1995. *An Odyssey in Anthropology and Public Health*. Tel Aviv: Tel Aviv University, Department of Anatomy and Anthropology, Sackler Faculty for Medicine.

Goldstein-Gidoni, Ofra. 1997. *Packaged Japaneseness: Wedding Business and Brides*. Honolulu: University of Hawaii Press.

———. 2005. "Fashioning Cultural Identity: Body and Dress in Japan." In *A Companion to the Anthropology of Japan*, edited by Jennifer Robertson, 153–66. Malden: Blackwell.

Goody, Jack. 1995. *The Expansive Moment: The Rise of Social Anthropology in Britain and Africa 1918–1970*. Cambridge: Cambridge University Press.

Gross, Nahum. 2001. *Mada'ai Hahevra Bauniversita Ha'ivrit ad 1948/49* [Social Sciences in the Hebrew University until 1948/49]. Jerusalem: Hebrew University.

Guba, Egon G., and Yvona S. Lincoln. 1998. "Competing Paradigms in Qualitative Research." In *The Landscape of Qualitative Research*, edited by Norman K. Denzin and Yvona S. Lincoln, 195–220. Thousand Oaks: Sage.

Guber, Rosana. 2008. "Committed or Scientific? The Southern Whereabouts of Social Anthropology and Antropologia Social in 1960–70 Argentina." In *Other People's Anthropologies: Ethnographic Practice on the Margins*, edited by Aleksandar Bošković, 110–24. New York: Berghahn.

Hajaj, Nurit, and Jafer Farah. 2005. "Idkun:Tguvatenu Lakenes Hashnati Shel Ha'aguda Hayisraelit Leantropologia [Update: Our Response to the Annual Meeting of IAA]." *Haoketz*. Last modified May 26. www.haokets.org/2005/05/26.

Hakak, Yochai. 2003. *Me'ohala shel Tora Le'ohel Tironim* [Yeshiva Learning and Military Training]. Jerusalem: Floersheimer Institute for Policy Studies.

Hallowell, Irving. 1965. "The History of Anthropology as an Anthropological Problem." *Journal of the History of Behavioral Sciences* 1 (1): 24–38.

Halper, Jeff, and Anita Nudelman. 1993. "Applied, Practicing, and Engaged Anthropology in Israel." *Practicing Anthropology* 15 (2): 3–4.

Handelman, Don. 1975. "The Anthropological Milieu in Israel." *Mental Health and Society* 2: 294–344.

———. 1977. *Work and Play among the Aged.* Assen: Van Gorcum.

———. 1998. *Models and Mirrors: Toward an Anthropology of Public Events.* New York: Berghahn.

———. 2004. *Nationalism and the Israeli State: Bureaucratic Logic in Public Event.* Oxford: Berg.

Handelman, Don, and Shlomo A Deshen. 1975. *The Social Anthropology of Israel: A Bibliographical Essay.* Tel Aviv: Tel Aviv University.

Handelman, Don, and Terry M. S. Evens. 2006. *The Manchester School: Practice and Ethnographic Praxis in Anthropology.* New York: Berghahn.

Hare, A. Paul, and Gideon M. Kressel, eds. 2009. *The Desert Experience in Israel: Communities, Arts, Science, and Education in the Negev.* Lanham: University Press of America.

Harris, Marvin. 1968. *The Rise of Anthropological Theory.* New York: Thomas Y. Crowell.

———. 1980. *Kanibalim Umlahim* [Cannibals and Kings]. Tel Aviv: Sifriyat Hapoalim.

———. 1987. *Parot Kdoshot Ve'hazirim Meshukatzim* [Cows, Pigs, War and Witches]. Tel Aviv: Masada.

———. 1991. *Bnei Minenu* [Our Kind]. Tel Aviv: Ma'ariv.

Hart, Mitchell. 2000. *Social Science and the Politics of Modern Jewish Identity.* Stanford: Stanford University Press.

Hartog Committee. 1934. "Report of the Survey Committee of the Hebrew University of Jerusalem." Jerusalem: Hebrew University.

Hasan-Rokem, Galit, and Eli Yassif. 1990. "Jewish Folklorists in Israel: Directions and Goals." In *Proceedings of the 10th World Congress of Jewish Folklore*, Vol. IX, Section B, 33–62.

———. 2001. "Yerushalayim shel Mala Veshel Mata—Folklore Ba'universita Ha'ivrit." Paper presented at the 13th meeting of Judaic Studies, Jerusalem.

Hazan, Haim. 1980. *The Limbo People—A Study of the Constitution of the Time Universe among the Aged.* London: Routledge and Kegan Paul.

———. 1992. *Managing Change in Old Age: The Control of Meaning in an Institutional Setting.* Albany: State University Press of New York.

———. 1994. *Old Age: Constructions and Deconstructions.* Cambridge: Cambridge University Press.

———. 1997. "Al Mehika Tarbutit [On Cultural Deletion]." In *Tikshoret Vedemocratia Be'israel*, edited by Dan Kaspi, 153–67. Jerusalem: Van Leer.

———. 2001. *Simulated Dreams: Israeli Youth and Virtual Zionism. New York:* Berghahn.

Hazan, Haim, and Esther Hertzog, eds. 2012. *Serendipity in Anthropological Research: The Nomadic Turn.* Surrey: Ashgate.

Heilman, Samuel C. 1980. "Jewish Sociologist: Native as Stranger." *American Sociologist* 15: 100–108.

Herskovits, Melville. 1947. "Din Ve'heshbon Beinleumi al Ha'antropologian [International Report on Anthropology]." *Edot* 2 (3–4): 292–96.

Hertzog, Esther. 1999. *Immigrants and Bureaucrats, Ethiopians in an Israeli Absorption Center.* Oxford: Berghahn.

———. 2008. *Life, Death and Sacrifice: Women and Family in the Holocaust.* Jerusalem: Gefen Publishing.

———. 2010. "Gender and Power Relations in a Bureaucratic Context: Female Immigrants from Ethiopia in an Absorption Center in Israel." In *Perspectives on Israeli Anthropology*, edited by Esther Hertzog, Orit Abuhav, Harvey Goldberg, and Emanuel Marx, 173–89. Detroit: Wayne State University Press.

———. 2012. "Migdar Ve'antropologia-Inyanei Nashim Ba'antropologia Ha'israelit [Gender and Anthropology—Woman Matters in Israeli Anthropology]." *Migdar* 1: 2–22.

Hertzog, Esther, Orit Abuhav, Harvey E. Goldberg, and Emanuel Marx, eds. 2010. *Perspectives on Israeli Anthropology*. Detroit: Wayne State University Press.

Hever, Hannan, Yehuda Shenhav, and Pnina Motzafi-Haller, eds. 2002. *Mizrahim Be'israel* [Mizrahim in Israel: A Critical Observation into Israel's Ethnicity]. Jerusalem: Van Leer Institute.

Hirschler, Gretrud. 1983. "Bibliography of the Published Writing of Raphael Patai." In *Fields of Offerings*, edited by Victor Sanua, 29–53. Rutherford, NJ: Fairleigh Dickinson University Press.

Horowitz, Avner. 1997. "Siegfrid Landshut Vehesronam shel Mada'ei Hevra Kanoniyim Bayeshuv [Siegfrid Landshut and the Dread of Political Sociology in Mandatory Palestine]." In *Toldot Ha'universita Ha'ivrit Biyrushalaim*, Vol. 1, edited by Shaul Katz and Michael Heyd, 660–71. Jerusalem: Magnes.

Humes-Schulz, Lisa. 2005. "Allegations Send Professor to UC Berkeley." *Daily Californian*, March 2.

Hutchinson, Sally. A. 1988. "Grounded Theory." In *Qualitative Research and Education: Focus and Methods*, edited by Robert Sherman and Rodman Webb, 123–40. London: Falmer.

Ivry, Tsipy. 2006. "At the Back Stage of Prenatal Care: Japanese OB-GYNns Negotiating Prenatal Diagnosis." *Medical Anthropology Quarterly* 20 (4): 441–68

———. 2010. *Embodying Culture: Pregnancy in Japan and Israel*. Rutgers University Press.

Jacobs-Bromberg, J. 1988. *Fasting Girls: Emergence of Anorexia Nurosa as a Modern Disease*. Cambridge: Harvard University Press.

Jackson, Andrew. 1987. "Reflections on Ethnography at Home and ASA." In *Anthropology at Home*, edited by Andrew Jackson, 1-14. ASA Monographs 25. London: Tavistock Publications.

Johanson, Donald C., and Maitland A. Edey. 1985 [1981]. *Lucy [Lucy: The Beginning of Humankind]*. Tel Aviv: Masada.

Kalifon, Zev S. 1997. "Applied Anthropology in Israel: Doing Applied Work without Really Trying." In *The Global Practice of Anthropology, Studies in the Third Word Societies*, edited by Marietta L. Baba and Carole E. Hill, 179–97. Pub. 58. Williamsburg: College of William and Mary.

Katriel, Tamar. 1985. "Griping as a Verbal Ritual in Some Israeli Discourse." In Dialogue: *An Interdisciplinary Approach*, edited by Marcelo Dascal, 373–87. Amsterdam: John Benjamins.

———. 1993. "'Lefargen': A Study in Israeli Semantics of Social Relations." *Research on Language and Social Interaction* 26 (1): 31–53.

———. 1997. "Lesaper Et Eretz Israel [To Tell Eretzisrael]." *Dvarim A'Khadim* 2: 56–76.

———. 2004. *Dialogic Moments: From Soul Talks to Talk Radio in Israeli Culture*. Detroit: Wayne State University Press.

Katz, Shaul. 1998. "Mada Tahor Beuniversita Leumit ['Pure Science' in a National University: Einstein Institute of Mathematic and Other Research]." In *Toldot Ha'universita Ha'ivrit Biyrushalaim*, Vol. 1, edited by S. Katz and M. Heyd, 397–456. Jerusalem: Magnes.

———. 2004. "Berlin Roots—Zionist Incarnation: The Ethos of Pure Mathematics and the Beginnings of the Einstein Institute of Mathematics at the Hebrew University of Jerusalem." *Science in Context* 17 (1–2): 1–36.

Katzir, Yael. 1993. "Yemenite Jewish Women in Rural Development: Female Power versus Male Authority." *Economic Development and Cultural Change* 32 (1): 45–61.

Kidron, Carol. 2009. "Towards an Ethnography of Silence: The Lived Presence of the Past among Holocaust Trauma Descendants in Israel." *Cultural Anthropology* 50(1): 5–27.

Kimmerling, Baruch. 2001. *The Invention of Israeliness: State, Society and the Military*. Berkeley: University of California Press.

Kirsh, Nurit. 2003. "Population Genetics in Israel in the 1950s: The Unconscious Internalization of Ideology." *Isis* 94 (4): 631–55.

———. 2007. "Genetic Studies of Ethnic Communities in Israel: A Case of Values Motivated Research Work." In *Jews and Sciences in German Contexts: Case Studies from the 19th and 20th Centuries,* edited by Ulrich Charpa, and Ute Deichmann, 181–94. Tübingen: Mohr Siebech.

———. 2009. "Rashita shel Hagenetica Bauniversita Ha'invrit [The Beginning of Genetics in the Hebrew University]." In *Toldot Ha'universita Ha'ivrit Beyrushalayim,* Vol. 2, edited by Hagit Lavski, 163–87. Jerusalem: Magnes.

Klausner, Joseph. 1899–1900. *Ha'adam Hakadmon: Yesodot Ha'antropologia* [The Ancient Man: The Foundations of Anthropology]. Warsaw: Tushiya.

Knorr-cetina, Karen D., and Michael J. Mulkoy, eds. 1983. *Science Observed: Perspectives on the Social Study of Science.* London: Sage.

Kressel, Gideon M. 1974. *"Mikol ehad lefi yecholto": Rivud mul shivion bakibbutz* ["From Each According to His Ability": Stratification versus Equality in a Kibbutz]. Tel Aviv: Tcherikover.

———. 1975. *Pratiut le'umat shivtiut* [Individuality versus Tribality]. Tel Aviv: Hakibbutz Hameuhad

———. 1983. *"Lekol ehad lefi tzerachav": Rivud mul shivion bakibbutz* ["To Each According to His Needs": Stratification versus Equality in a Kibbutz]. Tel Aviv: Tcherikover.

———. 1992. *Descent through Males: An Anthropological Investigation into the Patterns Underlying Social Hierarchy, Kinship, and Marriage among Former Bedouin in The Ramla-Lod Area (Israel).* Wiesbaden: Otto Harrassowitz Verlag.

———. 1996. "Mentaliyut: Inteligentzia, Musar Vehasihsuh Ha'aravi-Yehudi." *Teoria Ubikoret* 8: 72–84.

———. 2002. "Introduction." In *Siegfried Landshut, Hakvutza: Mehkar Sotziologi al Hayeshuv Hakibutzi Be'ertz Israel* [Hakvutza: Sociological Study on the Communal Settlements in Eretz Israel]. Jerusalem: The Jewish Agency.

———. 2010. *Anthropological Studies in Post-Socialist Micro-Economies in the Balkans: Creative Survival Adaptations in Bulgaria and Yugoslavia.* Edwin Mellen Press.

Kuklick, Henrika. 1983. "The Sociology of Knowledge: Retrospect and Prospect." *Annual Review in Sociology* 9: 287–310.

———. 1991. *The Savage Within: Social History of British Anthropology 1885-1945.* Cambridge: Cambridge University Press.

Kunda, Gideon. 1992. "Bikoret Bemivhan: Etnografia Vebikoret Tarbut Be'israel [Critics on Trial: Ethnography and culture criticism in Israel]." *Teoria Ubikoret* 2: 7–23.

———. 2000. *Mehandesim Tarbut* [Engineering Culture: Control and Commitment in a High-Tech Corporation]. Tel Aviv: Hargol.

Kuper, Adam. 1973. *Anthropologists and Anthropology: The British School: 1922–1972.* London: A. Lane.

———. 1996. *Anthropology and Anthropologists: The Modern British School.* London: Routledge.

Kushner, G. 1973. *Immigrants from India in Israel.* Tucson: University of Arizona Press.

Landshut, Siegfried. 1944. *Hakvutza: Mehkar Sotziologi al Hayeshuv Hakibutzi Be'ertz Israel* [Hakvutza: Sociological study on the Communal Settlements in Eretzisrael]. Jerusalem: The Jewish Agency.

———. 1950. *The Jewish Communities in the Muslims Countries of the Middle East. London:* Jewish Chronicle.

Lavie, Smadar. 2003. "Lilly White Feminism and Academic Apartheid in Israel." Anthropology News, *American Anthropological Association,* October.

Lavie, Smadar, and Ted Swedenberg. 1995. "Bein Ubetoch Gvulot Hatarbut [Between and Among the Culture's Borders]." *Teoria Ubikoret* 7: 67–86.

Leakey, Richard, and Roger Lewin. 1982. *Anshei Ha'agam* [People of the Lake]. Tel Aviv: Sifriat Maariv.

Lerner, Julia. 2008. "'We Teach Our Students to Do Science as in the West': Exploring the Mimetic University in Post-Soviet Russia." In *The Production of Educational Knowledge in the Global Era,* edited by Julia Resnik, 187–214. Rotterdam: Sense.

Lev, Tali, and Erez Cohen. 2010. "Mesima Be'israel: Bikura Shel Margaret Mead Be'israel Bekayitz 1965 [Margaret Mead's Visit to Israel in Summer 1965]." *Teorya Ubikoret* 7: 67-87.

Lévi-Strauss, Claude. 1955. *Tristes Tropiques.* New York: Atheneum.

———. 1973a. *Ha'hashiva Haprait* [La Pansée Sauvage]. Tel Aviv: Sifriyat Hapoalim.

———. 1973b [1955]. *Tristes Tropiques.* London: Jonathan Cape.

———. 2004. *Hana Vehamevushal* [Le Cru et la Cuit]. Tel Aviv: Nimrod.

Levy, André. 2010. "Playing for Control of Distance: Card Games between Jews and Muslims on a Casablancan Beach." In *Perspectives on Israeli Anthropology,* edited by Esther Hertzog, Orit Abuhav, Harvey Goldberg, and Emanuel Marx, 555–74. Detroit: Wayne State University Press..

Levy, André, and Alex Weingrod. 2005. *Homelands and Diasporas: Holy Lands and Other Places.* Stanford: Stanford University Press.

Lewis, Herbert S. 1989. *After the Eagles Landed: The Yemenite of Israel.* Boulder: Westview Press.

———. 1998. "The Misrepresentation of Anthropology and Its Consequences." *American Anthropologist* 100 (3): 716–31.

———. 2013. *In Defence of Anthropology: An Investigation of the Critique of Anthropology.* New Brunswick: Transaction.

Lieblich, Amia, et.al., eds. 1994. *Narrative Research: Reading, Analysis and Interpretation.* Thousand Oaks: Sage.

Lippert, Julius. 1904. *Toldot Hashlamat Ha'adam* [The History of Human Kind]. Warsaw: Ahiasaf.

Lissak, Moshe. 1996. "'Critical' Sociology and 'Establishment' Sociology in the Israeli Academic Community: Ideological Struggles or Academic Discourse?" *Israel Studies* 1 (1): 247–94.

Loewe, Ronald B., and Helene Hoffman. 2002. "Building the New Zion: Unfinished Conversations between the Jews of Venta Prieta, Mexico, and Their Neighbors to the North," *American Anthropologist* 104 (4): 1135–47.

Lomsky-Feder, Edna. 1998. *Ke'ilu Lo Hayta Milhama* [As if There Was No War]. Jerusalem: Magnes.

Lomsky-Feder, Edna, and Eyal Ben-Ari, eds. 1999. *The Military and Militarism in Israeli Society,* Albany: State University of New York Press.

Loss, Josef. 2001. "Antropologim, Mizrahim and Ha'academia Bishnot Hashishim Vehashiv'im [Anthropologies, Mizrahim and the Academia in the 60th and the 70th." M.A. thesis, Tel Aviv University.

Magnarella, Paul J., and Orhan Türkdoğan. 1976. "The Development of Turkish Social Anthropology." *Current Anthropology* 17 (2): 263–74.

Malinowski, Bronislav. 1967. *A Diary in the Strict Sense of the Term. New York:* Harcourt Brace.

Mannheim, Karl. 1952. *Essays on the Sociology of Knowledge.* London: Routledge and Kegan Paul.

Maoz, Daria. 2002. *Hodu To'hav Oti* [India Will Love Me]. *Jerusalem: Keter.*

Marcus, George E., and Michael Fischer. 1986. *Anthropology as Cultural Critique: An Experimental Moment in the Human Sciences.* Chicago: University of Chicago Press.
Markowitz, Fran. 1993. *A Community in Spite of Itself: Soviet Jewish Émigrés in New York.* Washington: Smithsonian Institution Press.
———. 2010. *Sarajevo: A Bosnian Kaleidoscope.* Urbana: University of Illinois Press.
———, ed. 2013. *Ethnographic Encounters in Israel: Poetics and Ethics of Fieldwork.* Bloomington: Indiana University Press.
Mars, Leonard. 1980. *The Village and the State: Administration, Ethnicity and Politics in an Israeli Co-operative Village.* Westmead: Gower.
Martin, Emily. 1987. *The Woman in the Body: A Cultural Analysis.* Boston: Beacon Press.
———. 1997. "Anthropology and the Cultural Study of Science: From Citadels to String Figures." In *Anthropological Locations: Boundaries and Grounds of a Field Science,* edited by Akil Gupta and James Ferguson, 146–85. Berkeley: University of California Press.
Marx, Emanuel. 1967. *Bedouin of the Negev.* Manchester: Manchester University Press.
———. 1975. "Anthropological Studies in a Centralized State: Max Gluckman and the Berenstein Israel Project." *Journal of Jewish Sociology* 17 (2): 131–50.
———. 1976. *The Social Context of Violent Behavior.* London: Routledge and Kegan Paul.
———, ed. 1980a. *A Composite Portrait of Israel.* London: Academic Press.
———. 1980b. "Introduction." In *A Composite Portrait of Israel,* edited by Emanuel Marx, 1–14. London: Academic Press.
———. 1980c. "Introduction." In *Y. Eilam: Hagruzinim Be'israel,* II–IV. Jerusalem: Hebrew University.
———. 1980d. "On the Anthropological Study of Nations." In *A Composite Portrait of Israel,* edited by Emanuel Marx, 15–28. London: Academic Press.
———. 1981. "The Anthropologist as Mediator." In *The Future of Pastoral People,* edited by J. G. Galaty et al., 119–26. Montreal: International Development Research Centre.
———. 1983. "The Future of Social Anthropology." Lecture in the IAA Meeting, Jerusalem.
———. 1985. "Hamehkar Ha'antropologi-Hevrati Be'israel Vehakarat Hahevre Ha'aravit [The Social Anthropology Research in Israel and the Knowledge of the Arabic Society]." In *Lachkor Amim Krovim,* edited by Aluf Hareven, 104–31. Jerusalem: Val Leer.
———, ed. 2001. "Employment and Unemployment among Bedouin." Special issue, *Nomadic Peoples,* 4(2). Oxford: Berghahn.
———. 2006. "The Political Economy of Middle Eastern and North African Pastoral Nomads." In *Nomadic Societies in the Middle East and North Africa: Entering the 21st Century,* edited by Dawn Chatty, 78–97. Leiden: Brill.
———. 2013. *The Bedouin of Mount Sinai: An Anthropological Study of Their Political Economy.* New York: Berghahn.
Massin, Benoit. 1996. "From Virchow to Fisher: Physical Anthropology and 'Modern Race Theories' in Wilhelmine Germany." In *Volkgeist as Method and Ethic: Essays on Boasian Ethnography and the German Anthropological Tradition,* edited by George Stocking Jr., 79–154. Madison: University of Wisconsin Press.
Mead, Margaret. 1956. "Report of visit in Israel."
———. 1960. "Problems of Cultural Accommodation." In *Assignment in Israel,* edited by Bernard Mandelbaum, 99–114. New York: Jewish Theological Seminary.
Mead, Margaret, and Rhoda Metraux, eds. 1953. *The Study of a Culture at a Distance.* Chicago: University of Chicago Press.

Melzer-Geva, Maya. 1983. "Hadinamica shel Bhirat Ben/Bat Zug Lenisu'in Bekerev Yehudei Gruzia [The Dynamic of Spouse Choice among Georgian Jews]." Master's thesis, Hebrew University, Jerusalem.

———. 2012. "Ein Antishemiyut Begruzia [No Anti-Semitism in Georgia: Constructing the Georgian Identity in the Israeli Society as an Inter-Cultural Learning Process]." *Mifgash* 35: 37–54.

Merton, Robert. 1973. *The Sociology of Science.* Chicago: Chicago University Press.

Messerschmidt, D. A., ed. 1981. *Anthropologists at Home in North America: Methods and Issues in the Study of One's Own Society.* Cambridge: Cambridge University Press.

Milson, Menachem. 1997. "Reshit Limudei Ha'arvit Veha'islam Ba'univerista Ha'ivrt [The Beginning of Arabic and Islamic Studies at the Hebrew of Jerusalem University]." In *Toldot Ha'universita Ha'ivrit Biyrushalaim,* Vol. 1, edited by Shaul Katz and Michael Hyed, 575–88. Jerusalem: Magnes.

Mizrahi, Beverly. 1995. "The Recruitment of Women into Strategic National Elite Positions in Israel." PhD thesis,Hebrew University, Jerusalem.

Montagu, Ashley. 1964. *H'adam: Milion Shnotav Harishonot* [Man: His First Million Years]. Jerusalem: Targumei Mada La'am..

Morris-Reich, Amos. 2006. "Arthur Ruppin's Concept of Race." *Israel Studies* 11 (3): 1–30.

Motzafi-Haller, Pnina. 1988. "Transformations in the Tswapong Region, Central Botswana: National Policies and Local Relations." PhD dissertation, Brandeis University, Massachusetts.

———. 1994. "Historical Narratives as Political Discourses of Identity." *Journal of South American Studies* 20 (3): 417–31.

———. 1997. "Yesh Lach Kol Otenti [You Have an Authentic Voice]." *Teoria Ubikoret* 11: 81–97.

———. 2001. "Scholarship, Identity and Power: Mirzrahi Women in Israel." *Signs* 26 (3): 697–734.

———. 2012. *Bekufsa'ot Habeton* [In Concrete Boxes]. Jerusalem: Magnes.

Mulkay, Michael. 1979. *Science and the Sociology of Knowledge.* London: George Allen and Anwin.

Nader, Laura. 1974. "Up the Anthropologist—Perspectives Gained from Studying Up." In *Reinventing Anthropology,* edited by Dell Hymes, 284–311. *New York:* Vintage.

Nakhleh, Khalil. 1979. "On Being a Native Anthropologist." In *The Politics of Anthropology,* edited by Gerrit Huizer and Bruce Mannheim, 343–52. The Hague: Mouton.

Narayan, Kirin. 1993. "How Native Is a 'Native' Anthropologist?" *American Anthropologist* 95: 671–86.

Nash, Dennison. 1963. "The Ethnologist as Stranger: An Essay in the Sociology of Knowledge." *Southwestern Journal of Anthropology* 19: 149–67.

Nashif, Esmail. 2008. *Palestinian Political Prisoners: Identity and Community.* London: Routledge.

Nevo, Naomi. 1993. "The Anthropologist in a Rural Bureaucracy: Chances for Survival." *Practicing Anthropology* 15 (2): 9–12.

Nordau, Max Simon. 1941. *Max Nordau to His People: A Summon and a Challenge.* New York: Scopus.

Noy, Dov. 1967. *Shiv'im Sipur Vesipur mipi Yehudei Luv* [70 Stories of Jews of Libya]. Jerusalem: WZA.

Ntarangwi, Mwenda. 2008. "Refacing Mt. Kenya or Excavating in Rift Valley? Anthropology in Kenya and the Question of Tradition." In *Other People's Anthropologies: Ethnographic Practice on the Margins,* edited by Aleksandar Bošković, 83–96. New York: Berghahn.

Ofaz, Aviva. ed. 2001. *Sefer Ha'hayim: Yomana shel Kvutzat Kiryat Anavim* [The Book of Life: The Diary of Kiryat Anavim]. Jerusalem: Yad Ben Zvi.

Oppenheimer, Jonathan. 1979. "Hadruzim Ke'aravim Vekelo Aravim [Druze as Arabs and Non-Arabs]." *Mahbarot Lemehkar Vebikoret* 41–57.

Özbudun-Demirer, Sibel. 2011. "Anthropology as Nation-Building Rhetoric: The Shaping of Turkish Anthropology (from 1850 till 1940)." *Dialectical Anthropology* 35: 111–29.

Paine, Robert. 1989. "Israel: Jewish Identity and Competition over Tradition." In *History and Ethnicity,* edited by Elizabeth Tonkin et al., 121–36. London: Routledge.

Palgi, Phyllis. 1993. "How It All Began . . . A Personal Saga." *Practicing Anthropology* 15 (2): 5–8.

Patai, Raphael. 1936. Hamayim: Mehkar Leyediat Ha'aretz Ulefolklore Eretzisraeli Betkufat Hamikra Vehamisna [The Water: Folkloristic Study in the Mikra and Mishna]. Tel Aviv: Dvir.

———. 1946. "Anthropology during the War: Palestine." *American Anthropologist* 48 (3): 477–82.

———. 1947a. Mada Ha'adam [The Science of Man: Introduction to Anthropology]. Tel Aviv: Yavne.

———. 1947b. *On Culture Contact and Its Working in Modern Palestine,* American Anthropological Association, Memoir no. 67.

———. 1949. "Hesegim Vetafkidim Be'etnologia Yehudit [Achievements and Roles of Jewish Ethnology]." *Edot* 3 (1–2): 19–27.

———. 1953. *Israel between East and West: A Study in Human Relations.* Philadelphia: Jewish Publication Society of America.

———. 1991. "Erich Brauer." In *International Directory of Anthropologists,* 77–78. New York: Garland.

———. 1992. *Journeyman in Jerusalem.* Salt Lake City: University of Utah Press.

———. n.d. "Anthropometric and Anthropology." Israeli Bureau of Statistics, file 9/4, p. 85532. Jerusalem: Israeli State Archive.

Peacock, James L., and Dorothy C. Holland. 1993. "The Narrated Self: Life Stories in Process." *Ethos* 21(4): 367–83.

Pels, Peter, and Oskar Salemink. 1994. "Five Theses on Ethnography as Colonial Practice." *History and Anthropology* 8 (1–4): 1–34.

Pringle, Dennis, and Oren Yiftachel, eds. 1999. *On Geography and Nation-State.* Be'er-Sheva: Ben Gurion University of the Negev Press.

Rabinow, Paul. 1991. "For Hire: Resolutely Late Modern." In *Recapturing Anthropology,* edited by Richard Fox, 59-72. Santa Fe: School of American Research Press.

———. 1999. *French DNA: Trouble in Purgatory.* Chicago: Chicago University Press.

Rabinowitz, Dan. 1997. *Overlooking Nazareth: The Ethnography of Exclusion in a Mixed Town in Galilee.* Cambridge: Cambridge University Press.

———. 1998. Antropologia vehapalestinim [Anthropology and the Palestinians]. Ra'anana: Institute for Israeli Arab Studies.

———. 2002. "Oriental Othering and National Identity: A Review of Early Israeli Anthropological Studies of Palestinians." *Identities* 9: 305–25.

Rabinowitz, Dan, and Khawla Abu Baker. 2002. Hador Hazakuf [The Stand Tall Generation]. Jerusalem: Keter.

Ram, Uri. 1995. *The Changing Agenda of Israeli Sociology: Theory, Ideology and Identity.* Albany: State University of New York Press.

———. 2008. *The Globalization of Israel: Mc'World in Tel Aviv, Jihad in Jerusalem.* London: Routledge.

Ram, Uri, and Oren Yiftachel. 1999. *"Etnocratia" Ve "Olamekomiyut"* ["Ethnocracy" and "Glocality"]. Be'er Sheva: Ben Gurion University Press.

Redfield, Robert. 1955. *The Little Community: Viewpoints for the Study of a Human Whole.* Chicago: Chicago University Press.

Roe, Anne. 1952. "A Psychological Study of Eminent Psychologists and Anthropologists and a Comparison with Biological and Physical Scientists." *Psychological Monographs* 67 (2): 1–55.

———. 1953. *The Making of a Scientist.* New York: Dodd, Mead.

Rosenfeld, Eva. 1952. "Social Classification in a 'Classless' Society." *American Sociological Review* 16: 766–74.

Rosenfeld, Henry. 1958. "Ir Ha'olim [The Olim City]." *Mibifmin* 87: 116–20.

———. 1964a. "From Peasantry to Wage Labor and Residual Peasantry: The Transformation of an Arab Village." *Process and Pattern in Culture* , 211–34. Chicago: Aldine.

———. 1964b. *Hem Hayu Falachim [They Were Peasants].* Tel Aviv: Hakibbutz Hameuchd.

———. 1968. "The Contradictions between Property, Kinship and Power as Reflected in the Marriage System of an Arab Village (Israel)." In *Contributions to Mediterranean Sociology,* edited by J. G. Peristiany, 247–60. Paris: Mouton.

———. 2002. "The Idea Is to Change the State, not the 'Conceptual' Terminology." *Ethnic and Racial Studies* 25 (6): 1083–95.

Rosenfeld, Henry, and Majid Al-Haj. 1990. *Arab Local Government in Israel.* Boulder: Westview.

Ruppin, Arthur. 1913. *Jews of To-day.* New York: H. Holt.

———. 1934. *Hasotziologia shel Hayehudim,* Vol. 1. Berlin: Shtibel.

Saar, Amalya. 2001. "Lonely in Your Firm Grip: Women in Israeli-Palestinian Families," *Royal Anthropological Institute* n.s., 7: 723–39.

———. 2009. "Low-Income 'Single Moms' in Israel: Redefining the Gender Contract," *Sociological Quarterly* 50: 450–73.

Sabar, Ben-Yehoshua Naama, ed. 2001. *Masorot Uzeramim Bamehkar Ha'eihuti* [Genres and Tradition in Qualitative Research]. Lod: Dvir.

Said, Edward. 1978. *Orientalism.* New York: Vintage.

Salamon, Hagar. 1997–8. "Gilgula shel Toda'a Gizit [The Metamorphosis of Racial Awareness]." *Mehkarei Yerushlaim Befolklore Yehudi* 19–20: 125–146.

———. 1999. *The Hyena People: Ethiopian Jews in Christian Ethiopia.* California: University of California Press.

Salamon, Hagar, and Steve Kaplan. 1998. *Ethiopian Immigrants in Israel: Experience and Prospects.* London: Institute for Jewish Policy and Research.

Saltman, Michael. 1977. *The Kipsidis: A Case Study in Changing Customary Law.* Cambridge: Schenkman.

———. 1991. *The Demise of the Reasonable Man: A Cross Cultural Study of a Legal Concept.* New Brunswick: Transaction.

———, ed. 2002. *Land and Territoriality.* New York: Berg.

Scheper-Hughes, Nancy. 1979. *Saints, Scholars and Schizophrenics: Mental Illness in Rural Ireland.* Berkeley: University of California Press.

Schnell, Izhak. 1994. *Perspectives on Israeli-Arabs Territoriality and Identity.* Aldershot: Avenbury.

———. 2000. "Israeli Geography in Search for National Identity." Paper Presented in the IGU conference, The Commission on the History of Geographical Thought, Seoul.

Scholem, Gershom. 1980. *From Berlin to Jerusalem.* New York: Schocken.

Schrire, Dani. 2010. "Raphael Patai, Jewish Folklore, Comparative Folkloristics, and American Anthropology." *Journal of Folklore Research* 47 (1–2): 7–43

Schumaker, Lyn. 2001. *Africanazing Anthropology: Fieldwork, Networks, and the Making of Cultural Knowledge in Central Africa.* Durham: Duke University Press.

Schwartz, Moshe. 1995. "Moshav and Kibbutz in the Anthropology and Sociology of Israel." In *Rural Cooperatives in Socialist Utopia*, edited by Susan Lee, Moshe Schwartz, and Gideon M. Kressel, 3–29. London: Praeger.

Schwartz, Shuly R. 1991. *The Emergence of Jewish Scholarship in America: The Publication of the Jewish Encyclopedia.* Cincinnati: Hebrew Union College Press.

Schwarzbaum, Haim. 1983. "The Oeuvre of Raphael Patai." In *Fields of Offerings*, edited by Victor Sanua, 19–28. Rutherford, NJ: Fairleigh Dickinson University Press.

Shabtai, Malka. 1999. *"Hachi ahi": Masa Hazehut shel hayalim 'Olim mietiopia* ["Best Brother": The Identity Journey of Ethiopian Immigrant Soldiers]. Tel Aviv: Tcherikover.

———. 2001. *Bein reggae lerap: Etgar hahishtaychut shel no'ar yotze Etiopia Be'israel* [Between Reggae and Rap: The Integration Challenge of Ethiopian Youth in Israel]. Tel Aviv: Tcherikover

Shabtai, Malka, and Yoni Mizrahi, eds. 2004. *Profilim shel Antropologim Yisumiyim Be'israel* [Profiles of Applied Anthropologists in Israel]. Afula: Yezreel Valley College.

Shai, Dona. 1970. *Neighborhood Relations in Immigrants Quarter.* Jerusalem: Szold Institute.

Shamgar-Handelman, Lea, and Don Handelman. 2010. "Celebrations of Bureaucracy: Birthday Parties in Kindergartens." In *Perspectives on Israeli Anthropology*, edited by Esther Hertzog, Orit Abuhav, Harvey Goldberg, and Emanuel Marx, 111–56. Detroit: Wayne State University Press.

Shamir, Ronen, and Dan Avnon. 2009. "Martin Buber Vehasotzyologya Hayisraelit [Martin Buber and the Israeli Sociology]." *Hamishim Learbaim Ushmone*, edited by Adi Ophir, 47-55. Jerusalem: Van Leer.

Shapira, Ovadya. 1972. *Moshvei Olim Be'israel* [Workers' Moshavim in Israel], 171-81. Jerusalem: The Jewish Agency.

Shapira, Reuven. 1990. "Rottatzya 'Otomatia' Veshamranut Irgunit Bakibbutz [Ratation and Organizational Conservativeness in the Kibbutz]." *Megamot* 33(4):522-36.

Shavit, Yaacov. 1997. "Archaeology, Political Culture and Culture in Israel. Constructing the Past, Interpreting the Present," Supplement series, *Journal of the Study of the Old Testimony* 237: 48–61.

Shavit, Zeev. 2003. "Hamerkaz Leshiluv Moreshet Yahadut Sefarad Vehamizrach Kesochen Leshinuy Hevrati Be'israel [The Center for Integration of the Oriental Jewish Heritage as an Agent for Social Change in Israel]." *Peamim* 94–95: 95–103.

Sheehan, Elizabeth A. 1993a. "The Academic as Informant: Methodological and Theoretical Issues in the Ethnography of Intellectuals." *Human Organization* 52 (3): 252–59.

———. 1993b. "The Student of Culture and the Ethnography of Irish Intellectuals." In *When They Read What We Write: The Politics of Ethnography*, edited by Caroline B. Brettell, 75–90. Westport: Bergin and Garvey.

Shepher, Israel. 1983. *The Kibbutz: An Anthropological Study.* Norwood: Norwood Editions.

Shepher, Joseph, and Lionel Tiger. 1975. *Women in the Kibbutz.* New York: Harcourt Brace.

Shenhav-Keller, Shely. 2005. "'Medabrim Avar'—'Medabrim Hove': Siyakh Parshani shel Avar Betetzuga Muzeonit ['Talking on the Past'—'Talking on the Present': Interpretative Discourse on the Past.]" In museum exhibition.

Shilo, Ailon, ed. 1969. *Peoples and Cultures in the Middle East.* New York: Random House.

Shkedi, Asher. 2003. *Milim Hamenasot Laga'at* [Words of Meaning]. Tel Aviv: Ramot.

Shokeid, Moshe. 1971a. *The Dual Heritage: Immigrants from the Atlas Mountains in an Israeli Village.* Manchester: Manchester University Press.

———. 1971b. "Fieldwork as Predicament rather than Spectacle." *European Journal of Sociology* XII: 111–22.

———. 1976. "M. Gluckman and the Establishment of Israeli Anthropology." In *In Memoriam: Professor Max Gluckman,* edited by S. N. Eisenstadt et al., 10–13. Jerusalem: Faculty of Social Sciences, Hebrew University.

———. 1988. *Children of Circumstances: Israeli Emigrants in New York.* Ithaca: Cornell University Press.

———. 1988/89. "'The Manchester School in Africa and Israel' Revisited: Reflections of the Sources and Method of an Anthropological Discourse." *Israel Social Science Research* 6 (1): 9–24.

———. 1992a. "An Anthropologist Work between Moving Genres." *Ethnos* 57 (3–4): 233–44.

———. 1992b. "Commitment and Contextual Study in Anthropology." *Cultural Anthropology* 7 (4): 464–77.

———. 1995. *A Gay Synagogue in New York.* New York: Columbia University Press.

———. 2001. "For the Sin We Did Not Commit in the Research of Oriental Jewry." *Israel Studies* 6 (1): 15-33.

———. 2002. *Massa Israeli* [Israeli Journey]. Tel Aviv: Yediot Akhronot.

———. 2003. "Hatext Haetnografi Bimevukhot Hazman [The Ethnographical Text in the Time Confusions]." *Mikarov* 11: 67-73.

———. 2009. *Three Jewish Journeys through an Anthropologist's Lens.* Brighton: Academic Studies Press.

———. 2012. *Mabat Mikarov Umerahok* [A View from Near and Far]. Tel Aviv: Resling.

Shokeid, Moshe, and Shlomo Deshen, eds. 1999. *Hakhavaya Habeintarbutit* [The Cross-Cultural Experience]. Tel Aviv: Schoken.

Shokeid, Moshe, Emanuel Marx, and Shlomo Deshen, eds. 1980. *Prakin Be'antropologia Khevratit* [Chapters in Social Anthropology]. Tel Aviv: Schoken.

Shuval, Judith T., and Elazar Leshem. 1998. "The Sociology of Migration in Israel: A Critical View." In *Immigration to Israel: Sociological Perspectives,* Studies of Israeli Society, Vol. VIII, edited by Elazar Leshem and Judith T. Shuval, 3–50. New Brunswick: Transaction.

Silberman, Neil, and David Small, eds. 1997. *Archaeology of Israel: Constructing the Past, Interpreting the Present.* Sheffield: Sheffield Academic Press.

Simhai, Dalit. 2000. *Hashvil Haze Matkhil Kan: Tarmilaut Shel Yisraelim Bamizrah Harakhok* [This Road Starts Here: Israeli Backpacking in the Far East]. Tel Aviv: Prague.

Simpson, George Eaton. 1973. *Melville J. Herskovits.* New York: Columbia University Press.

Siskin, Edgar E. 1983. *Washo Shamans and Peyotists Religious Conflict in an American Indian Tribe.* Salt Lake City: University of Utah Press.

Smooha, Sami. 1985. "Bikoret al Girsa Mimsadit Adkanit shel Hgisha Hatarbutit Besotziologia Yakhasey Edot Be'israel [Critique on the Current Establishment's Version of the Cultural Approach to Ethnic Relationships in Israel.]" *Megamot* 29 (1): 73-92.

Spector-Mersel, Gabriela. 2006. "Never-Aging Stories: Western Masculanity Scripts." *Journal of Gender Studies* 15 (1): 67–82.

Spiro, Melford E. 1963. *Kibbutz, Venture in Utopia.* New York: Schocken.

———. 1972. *Children of the Kibbutz.* New York: Schocken.

Stadler, Nurit. 2007. "Ethnography of Exclusion: Initiating a Dialogue with Fundamentalist Men." *Nashim: A Journal of Jewish Women's Studies and Gender Issues* 14: 185-208.

Stillman, Noam. 2002. "Miheker Hamizrah Umichochmat Israel Lerav-Tkhumiut." *Peamim* 92: 63–82.

Stocking, George Ward Jr., ed. 1974. *A Franz Boas Reader: The Shaping of American Anthropology, 1883–1911*. Chicago: University of Chicago Press.

———. 1982. *Race, Culture and Evolution: Essays in the History of Anthropology*. New York: Free Press.

———. 1987. *Victorian Anthropology*. New York: Free Press.

———, ed. 1991. *Colonial Situations: Essays on the Contextualization of Ethnographic Knowledge, History of Anthropology*, Vol. 7. Madison: University of Wisconsin Press.

———. 1996. *After Tylor: British Anthropology 1888–1951*. London: Athlone Press.

———. 2000. "'Do Good, Young Man': Sol Tax and the World Mission of Liberal Democratic Anthropology." In *Excluded Ancestors, Inventible Traditions*, edited by Richard Handler, 171–264. Madison: University of Wisconsin Press.

Sugishita, Kaori. 2008. "Japanese Anthropology and the Desire for the West." In *Other People's Anthropologies: Ethnographic Practice on the Margins*, edited by Aleksandar Bošković, 142–55. New York: Berghahn.

Swedenberg, Ted. 1993. "Occupational Hazards Revisited: Reply to Moshe Shokeid." *Cultural Anthropology* 7 (4): 478–95.

Swidler, Ann, and Jorge Arditi. 1994. "The New Sociology of Knowledge." *Annual Review of Sociology* 20: 305–29.

Swirski, Shlomo. 1978. "He'arot Lasotziologia shel Tkufat Hayeshuv [Notes on the Sociology of the Yeshuv Era]." *Mahbarot Lemehkar Ulebikoret* 2: 5–42.

Talmon-Gerber, Yanina. 1970. *Yakhid Vekhevra Bakibbutz* [The Kibbutz: Sociological Studies]. Jerusalem: Magnes.

Tandoğan, Zerrin G. 2008. "Anthropology in Turkey: Impressions for an Overview." In *Other People's Anthropology: Ethnographic Practice on the Margins*, edited by Aleksandar Bošković, 97–109. New York: Berghahn.

Tene, Ofra. Forthcoming. "The New Immigrant Must Not Only Learn, He Must Also Forget: The Making of Eretz-Israeli Ashkenazi Cuisine." *Studies in Contemporary Jewry*.

Thomas, Nicolas. 1994. *Colonialism's Culture: Anthropology, Travel and Government*. Cambridge: Polity Press.

Tohn, Chana Helena. 1957. *Ha'edot Be'israel* [The Ethnic Groups of Israel]. Jerusalem: Reuven Mass.

Topel, Marta F. 1996. "Uma tradicao milenar, uma ciencia moderna: a antropologia israelense, autores e leitores." PhD dissertation, University of Campinas (UNICAMP), São Paulo.

Trencher, Susan R. 2002. "The American Anthropological Association and the Values of Science 1935–1970." *American Anthropologist* 104 (2): 450–62.

Tsing, Anna. 2000. "The Global Situation." *Cultural Anthropology* 15 (3): 327–60.

Turner, Victor. 1980. "Muchona Hatzir'a [Muchona the Hornet]." In *Prakim Beantopologia Hevratit*, edited by Moshe Shokeid et. al., 268–80. Tel Aviv: Schoken.

Tylor, Edward B. 1878. *Researches into the Early History of Mankind and the Development of Civilization*. Boston: Estes and Lauriat.

Tzur, Yaron. 2003. Hahisotiografia Hayisraeli Vehabe'aya Ha'adatit [The Israeli Historiography and the Ethical Issue]. *Peamim* 94-95:7-55.

Urry, James. 1993. *Before Social Anthropology: Essays on the History of British Anthropology*. Chur: Harwood Academic.

Van Bremen, Jan, Eyal Ben Ari, and Syed Faris Al-Atas, eds. 2005. *Asian Anthropology*. London: Routledge Curzon.

Van Teeffelen, Toin. 1977. *Anthropologists on Israel: A Case Study in the Sociology of Knowledge.* Papers on European and Mediterranean Societies, no.9, University of Amsterdam, Amsterdam.

———. 1980. "The Manchester School in Africa and Israel: A Critique." In *Anthropology: Ancestors and Heirs,* edited by Stanley Diamond, 347–75. The Hague: Mouton.

Vermeulen, Han, and Arturo Alvarez Roldan, eds. 1995. *Fieldwork and Footnotes: Studies in the History of European Anthropology.* London: Routledge.

Wasserfall, Rachel. 2010. "Menstruation and Identity: The Meaning of Niddah for Moroccan Women Immigrants." In *Perspectives on Israeli Anthropology,* edited by Esther Hertzog, Orit Abuhav, Harvey Goldberg, and Emanuel Marx, 611–26. *Detroit: Wayne State University Press.*

Watson, Lawrence C. 1976. "Understanding Life History as Subjective Document: Hermeneutical and Phenomenological Perspectives." *Ethos* 4 (1): 95–131.

Weil, Shalva, in collaboration with Michael Weil. 1987. "Anthropology Becomes Home; Home Becomes Anthropology." In *Anthropology at Home,* edited by Andrew Jackson, 196–212. New York: Tavistock.

Weil, Shalva. 1997. "Religion, Blood and the Equality of Rights: The Case of the Ethiopian Jews in Israel." *International Journal on Minority and Group Rights* 4: 397–412.

Weingrod, Alex. 1966. *Reluctant Pioneers: Village Development in Israel.* Ithaca: Cornell University Press.

———, ed. 1985. *Studies in Israeli Ethnicity. New York:* Gordon and Breach Science.

———. 1998a. "Hatzadikim Doharim Kadima [The Saints Marching Ahead]." In *Israel—Anthropologia Mekomit,* edited by Orit Abuhav et al., 625–41. Tel Aviv: Tcherikover.

———. 1998b. "Working at Home: Some Reflections on Reflexivity." Lecture at 50th Jubilee of Brandeis University, Waltham.

———. 2002. "Dry Bones: Nationalism and Symbolism in Contemporary Israel." In *The Best of Anthropology Today,* Jonathan Benthall. London: Routledge.

———. 2004. "Anthropology in a Stormy Pond." *Ethnos* 69 (3): 411–28.

Weir, Shelagh. 1975. "Hilma Granquist and Her Contribution to Palestine Studies." *British Society for Middle Eastern Studies Bulletin* 2 (1): 6–13.

Weiss, Meira. 1994. *Conditional Love: Parents' Attitudes toward Handicapped Children.* Westport, CT: Bergin and Garvey.

———. 2002. *The Chosen Body: The Politics of the Body in Israeli Society.* Stanford: Stanford University Press.

Weiss, Ruhama. 2010. *Ochlim Lada'at* [Meal Tests: The Meal in the World of the Sages]. Tel Aviv: Hakibbutz Hameuhad.

Weitman, Sasha. 2002. "Al 'Hahavana' Etzel Bourdieu." *Sotziologia Israelit* 4 (2): 411–25.

Werczberger, Rachel. 2012. "Dynamic Belonging of Younger Jews and the Transformation of the Jewish Self." In *Dynamic Belonging: Contemporary Jewish Collective Identities,* edited by Harvey E. Goldberg, Steven M. Cohen, and Ezra Kopelowitz, 165–72. New York: Berghahn.

Willner, Dorothy. 1956. "He'arot al Trumata shel Ha'anthropologia ve'al Kama Megishoteha Labe'aya shel Klitat Hagira [Notes on the Field of Anthroplogy and Some of Its Approaches to the Problem of Absorption of Immigration]." *Megamot* 7: 86–92.

———. 1969. *Nation-Building and Community in Israel.* Princeton: Princeton University Press.

Wolcott, H. F. 1995. *The Art of Fieldwork.* Walnut Creek, CA: AltaMira Press.

Wolf, Eric. 1969. "American Anthropologists and American Society." In *Reinventing Anthropology*, edited by Dell Hymes, 252–63. *New York:* Random House.

Wolf, Margery. 1972. *Women and the Family in Rural Taiwan.* Stanford: Stanford University Press.

Yacobson, Yehuda. 1987. "Tzalyanut Hilonit." Master's thesis, Tel Aviv University, Tel Aviv.

Yassif, Ali. 1998. "Legalot et Israel Ha'akheret [Discover the Other Israel]." In *Israel—Anthropologia Mekomit*, edited by Orit Abuhav, 525–52. Tel Aviv: Tcherikover.

Yassur, Yosi. 1990. *Tehum Hamoshav* [The Moshav Reservatior]. Tel Aviv: Ramot.

Zborowski, Mark, and Elizabeth Herzog. 1952. *Life Is with People: The Culture of the Shtetl.* New York: Schocken.

Zilberman, Yifrah. 1991. Hilma Granquist and Artas. *Cambridge Anthropology* 15(1): 56.

INDEX

www.ingramcontent.com/pod-product-compliance
Lightning Source LLC
LaVergne TN
LVHW010355080826
844660LV00016B/978/J

* 9 7 8 0 8 1 4 3 3 8 7 3 5 *